Shakespeare's Comic Rites

SHAKESPEARE'S COMIC RITES

EDWARD BERRY
University of Victoria

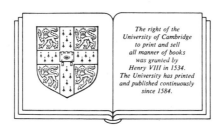

CAMBRIDGE UNIVERSITY PRESS

CAMBRIDGE

LONDON   NEW YORK   NEW ROCHELLE
MELBOURNE   SYDNEY

Published by the Press Syndicate of the University of Cambridge
The Pitt Building, Trumpington Street, Cambridge CB2 1RP
32 East 57th Street, New York, NY 10022, USA
296 Beaconsfield Parade, Middle Park, Melbourne 3206, Australia

First published 1984

Printed in Great Britain at the University Press, Cambridge

Library of Congress catalogue card number: 84-3229

British Library Cataloguing in Publication Data
Berry, Edward
Shakespeare's comic rites.
1. Shakespeare, William – Comedies
I. Title
822.3'3 PR2981

ISBN 0 521 26303 4

CE

To My Parents

Contents

Preface

I discuss the rationale for this study in the introduction, but it may be helpful at the outset to explain its organization. My title, *Shakespeare's Comic Rites*, is intended to suggest a remarkable affinity between the structure of Shakespeare's romantic comedies and that of rites of passage. The order of my chapters therefore follows Arnold van Gennep's description of the three phases of such rites: separation, transition, and incorporation. Chapter 1, "Comic Rites," introduces these phases and their relevance to Elizabethan society and Shakespeare's comedies. Chapter 2, "Separations," discusses the first phase. Chapters 3 and 4 explore courtship as a transitional experience – Chapter 3, "Natural Transitions," focusing on the follies of love; Chapter 4, "Artificial Transitions," on a special instance of those follies, female disguise. Chapters 5 and 6 also deal with transitional matters, although not so exclusively and from different perspectives: Chapter 5, "Natural Philosophers," discusses the role of clowns and fools; Chapter 6, "Time and Place," the temporal and spatial dimensions of the comic experience. Chapter 7, "Incorporations," considers the rites of incorporation that end the plays. A brief conclusion reviews the course of the study and highlights some of its implications. As this outline suggests, my aim is not to interpret individual plays, although interpretations are implicit, but to explore the dynamics of the genre as a whole.

Despite my restriction of discussion to the romantic comedies, I do not intend to suggest that the concept of rites of passage is inapplicable to other plays or genres. Quite the contrary. The pattern of experience that van Gennep defines, particularly as elaborated by recent anthropologists, may offer insights into a wide range of characteristic Shakespearean techniques. I focus on the romantic comedies as an unusually tight-knit genre based on specific ritual structures – those of initiation, courtship, and marriage.

Because of the peculiar nature of this study, my recorded debts to Shakespeare critics and scholars are relatively few. I have shied away from controversy and resisted my more idiosyncratic interpretations in the interests of the broad design. Careful readers will recognize numerous debts, some no doubt unconscious. For these I express *en masse* my appreciation. I regret that my broad scope has made it impossible to engage in dialogue (if one can use that word of notes) with many excellent critics and scholars who have fueled my interest in the comedies and deepened my understanding and appreciation.

In documenting the social history behind the plays, I have tried to stay within the boundaries of Shakespeare's lifetime. This has not always been possible; the records of Elizabethan and Jacobean social custom are sparse and fragmentary. Since my argument does not depend upon single details, I have avoided constant weighing of the evidence but have indicated dates for material that is not widely known. In citing old texts, I have normalized *u*, *v*, *i* and *j* to conform with modern practice. For Shakespeare's text, I have used *The Riverside Shakespeare*, ed. G. Blakemore Evans (Boston: Houghton Mifflin, 1974), except that I have omitted as unnecessarily distracting the square brackets indicating emendations.

Although I did not realize it at the time, this study began many years ago in Freetown, Sierra Leone, with students whose delight in Shakespeare taught me that the clichés of his universality hold a special truth; to them I owe a continuing obligation. More recently, I am indebted to the University of Victoria and the Social Sciences and Humanities Research Council of Canada for their invaluable support; to the University of Liverpool for a generous appointment as Visiting Scholar; and to the staffs of the Huntington and Folger Libraries for their kind assistance. To Professor Philip Edwards and the Department of English Literature at the University of Liverpool, I owe thanks for the opportunity to test my ideas at an early stage before a skeptical yet sympathetic audience. To Professors Sherman Hawkins and Terry Sherwood, both of whom read the entire manuscript of this study, I owe not only my thanks but my apologies for certain weaknesses that remain. Finally, I must thank my wife, Margaret, who has taught me much about the rites of marriage, and my children, Michelle and David, who have initiated me into the mysteries of adolescence.

Introduction: Comic Rites

This book brings together eight of Shakespeare's plays, those commonly called the romantic comedies: *The Comedy of Errors, The Taming of the Shrew, Two Gentlemen of Verona, Love's Labor's Lost, A Midsummer Night's Dream, Much Ado About Nothing, As You Like It,* and *Twelfth Night.* These plays are "romantic" not so much because they exploit the conventions and themes of romance, although many do, but because they share a central "romantic" action: they chart the tortuous course of pairs of lovers through courtship to marriage. It is this simple, dynamic, and infinitely variable structure that shapes most profoundly our experience of these plays, defines them as a genre, and differentiates them from other, related groups such as the problem comedies or late romances.[1]

To explore the nature of this genre and its distinctive appeal, I should like to begin some distance from Shakespeare, in the remote world of primitive ritual. The structure that informs Shakespearean comedy and creates its most distinctive effects is not only esthetic but social and psychological. In the form of rites of passage this structure exists in nearly all cultures, including that of Elizabethan England. To pursue its significance in Shakespeare's comedies is to venture into three very different fields – anthropology, social history, and literary criticism. The journey, admittedly, is hazardous; yet it may also be rewarding, for if at all successful it may tell us something, not only about the central experience of Shakespearean comedy, but about its relation to Elizabethan culture and to cultural patterns common to all mankind. It may illuminate, in short, some of the ways in which the comedies are at once Shakespearean, Elizabethan, and universal. Since the terrain I intend to explore is still relatively uncharted, it may be useful to begin not with the comedies but with a broad survey of our route.

In his anthropological classic, *The Rites of Passage*, Arnold van Gennep analyzes the various rites by means of which societies effect transitions in the life of an individual from one social identity to another – rites of birth, initiation, marriage and death. These celebrations of crises in the life cycle occur in societies throughout the world and at different stages of historical development. Their precise significance varies from culture to culture. As van Gennep demonstrates, however, they share a common structure, unfolding in three movements: an initial stage of separation, in which the individual is divorced from his familiar environment; a transitional stage, in which his old identity is destroyed and a new one created; and a final stage of incorporation, in which he is reintegrated into society in his new role.

In practice, rites of passage are naturally more complicated than this schema suggests: in some cases one phase may be insignificant or even missing; in others, a phase may so dominate that it monopolizes the entire rite; in still others, a phase may itself contain elements of other phases. An Elizabethan wedding, for example, may be viewed as a series of rites of passage – with separations, transitions, and incorporations. The couple move from the bride's house to the church, where they are joined as man and wife, then move from the church to the bride's house, where they are feasted, and finally move from the banquet to the bridal chamber, where the marriage is consummated. Viewed as the culmination of a courtship, however, the entire ceremony becomes a rite of incorporation.[2] Despite the recalcitrance of life to scholarly order, van Gennep's schema, flexibly applied, offers a meaningful approach to a wide variety of phenomena. Its impact on modern anthropology has been profound.[3]

Since I shall focus on initiation,[4] courtship, and marriage, it may be helpful to flesh out van Gennep's skeletal structure with illustrations from these rites. The phase of separation, as the name implies, marks the first stage in the loss of a sense of identity. Usually abrupt, and sometimes violent, rites of separation rupture the individual's ties to his former self, his family, his community, his familiar routine and environment. In initiation, separation is effected by such actions as whipping or intoxication, and most often by literal journeys into the bush or into seclusion; the event is sometimes characterized as a symbolic death. In marriage, separation occurs through such rites as mock-abduction, in which the bride is "captured"; by a movement across boundaries, such as crossing a threshold; or by a variety of other actions, many of which symbolize separation in other rites as well – changing clothes, destroying or throwing away something linked to the former identity, cutting the hair or beard, insulting or beating childhood companions, washing or being washed, losing one's name. Whatever their specific form or intensity, each of these rites dramatizes a process of alienation.

Transitional rites, or liminal rites, as they are often called (from the Latin *limen*, threshold), are usually more complicated and extensive than rites of separation, especially during initiation, when they sometimes last for years. In general, the liminal phase can be characterized as one of confusion, testing, and education, although "confusion" is too trivial a word for the fundamental dislocation of self sometimes experienced. In initiation, this disorientation occurs in such activities as dying symbolically; losing one's name, language, and customary diet; disguising oneself, or mutilating or painting one's body; and engaging in sex reversal, or in other modes of behavior, such as stealing, that are ordinarily taboo. The testing in initiation rites includes physical and mental ordeals of various kinds, such as beating, fasting, sleeplessness, scarification, and circumcision. The process is educational in many senses. Formal instruction is often provided in the religion, customs, and skills of the society, but this seems usually less important than the symbolic re-enforcement of tribal values of which the individual is already aware. At times, the liminal phase culminates in a moment of insight; in some North American and Australian cultures, for example, the "gods" who torment the novices are unmasked at the end of the rite.

The liminal phase of marriage rites, or courtship, as we know it, is usually less traumatic than that of initiation. In most societies, the period of betrothal is chiefly one of testing and education. The families and future partners exchange visits and gifts, and often the betrothed couple serve their respective in-laws, demonstrating their worth and learning the behavior appropriate to married adults. The disorientation and confusion which are so dramatic in initiation rites are less pronounced in courtship, although a kind of festive misrule is not uncommon. In Zulu wedding ceremonies, for example, brides wear men's weapons, run away from their husbands, and endure for long periods the insults of their husband's kin.[5] In Western societies, since roughly the time of Shakespeare, when the conventional symptoms of romantic love became a prelude to marriage, courtship has been a period of high trauma, as painful and elaborate as many rites of initiation. The liminal phase is a period of indeterminate identity, full of ambiguity and paradox; in it, as van Gennep observes, the individual "wavers between two worlds."[6] Since the notion of liminality is crucial to the comedies – and, indeed, immensely suggestive for many of Shakespeare's plays – it may be worth pausing for a moment over a synoptic description provided by the anthropologist Victor Turner:

... the most characteristic midliminal symbolism is that of paradox, or being *both* this *and* that. Novices are portrayed and act as androgynous, or as both living *and* dead, at once ghosts and babes, both cultural and natural creatures, human *and* animal. They may be said to be in a process of being ground down into a sort of homogeneous social matter, in which possibilities of differentiation may be still glimpsed, then later positively refashioned into specific shapes compatible with their new postliminal duties and rights as incumbents of a new status and state. The grinding down process is accomplished by ordeals: circumcision, subincision, clitoridectomy, hazing, endurance of heat and cold, impossible physical tests in which failure is greeted by ridicule, unanswerable riddles which make even clever candidates look stupid, followed by physical punishment, and the like. But reducing down overlaps with reconstruction. The rebuilding process is by instruction, partly in practical skills, partly in tribal esoterica, and proceeds both by verbal and nonverbal symbolic means. Sacred objects may be shown, myths recited in conjunction with them, answers may be given to riddles earlier left unexplained.[7]

In several provocative studies, particularly *The Ritual Process* and *The Forest of Symbols*, Turner has explored the nature of liminality and its function in a wide variety of social contexts, ranging from political rites among the Ndembu to the social customs of modern hippies.

Rites of incorporation integrate the individual into society in his new role. In both initiation and marriage, the most common of these rites are a religious ceremony and a communal meal. They are often supplemented by the exchange of gifts and visits, and by ritual dancing. Although the community as a whole participates in these rites, they center on the initiates or the married pair, who often receive emblems of their new status, such as a ring, new clothing, or a new name. Marriage includes not only the collective rites of a communal meal and religious ceremony but many personal rites which join bride and bridegroom to each other, such as exchanging belts, bracelets, or rings; being bound to one another, or wrapped together in a veil or piece of clothing; or eating from the same dish. The incorporation symbolized in these personal rites culminates in sexual consummation. Bonding tends to be more complicated in marriage than initiation because spouses must be joined not only to their community but to each other and their immediate kin; the network of marital relations is thus particularly elaborate and extensive.

In some societies, initiation and marriage form a single process, especially in the case of girls. Among the Vai in Liberia, for example, young girls are initiated by being taken to the *sande*, a sacred place in the forest, where they are considered dead and are instructed in domestic and sexual behavior by old women. Often, a girl's parents arrange her marriage while she is in the *sande*; in such cases she is not permitted to leave until her first menstruation. At that point, after being presented with gifts from her betrothed, she is perfumed, adorned, and taken to meet her parents at the entrance to the sacred place. After a ceremonial meal, she accompanies her mother to the hut of her intended. While the couple consummate their marriage inside the hut, their parents and guests sit outside, sharing a meal. After the consummation, the husband joins them.[8] In such instances, maturity and marriage coincide, the initiate being transformed in one step from unmarried child to married adult. A similar integration of initiation and marriage rites, as we shall see, occurs in Elizabethan society and Shakespeare's comedies.

In its broad outlines, the initiatory process that van Gennep describes parallels that of Shakespeare's comedies. The shipwrecks, banishments, and journeys that begin the plays may be compared with rites of separation, breaking apart lovers, families, and friends, and placing the protagonists in states of social and psychological alienation. The consistent use of symbolic geography in the plays – the movement of characters into the "holiday" or "green" worlds so important in the criticism of C. L. Barber and Northrop Frye – creates mysterious landscapes analogous to the sacred forests of initiation. In these enchanted places, Shakespeare's protagonists experience the dislocations and confusions of identity, the ordeals, and the education characteristic of the liminal phase; as Leo Salingar observes, they "are led through a passage of illusion, as in a rite of initiation."[9] The conclusions of the plays not only announce the joining of lovers in marriage but in many cases dramatize the actual rites of incorporation prominent in Elizabethan weddings – the exchanging of rings and oaths, kissing, feasting, and dancing. Since Shakespeare's successful lovers are invariably young lovers, these rites mark not only the end of a single state but the end of adolescence. The comedies, in short, might be called comic rites of passage.

If this analytic schema is to be useful, however, it is important to recognize its limitations. It is not intended as a formula. In their diversity and complexity, Shakespeare's comedies resist scholarly strait-jackets more successfully, and more delightfully, than the rites that van Gennep defines. The comic pattern varies from play to play, and the schema fits some plays better than others. If van Gennep's initiatory pattern does not provide a formula for interpretation, however, it does offer a framework, flexible enough to relate the plays to each other without, I hope, suppressing their individuality, and broad enough to tell us something important about the sources of their dramatic appeal.

The parallels between Shakespeare's comic structure and that of rites of passage are strikingly exact but difficult to explain. Why should Shakespeare reproduce in his comedies an ancient ritual pattern? One place to look for answers, although it lies beyond my scope, is in the nature of comedy itself. Although Shakespeare exploits the threefold pattern of rites of passage more consistently, more precisely, and more profoundly than any other comic dramatist, it is clear that in an abstract form it can be detected in most conventional comedy from Aristophanes to Neil Simon. Shakespeare's romantic comedy, after all, is based on a comic formula, still very much alive, that inevitably entails separation, transition, and incorporation: a young man and woman fall in love, endure and eventually overcome a variety of obstacles to their union, and finally get married. Romantic comedy of this kind is a specialized and apparently immortal version of a structure that Susanne Langer, the most persuasive modern theorist of comedy, defines as the "upset and recovery of the protagonist's equilibrium." One of the few writers on comedy to be more concerned with comic structure than with the nature of laughter, Langer defines comedy in a way that may help explain its general resemblance to a rite of passage.

Langer locates the impulse behind comic form in biology, in what she calls "the round of conditioned and conditioning organic processes that produces the life rhythm." "When this rhythm is disturbed," she observes, "all activities in the total complex are modified by the break; the organism as a whole is out of balance. But, within a wide range of conditions, it struggles to retrieve its original dynamic form by overcoming and removing the obstacle, or if this proves impossible, it develops a slight variation of its typical form and activity and carries on life with a new balance of functions – in other words, it adapts itself to the situation." It is this periodic alternation of disequilibrium and equilibrium, according to Langer, that determines the form of comedy: "Destiny in the guise of Fortune is the fabric of comedy; it is developed by comic action, which is the upset and recovery of the protagonist's equilibrium, his contest with the world and his triumph by wit, luck, personal power, or even humorous, or ironical, or philosophical acceptance of mischance. Whatever the theme ... the immediate sense of life is the underlying feeling of comedy, and dictates its rhythmically structured unity, that is to say its organic form."[10] Langer's description of the comic process is analogous to van Gennep's of rites of initiation and marriage: in both cases the protagonists move from an initial state of equilibrium into a state of disequilibrium, and finally into a new and more complicated state of equilibrium. In comedy or in life the triumph of the protagonists may be short-lived – there is a certain hopeful oversimplification in calling marriage a state of equilibrium – but it is a triumph nonetheless and testifies to man's capacity for renewal and re-creation.

While Langer locates the structure of comedy in fundamental biological rhythms, van Gennep uses the same rhythms to explain the function of rites of passage. Such rites are necessary, he argues, because individuals, like other organisms, experience periodically the need for renewal:

The phenomenon of a *transition* may be noted in many other human activities, and it recurs also in biological activity in general, in the applications of physical energy, and in cosmic rhythms. It is necessary that two movements in opposite directions be separated by a point of inertia, which in mechanics is reduced to a minimum by an eccentric and exists only potentially in circular motion. But, although a body can move through space in a circle at a constant speed, the same is not true of biological or social activities. Their energy becomes exhausted, and they have to be regenerated at more or less close intervals. The rites of passage ultimately correspond to this fundamental necessity, sometimes so closely that they take the form of rites of death and rebirth.[11]

If both rites of passage and comic dramas have their source in man's unity with nature, it is not surprising that they share a common, evolutionary form – a form in which periodic forays into chaos lead to new kinds of integration.

Because of these structural parallels, interpretations of rites of passage are often applicable to comedy as a structure of experience, both for the characters within a play and the audience outside it. For the most part, anthropologists have approached rites of passage, as they have approached all ritual, in terms of their social function.[12] The dominant view, argued forcefully by A. R. Radcliffe-Brown in his influential study of the Andaman Islanders, has been that rituals express and thereby perpetuate the basic values of a society: "the social function of the Andaman Islanders is to maintain and to transmit from one generation to another the emotional dispositions on which the society (as it is constituted) depends for its existence."[13] Although by no means abandoned, this view has been qualified considerably by more recent anthropologists, who have stressed the role of ritual in expressing and resolving, if only partially and temporarily, underlying social tensions and conflicts. Interpreting the social disorder and sexual inversions that characterize marriage rites among the Zulu, for example, Max Gluckman observes that the rites state "in advance the conflicts that will hinge on [the bride's] position, and this statement is believed to bless the marriage."[14] Although Gluckman links this process to Aristotle's conception of catharsis, he admits that we understand very little about how, or to what extent, it works.[15] Instead of ending social conflict, Gluckman suggests, such rituals lead to "temporary truces, and at times conceal the basic conflicts between competitors."[16]

From a sociological perspective, then, rites of passage may be seen as symbolic forms for the perpetuation of social values and for the expression and partial resolution of social tensions and conflicts. Both of these functions seem pertinent to the experience of comedy. In a recent monograph, for example, Monika Vizedom has demonstrated how Gluckman's approach might be applied to a particular set of social tensions with obvious relevance to romantic comedy – those between age and youth. Many rites of passage, Vizedom finds, especially those of initiation and marriage, involve generational conflict. Some, she notes, stress the submission of youth to age, the inviolability of the authority of the elders; others, however, such as the "coming out ceremony" of the Nyakusa, seem to "enact the triumph of youth over age."[17] This conflict between youth and age figures prominently in Northrop Frye's view of comedy: "At the core of most Renaissance comedy, including Shakespeare's, is the formula transmitted by the New Comedy pattern of Plautus and Terence. The normal action is the effort of a young man to get possession of a young woman who is kept from him by various social barriers: her low birth, his minority or shortage of funds, parental opposition, the prior claims of a rival. These are eventually circumvented, and the comedy ends at a point when a new society is crystallized, usually by the marriage or betrothal of hero and heroine."[18]

To view Shakespearean comedy from an exclusively sociological perspective, however, is to miss its most distinctive quality. As Leo Salingar observes, "Shakespeare's great innovation was to treat comedy lyrically as an emotional and imaginative experience, an inward metamorphosis."[19] The obstacles that stand between lovers in most romantic comedy from Terence and Plautus to Dekker and Greene, as Frye observes, are external – if not social, then metaphysical. While parental opposition and the vagaries of Fortune are by no means absent in Shakespearean comedy, the most important obstacles, and those that create the most delightful entanglements, are internal and self-imposed. Egeus, the archetypal *senex* of *A Midsummer Night's Dream*, is no more instrumental in keeping Hermia and Lysander apart than their own folly, exposed in their flight through the wood. And pairs like Rosaline and Berowne, Kate and Petruchio, Beatrice and Benedick, and Orsino and Viola are separated primarily by their own divided minds. In Shakespearean comedy the crucial obstacles are usually psychological, not social or metaphysical.

Rites of passage too have an important psychological dimension, for at their center, at least in initiation and marriage, is not society at large but the individual, in a state of crisis. Hence the sociological perspective dominant in anthropology seems not only insufficient for Shakespearean comedy but, as Gluckman is aware, for rites of initiation and marriage as well. Anthropologists, however, for understandable reasons, have been reluctant psychoanalysts, with the result that the effects of these rites upon the individuals involved, and the needs they fulfill, remain largely unknown and unexplored. Two studies, however, one by the anthropologist Claude Lévi-Strauss, and the other by the psychoanalyst Bruno Bettelheim, offer insights into the psychology of such rites that are suggestive for the experience of comedy in general and Shakespearean comedy in particular.

The rite that Lévi-Strauss "psychoanalyzes" is a curing rite, not a rite of passage, but as Monika Vizedom observes, the process involved seems applicable to other rituals, especially those of initiation.[20] The rite is used by the Cuna Indians of Panama to ease difficulties in childbirth. In the mythology of the tribe, the afflictions are caused by Muu, the "power responsible for the formation of the fetus," who has captured the sick woman's *purba*, or "soul." The cure is effected through a long incantation, sung by a shaman, which tells the story of his struggle to free the woman from Muu's power:

Thus the song expresses a quest: the quest for the lost *purba*, which will be restored after many vicissitudes, such as the overcoming of obstacles, a victory over wild beasts, and, finally, a great contest waged by the shaman and his tutelary spirits against Muu and her daughters, with the help of magical hats whose weight the latter are not able to bear. Muu, once she has been defeated, allows the *purba* of the ailing woman to be discovered and freed. The delivery takes place, and the song ends with a statement of the precautions taken so that Muu will not escape and pursue her visitors.

The woman is cured, then, through a symbolic narrative in which the obstacles that prevent her childbirth are overcome by her physician.

After a lengthy analysis of the symbolism of the narrative, Lévi-Strauss concludes that the psychological dynamics of the rite are analogous to those of traditional psychoanalysis:

In both cases the purpose is to bring to a conscious level conflicts and resistances which have remained unconscious, owing either to their repression by other psychological forces or – in the case of childbirth – to their own specific nature, which is not psychic but organic or even simply mechanical. In both cases also, the conflicts and resistances are resolved, not because of the knowledge, real or alleged, which the sick woman progressively acquires of them, but because this knowledge makes possible a specific experience, in the course of which conflicts materialize in an order and on a level permitting their free development and leading to their resolution.[21]

Lévi-Strauss's psychoanalytic explanation of the Cuna curing rite complements Gluckman's sociological explanation of the Zulu wedding rites. Both center upon the mysterious way in which the symbolic expression of conflict may allay or resolve it; both edge close to a cathartic view of ritual reminiscent of Aristotle's conception of tragedy.

The notion that rites of initiation and marriage might be cathartic, enabling the expression and resolution of psychological conflicts, is not difficult to translate into comic terms.[22] In Shakespeare's comedies, the romantic disorders of the liminal phase – the confusions, betrayals, even the games – reflect the psychological instability that accompanies a transformation of identity. The characters who live through this confusion – at least some of them – not merely bring their conflicts to a conscious level, acknowledging their folly, but seem to purge themselves of them in the process. The kind of experience that Lévi-Strauss describes, as we shall see later, is particularly suggestive for those comedies, like *A Midsummer Night's Dream*, in which the mysterious suspended acceleration of liminal time enables lovers to play out in dream, enchantment, or game the futures they fear. To be betrayed in dream or in sport is in some sense to undergo a catharsis without the tragedy. Perhaps this is why the symbolic expression of conflicts that Gluckman detects in Zulu wedding rites "is believed to bless the marriage."

The most provocative and thorough application of psychoanalysis to rites of passage is that of Bruno Bettelheim in *Symbolic Wounds*, a study of male and female initiation rites. For Bettelheim, these rites fulfill the need of adolescents to express and resolve the conflicts that arise through their envy of the attributes of the opposite sex. Countering a tendency he finds in anthropology to stress the progressive elements in initiation rites, Bettelheim insists upon their ambiguity, their paradoxical conjunction of destruction and creation:

Among anthropologists, initiation rites are considered predominantly progressive phenomena. To the psychoanalyst, they can as easily be considered either regressive or id-motivated. Probably they are all of this. Some parts of the rituals, such as learning tribal customs, may have mainly progressive meanings and accord with ego and super-ego strivings. Others, such as subincision, may be the result of a "regressive" breaking through of pregenital desires and serve mainly to satisfy id strivings. Still others may be both at once.

If, as I believe, man's envy of the other sex is a major factor, the participant may well act out such "regressive" tendencies; but where the ceremonies result in a better adjustment to his own sex role, this constitutes an integrative, progressive aspect.[23]

The regressive tendencies in these rites, according to Bettelheim, return the individual to the undifferentiated sexuality of child-hood, the state of "'polyvalence' in which Jung found the seeds of 'vital spiritual functions'".[24] When initiation rites fulfill their integrative ends, they do so because they enable "an actual or symbolic understanding of the functions of the other sex and a psychological mastery of the emotions they arouse."[25] As we shall see later, Bettelheim's discussion of initiation, particularly of transvestism and other role reversals, illuminates certain features in Shakespeare's treatment of female disguise.

For a final example of the way in which initiatory, comic, and biological structures converge, we might turn to one of the most influential modern handbooks of child psychology. In *Infant and Child in the Culture of Today*, co-authored by Arnold Gesell and Frances L. Ilg, the "fluctuations" in normal child development are described in terms similar to those of van Gennep, Langer, and Bettelheim: "A developmental philosophy sees a manifestation of natural law in these fluctuations. A ship cannot always sail on even keel. It must dip with the waves. The organism of the growing child has comparable ups and downs. It cannot remain in stable balance indefinitely; it may come to relative rest, but then it must again forge ahead. More or less rhythmically it comes into relative equilibrium, passes into disequilibrium, and then returns again to relative equilibrium." Although they make no mention of rites of passage, Gesell and Ilg describe transitions in child development in a manner that recalls the rites defined by van Gennep:

This form of disequilibrium is a transitional phase, during which the organism is creating a new ability or achieving a reorientation of some kind. It is a phase of *innovation*. The child withdraws from his former self, and also somewhat from his environment, as though to gather strength for a forward thrust, which may be so vigorous that it has the appearance of aggression. But even during the aggressive thrust new patterns are being incorporated into the old. A working balance is achieved between the new and the old and presently the organism settles down into a period of relative equilibrium, of assimilation, and of consolidation.[26]

Here we have the familiar pattern of van Gennep – separation, transition, incorporation – expressed in a vocabulary that recalls

Langer's description of comic structure. For mid-twentieth-century American parents, one might say, Gesell and Ilg made it possible to see the chaotic behavior of their children as a comic rite of passage.

Whether seen from a sociological or psychological perspective, then, rites of initiation and marriage seem to be essentially "comic" rites. From one perspective the process involves social conflict and resolution, from the other psychological conflict and resolution. The pattern remains much the same from a religious point of view. Mircea Eliade, who focuses not on marriage but on rites of initiation, finds in the initiatory experience a symbolic movement into chaos that culminates in the creation of a new order.[27] In each case, to adopt Langer's vocabulary, these writers describe a movement from a state of equilibrium into disequilibrium, and then into a new and more complicated equilibrium. Both the ritual and comic structures are dynamic and progressive, precipitating a breakdown of order that creates, paradoxically, the conditions for a more perfect kind of integration. This integration is not always achieved in the same way or to the same extent. In some cases the process can be aborted, leading to psychological regression or social disruption. In others, it can be effected as "mere" ritual, as a series of external signs which have no relation to internal realities. The aim implicit in the rite, however, is a meaningful change in status – a change in which the individual understands and accepts his new role and in which society is renewed by accepting him in it. This too is the aim implicit in the structure of Shakespeare's comedies.

Since Northrop Frye and C. L. Barber have both stressed the relevance of another kind of ritual to the comedies – seasonal or "cyclic group rites," as they are sometimes called[28] – it may be useful to distinguish between the two kinds of structures and their implications. In his *Anatomy of Criticism*, Frye develops analogies between the major literary genres and the seasons of the year and observes in Shakespeare's comedies a pattern derived from seasonal ritual. In *A Natural Perspective*, Frye briefly develops resemblances between Shakespeare's comic structure and three phases of seasonal ritual: a somber and gloomy period of preparation; a period of license; and a period of festivity.[29] More central to my purpose, and more systematic, is the approach of C. L. Barber, whose classic study traces Frye's archetypal pattern to its local habitation in Elizabethan culture in popular seasonal rites such as Twelfth Night, May Day, and Midsummer's Eve. Barber defines the dynamics of these rites, and the plays based upon them, in terms of a movement through "release" to "clarification." In the "festive" comedies, he argues, the experience of release is akin to that of the Saturnalian license that separates holiday from everyday. The clarification that results "is concomitant to the release they dramatise: a heightened awareness of the relation between man and 'nature' – the nature celebrated on holiday."[30]

In many respects, seasonal rites and rites of passage are complementary. The pattern that Barber so brilliantly defines can be translated roughly into that of a rite of passage – the period of release corresponding to the disequilibrium of the liminal phase, the clarification matching the awareness of a new identity that comes with adulthood and marriage. The structure of certain of the Elizabethan festivals that Barber draws upon, moreover, might be easily described to fit van Gennep's tripartite scheme. The Elizabethan rites of May, for example, involve separation – the flight of young couples into the wood; transition – the merriment of gathering hawthorn and indulging in the wooing games appropriate to the season; and incorporation – the decking of the houses and church with hawthorn and the dancing around the Maypole. Seasonal festivals of this kind, in addition, are almost always rites of courtship, as Herrick makes delightfully clear in "Corinna's going a Maying":

> And some have wept, and woo'd, and plighted Troth,
> And chose their Priest, ere we can cast off sloth:
> Many a green-gown has been given;.
> Many a kisse, both odde and even:
> Many a glance too has been sent
> From out the eye, Loves Firmament:
> Many a jest told of the Keyes betraying
> This night, and Locks pickt, yet w'are not a Maying.

The "release" of holiday provides in many cases a setting for the release of love.

Although he does not analyze seasonal rites, van Gennep sees in them the same rhythms that characterize rites of passage: "For groups, as well as for individuals, life itself means to separate and to be reunited, to change form and condition, to die and to be reborn. It is to act and to cease, to wait and rest, and then to begin acting again, but in a different way. And there are always new thresholds to cross: the thresholds of summer and winter, of a season or a year, of a month or a night; the thresholds of birth, adolescence, maturity, and old age; the threshold of death and that of the afterlife – for those who believe in it."[31] For van Gennep, seasonal rituals are to society as a whole what rites of passage are to the individual – a means of effecting a transition from one kind of status to another; like rites of passage, seasonal rites are also based on fundamental biological rhythms. In his study of rituals of rebellion in South-East Africa, Max Gluckman adopts a similar point of view. Breaks in the seasons give rise to rituals of Saturnalian misrule, he argues, because they inevitably bring a period of social instability.[32] In this sense, too, seasonal rites are analogous to rites of passage, which arise at points of transition in the life-cycle of the individual.

Despite these similarities, the two kinds of rites are not identical; nor do they have the same implications if applied to Shakespearean comedy. As van Gennep's description makes clear, seasonal rites are communal; their protagonist is society as a whole. Rites of passage, on the other hand, are both communal and personal; they mark a crisis in the life of an individual and redefine his role in society. Rites of passage, like seasonal rites, might be said to renew the community, but they do so indirectly, through the renewal of the individual or, in marriage, the pair. In rites of passage, the integration of society follows upon the integration of individuals. For this reason, rites of passage take us to the heart of Shakespeare's comedies. As Leo Salingar observes, Shakespeare is not "a recorder of fêtes": "the festive strains in his comedies always subserve or support the theme of love as initiation to marriage."[33]

If we consider the nature of the transitional phase in both kinds of ritual, moreover, further differences emerge. In the seasonal rites that Barber describes, the transitional experience is that of holiday – a period of licensed misrule, in which the cares and responsibilities of daily life are tossed aside. The transitional experience of rites of passage, however, as we have seen in the descriptions of van Gennep and Turner, is of a more paradoxical and ambiguous kind. The disorientations of this phase are often more radical, and more painful, than any we associate with holiday. Circumcision, to take an extreme example, is no rite of

May. Although Barber excludes the darker comedies from his survey, even a play like *A Midsummer Night's Dream*, as we shall see, dramatizes anxieties that strain the metaphor of holiday, making it more appropriate to the experience of the audience than to that of the characters within the play. To account for these disturbing elements, Barber includes within his definition of holiday the destructive and anti-social behavior that often accompanies it but is hardly inevitable – the kind of behavior that characterizes a party run wild. Consider, for example, Barber's view of the lovers' "fierce vexation" in *A Midsummer Night's Dream*: "Shakespeare's young men and maids, like those Stubbes described in May games, 'run gadding over night to the woods, . . . where they spend the whole night in pleasant pastimes' – and in the fierce vexation which often goes with the pastimes of falling in and out of love and threatening to fight about it."[34] While holiday release may provide the occasion for conflict, as Barber observes, the two are not inseparable. In rites of passage, however, as Victor Turner reminds us, "the most characteristic midliminal symbolism is that of paradox, or being *both* this *and* that." In the liminal experience, elements of creation and destruction clash and become confused. It is this paradoxical state of mind, as we shall see, that characterizes the middle phase of Shakespeare's comedies.

Rites of passage, finally, seem more relevant to the comedies than seasonal rites because they are non-recurrent. While seasonal rites return at fixed points in the calendar, rites of passage occur only once in the life of an individual, at a unique point of crisis. Hence the change in status they mark is permanent; once lost, childhood or bachelorhood cannot be regained. To marry, as the Princess shrewdly observes in *Love's Labor's Lost*, is to "make a world-without-end bargain" (V.ii.789). The "clarification," to use Barber's word, that results in seasonal rites may recur, but that of rites of passage is permanent, or at least has permanent consequences. In the comedies, moreover, as in rites of courtship and marriage, whatever clarification occurs illuminates not merely the protagonists' relation to "the nature celebrated on holiday" but to the nature of love. To focus on clarification, indeed, is to blur the ritualistic quality of Shakespeare's comic endings; self-recognition is the first stage in a rite of incorporation that binds lovers to each other and to society, in their new roles as married adults. The dancing, feasting, and betrothing that end the comedies are specifically rites of marriage. In some cases, indeed, marriage occurs without clarification, as in life.

Rites of passage, then, unlike seasonal rites, effect permanent changes in status. They do so, moreover, in ways that seem peculiarly compatible with Shakespeare's comic method. It is conventional to distinguish between tragedy and comedy in terms of characterization: the one genre presents characters who are complex and who change and develop, the other characters who are simple and static. While the distinction holds for most comic playwrights, it oversimplifies Shakespeare. As Leo Salingar observes, Shakespeare's characterization sets his comedies apart: "Shakespeare's characters are not merely capable of being surprised by what happens to them, dismayed or delighted, like the people in Italian comedies; they can be carried out of their normal selves, 'transformed', observe themselves passing into a new phase of experience, so strange that it seems like illusion. This is only part, indeed, of a more fundamental innovation which in its general effect distinguishes Shakespeare's plays from all previous comedies, that he gives his people the quality of an inner life."[35] Shakespeare's tragic protagonists may have more complicated inner lives than his comic protagonists, but the difference is only of degree, not kind. The more useful distinction, for Shakespeare, is one of technique. While the comic protagonists, like their tragic counterparts, are complex and dynamic characters, their psychology is depicted in less straightforward ways. The tragedies take us directly into the minds of the protagonists, through soliloquies and other reflective speeches; the comedies work obliquely, suggesting psychological conflict and development through symbols, such as masks, magic, and dreams. And this is precisely the method of rites of passage.

One of the persistent problems in criticism of the comedies has been an unresponsiveness to the dynamic implications of comic symbols. The problem becomes especially acute in criticism of the most complicated characters, the romantic heroines, who tend to be idealized as static types of human perfection. Rosalind, for example, in *As You Like It*, has been described by different critics as an "ideal woman," a synthesis of "conflicting attitudes of love," an embodiment of "the ideals of love and the values of pastoral," and a "seemingly impossible reconciliation of opposites."[36] While we can recognize something of Rosalind in each of these descriptions, they tend to subordinate her character to an abstract and static idea. Even C. L. Barber's sensitive analysis of Rosalind's role underplays its dynamic qualities, celebrating instead her sustained and "inclusive poise."[37] Rosalind, however, like other romantic heroines, puts on a disguise, a familiar symbol of transition in rites of initiation, and while in disguise, she undergoes a comic ordeal that prepares her for marriage.[38] The ordeal itself, of course, is a familiar feature of courtship. And when Rosalind takes off her disguise she does not return to her everyday role but assumes a new one. Hence the liminal symbolism of rites of passage, as we shall see, may help us to appreciate more fully the dynamics of Shakespeare's comic characterization.

To say that in their structure and symbolic techniques Shakespeare's comedies resemble rites of passage is not to suggest that the plays are themselves rites. As modes of performance, ritual and drama share much in common, but they are not identical, and I do not intend to imply that the presence of a ritual structure or technique transforms drama into rite. Although Shakespeare's comedies may strike one as more ritualistic than Shaw's, they are plays nonetheless: they present rather than re-present actions; they depend upon actors who play rather than become their roles; they work upon their audiences through surprise rather than certainty; they encourage critical detachment as well as emotional involvement.[39] Shakespeare wrote his comedies as plays, not rituals, and the extent to which he was even aware of ritual as a dramatic influence is uncertain.

Why Shakespeare should have developed a distinctive comic structure with such deep affinities to rites of passage is, as Falstaff might say, a "question to be asked." We know so little about Shakespeare as a man and so much about the universality of his appeal that the better part of valor may lie in simply acknowledging the mysterious ability of a great artist to draw upon one of the most potent and universal patterns of human experience[40] – a pattern that seems to have left its mark upon comedy from the very beginning. Yet what lies between even a great artist and archetypes is his culture, and of this questions may be asked. I have thus attempted a historical anthropology, not in the interest of explaining Shakespeare's comedies as the products of Elizabethan society, 'but in the hope of placing them within that society, creating a context of social patterns with which they interact. Shakespeare's comedies do not so much reflect these patterns as re-create them. My aims have much in common with those of Stephen Greenblatt, who in *Renaissance Self-Fashioning* defines his goal as a "poetics of culture." "Such an approach," he observes, "is necessarily a balancing act ... and necessarily impure: its central concerns prevent it from permanently sealing off one type of discourse from another or decisively separating works of art from the minds and lives of their creators and audiences."[41]

In establishing a social context for Shakespeare's comedies, I shall be concerned with patterns of thought and behavior that illuminate their structure – the distinctive ritual structure we have already examined. These social patterns are not to be found in any single Elizabethan rite; nor are they restricted to rites. They include a wide variety of rites, customs, and conventions, all of which figure in the stylized progression from adolescence to adulthood and from courtship to marriage. Although they will be discussed at length in their appropriate contexts, it may be useful to survey the more important practices here. Before doing so, however, we should consider briefly the role of ritual in Elizabethan society, for its centrality helps explain why ritual structures might be likely to inform Elizabethan works of art. To discuss the role of ritual, however, it is first necessary to clarify my use of the term.

Social scientists vary widely in their definitions of "ritual." Some restrict the word to a religious context. Victor Turner, for example, defines ritual as "formal behavior for occasions not given over to technological routine, having reference to beliefs in mystical beings or powers."[42] Others include secular actions; for Jack Goody, ritual is "a category of standardized behavior ... in which the relationship between the means and the end is ... either irrational or non-rational."[43] Still others define ritual not as a limited category of standardized behavior but as an aspect of all standardized behavior – for Edmund R. Leach, the "communicative aspect."[44] Semiotic theorists pursue Leach's line of thought, interpreting the whole of society as a system of signs.[45]

As a starting point for the interpretation of ritual, Leach's definition seems to me the most logical and, in the present context, the most useful. By defining ritual as a mode of communication, however, Leach excludes two other functions that are sometimes equally important – expression and transformation. A private rite may not communicate but may be deeply expressive. A public rite may communicate but also alter an individual's identity, as in a wedding. Hence I define ritual as an aspect of standardized behavior that serves at least one of the following functions – expression, communication, and transformation. The more elaborate kinds of rituals, such as the marriage ceremony, are likely to serve all three.

Perhaps some of the interpretative problems that arise in the study of ritual may become clear with a simple illustration, the making of tea. For one person this elaborately standardized behavior may be merely "technological routine." For this person the boiling of the water just to the size of frog's eyes, the "hotting" of the pot, the steeping of the tea in one place for just the right time, the careful covering of the pot with the tea cozy are important simply because they result in a potable beverage. For another person the action may be important as ritual: it may vent satisfying emotions; it may convey to a companion an atmosphere of ease and well-being; it may make one feel "a new person." Whether one makes tea as "technological routine" or ritual, the beverage may taste better for following a standardized behavior; the difference lies in the explanation. And the explanation may differ from participant to observer: watching someone make tea, we may conclude that although he believes his action is merely technological, the real source of his satisfaction, of which he is unconscious, is its symbolic power.

Since the focus of this study is Shakespeare's comedies and not the role of ritual in Elizabethan society, the difficulties of definition and interpretation need not detain us for long. Some of the social patterns I shall explore, such as weddings, are rites by anyone's definition. Others, such as the female role of coyness in courtship, may seem insufficiently standardized to be called ritual, even though they may fulfill certain ritual functions. Still others, such as the sending out of adolescents, may seem unlike ritual on both counts. For such doubtful cases I shall use the words "custom" or "convention" – words that imply less rigorous formalization than "ritual," and less symbolic significance. It is useful to recognize, however, as Leach's definition makes clear, that custom and ritual are not separate categories of experience but part of a continuum.

Given the broadest definition of the term, all societies become ritualistic — ours as well as Elizabethan. But this is to blur important distinctions. As Mary Douglas has demonstrated, we live in an age which is profoundly hostile to ritual.[46] The word is used almost exclusively in a negative sense, as when we characterize cocktail parties and graduations as social "rituals." To most moderns, it seems, all rituals are empty rituals, meaningless observances of external forms; we lack even a word to express the possibility that a ritual may be full. Hence our sense of shock when a sociologist exposes our ritual behavior — as if our unconscious actions linked us to a primitive past with which we would rather not be associated. Elizabethans were capable of empty rituals, of course, and Elizabethan Puritans were violently anti-ritualistic, but the dominant attitude of the society expressed what Mary Douglas has called "ritualism" — a "heightened appreciation of symbolic action" that is manifested in a "belief in the efficacy of instituted signs" and a "sensitivity to condensed symbols."[47] When Elizabethan men walked a step behind their superiors, they did so not as an instinctive gesture of subordination but as a conscious symbol of their place in the social hierarchy. In Elizabethan culture, unlike our own, ritual was conscious, valued, and pervasive. Such a culture is likely to endow even the minutiae of daily life — what we would call customs or social habits — with symbolic significance.

In his continuation of Marlowe's "Hero and Leander," George Chapman celebrates the goddess Ceremony. "She was all presented to the sence," he writes,

Devotion, Order, State, and Reverence
Her shadowes were; Societie, Memorie;
All which her sight made live, her absence die.

In praising this "all-states-ordering *Ceremonie*," as he calls her, Chapman not only articulates a central Elizabethan value but idealizes a way of life. The whole year was ordered by the daily, weekly, and seasonal rituals of the church. The rituals of Elizabeth's court affected the entire society, either directly or indirectly. Seasonal festivals touched all classes, both rural and urban. Civic pageants, such as the Lord Mayor's procession in London, were important annual events. Schools, universities, and guilds had their own elaborate ceremonies. Rogues and vagabonds celebrated rites of initiation, if we can believe Thomas

Harman's account in *Caveat for Commen Cursetors*; and even if we cannot, the assumption that they should is itself revealing.[48] The decorum of daily life, in speech, gesture, and apparel, enforced by custom in the family but by guild regulation and law in public, gave to common personal relationships some of the qualities of ritual events.

The most important centers of ritual in Elizabethan society were the court and church. Those with access to the court could experience at first hand the ceremonies by means of which Elizabeth cemented her power: the Accession Day tournaments, the royal progresses, the triumphal entries, the celebration of the Order of the Garter, and others. As Roy Strong has argued, many of these rites endowed Elizabeth's rule with something of the mystical potency of the pre-Reformation church:

> The cult of Gloriana was skilfully created to buttress public order and, even more, deliberately to replace the pre-Reformation externals of religion, the cult of the Virgin and saints with their attendant images, processions, ceremonies and secular rejoicing. So instead of the many aspects of the cult of Our Lady, we have the "several loves" of the Virgin Queen; instead of the rituals and festivities of Corpus Christi, Easter or Ascensiontide, we have the new fêtes of Elizabeth's Accession Day and birthday.[49]

A particularly striking instance of Elizabeth's ability to tap the emotional power of ritual, at least for my purposes, centered on the mystique of marriage rather than virginity. In February 1559, being urged by Parliament to marry, Elizabeth reportedly reminded her audience that she already had a husband:

> Yea, to satisfie you, I have already joyned my self in Marriage to an Husband, namely, the Kingdom of England. And behold (said she, which I marvell ye have forgotten,) the Pledge of this my Wedlock and Marriage with my Kingdom. (And therewith she drew the Ring from her Finger, and shewed it, wherewith at her Coronation she had in a set form of words solemnly given her self in Marriage to her Kingdom).[50]

Her subjects, Elizabeth went on to say, were the children of this marriage.

As the ritual of politics became more prominent, it seems, that of religion became more problematic. The continuing controversies of the sixteenth century among Catholics, Anglicans, and Puritans resulted in radically different attitudes and practices. At one extreme were the Catholics, who stressed the efficacy of the sacraments and the value of ritual in drawing people together in the worship of God. In *A Catechisme or Christian Doctrine* (1599), Lawrence Vaux states the typical Catholic position: "It is therefore first to bee knowen, that no company of men canne meete together in one minde and consent of heart, for the true service of God, except they have certaine holy signes, whereby both their worshippe towards GOD may be stirred up, and the profession thereof towards their Neighbour may be seene."[51] At the other extreme were the Puritans, whose objections towards ritual culminated in the pronouncements of *A Directory for the Publique Worship of God*, published in 1644 as a result of the Westminster Assembly. The *Directory*'s instructions for funeral services are representative: "When any person departeth this life, let the dead body, upon the day of Buriall, be decently attended from the house to the place appointed for Publique Buriall, and there immediately interred, without any Ceremony."[52] The Anglicans struggled to define a middle ground, retaining many of the Catholic ceremonies but only two of the seven sacraments, and upholding the value of ritual against the Puritans, but with an apologetic and defensive attitude. The *Book of Common Prayer* (1559) explains that certain Catholic ceremonies have been preserved in the Anglican service because "without some ceremonies it is not possible to keep any order or quiet discipline in the Church";[53] nothing is said of the capacity of ritual to stir up emotion or fuse people into a spiritual community.

These divergences in the theory and practice of the age's most important ritual, that of the Church, had far-reaching consequences, the most notable being civil war. One would like to know something of the subtler effects, however – whether, for example, the decorum of family life differed significantly in Catholic, Anglican, and Puritan households. But the history of ritual in the period is beyond my scope. One thing seems certain, however: controversy made ritual highly self-conscious. Consider, for example, the habit of mind reflected in William Harrison's account of Anglican worship in 1577. As he describes the liturgy, Harrison is constantly deflected by the controversies that surround it:

After Morning Prayer also we have the Litany and Suffrages, an invocation in mine opinion not devised without the great assistance of the spirit of God, although many curious, mind-sick persons utterly condemn it as superstitious and savoring of conjuration and sorcery.

This being done, we proceed unto the Communion, if any communicants be to receive the Eucharist; if not, we read the Decalogue, Epistle and Gospel, with the Nicene Creed (of some in derision called the "dry communion"), and then proceed unto an homily or sermon ...[54]

This kind of self-consciousness was pronounced in the period and had been building since the Reformation; the rapid alternations between Catholic and Anglican ceremonies at mid-century must have been particularly dizzying. As late as 1581, when Anglicanism was firmly established, one Christopher Smyth of Pateley Bridge in Yorkshire, clearly a local wit, was ordered to make a declaration of penance: he had sold a New Testament in the Tyndale translation for ten shillings, to be paid "when masse shal be said within this realme."[55] The extent to which this self-consciousness towards religious ritual affected secular ritual is an intriguing and open question.

With the ascendancy of Puritanism in the seventeenth century, a nostalgia for a ritualistic past is often poignantly expressed. In *Pasquil's Palinodia* (1619), for example, the Maypole is celebrated as a symbol of a communal spirit that no longer exists:

> Happy the age, and harmlesse were the dayes,
>   (For then true love and amity was found,)
> When every village did a May-pole raise,
>   And *Whitson-ales* and *May-games* did abound:
> And all the lusty Yonkers in a rout,
> With merry Lasses daunc'd the rod about,
> Then friendship to their banquets bid the guests,
> And poore men far'd the better for their feasts.[56]

When the Puritans drastically simplified the procedure for marriage by substituting a brief civil declaration for a religious ceremony, most people, according to Godfrey Davies, arranged a religious ceremony anyway. Davies cites the case of Sir James Halkett and Anne Murray, who were married both by civil and religious ceremony; of her wedding, Lady Anne writes, "if itt had nott beene done more solemnly afterwards by a minister I should nott [have] beleved it lawfully done."[57] Even the Puritans themselves were susceptible to this nostalgia. As David E. Stannard has shown, the early settlers of New England conducted their funerals in the manner prescribed by the *Directory*, "without any Ceremony," but as the century wore on "increasing numbers of Puritan funerals were conducted with an air of elaborate and formal ritual."[58]

Thus, if Shakespeare lived in a ritualistic culture, in which ceremony gave conscious shape even to the reflexes of daily life, he also lived in a culture in which the role of ritual was becoming increasingly problematic, even to the point of fragmenting the very community it should have sustained. A concern with the power of ritual, both positive and negative, runs throughout Shakespeare's plays. While the comedies, for the most part, use ritual to celebrate personal and social concord, the histories and tragedies link it to division and destruction. In *1 Henry VI* the Wars of the Roses begin with the paradox of an invented ritual, as Yorkists and Lancastrians choose their emblems in the Temple Garden. In *Richard II*, Richard creates his own rite of deposition. In *Henry V*, Henry rails against the "idol Ceremony"(IV.i.240). King Lear, having ceremonially yielded the power of his office, attempts in vain to keep its ceremonial attributes – "the name, and all th'addition to a king" (I.i.136). And both Brutus and Othello struggle to justify murder as ceremony, killing those they love as sacrifices to a noble cause. Ritual is not only a mode of action in Shakespeare's plays, but a continuing human need, explored in all its ramifications. Ritual structures were deeply embedded in Shakespeare's imagination.

Of all the rituals that touched Elizabethans on a regular basis, the most prominent and elaborate, with the exception of weekly attendance at church, were rites of passage – birth, marriage, and death. Birth was celebrated in three stages: the delivery of the infant, baptism, and the churching of the mother. Although the entire sequence can be considered a rite of passage for both infant and mother, each stage had its own tripartite structure. The delivery included the use of various lucky charms, such as eagle-stone, to ease the process; the participation not only of a midwife but of numerous "gossips"; and the husband's provision of a modest feast, the so-called "groaning cake" and cheese. The ceremony of baptism included the more formal and public rituals of naked immersion of the infant; the anointing with "chrism" oil; the wrapping in the "chrism" cloth; the presentation of gifts, such as plate, gilt spoons, or christening shirts; and a christening feast. The churching of the woman began with her period of confinement, which was followed by gifts of new clothes, attendance at a special church service, and a feast. When one considers the average number of births in an Elizabethan household, and the fragility of early life, the expense lavished on these rites is astonishing. In 1642, to take a striking example, Ralph Josselin, a Puritan clergyman (and therefore unlikely to indulge in ritualistic excesses), spent six pounds, thirteen shillings, and fourpence on the baptism of his daughter Mary – roughly ten percent of his annual salary.[59]

Death too was observed with elaborate ceremonies, not only in the funerals of the great, like that of Sir Philip Sidney, but in those of ordinary people. In the deathbed scenes so important in the period, dying itself became a ritual act, with the protagonist conducting his own rite of passage – settling his last affairs, blessing his family and friends, and reconciling himself to God. Once death occurred, the corpse was bathed, embalmed, wrapped in a winding sheet, and placed in a coffin. The funeral procession, often a pageant among the nobility, included mourners and pallbearers in prescribed attire, musicians playing dirges, and the coffin itself, decorated with herbs and flowers. The procession stopped at the church for the funeral service, and then continued to the grave, where the last rites were conducted. This ceremony too ended with a feast.

The rites of marriage were curiously parallel to those of death and involved the preparation of the protagonists, an elaborate procession, a church service, a return procession, and a feast. Since these rites will be discussed later, there is no need to recount them here. It might be useful, however, to pause over one of the rare documents of the period that describes courtship and marriage practices, for it illuminates more fully than any other their ritualistic nature. In his farming and account books for 1641, Henry Best, a Yorkshire farmer, describes in great detail "our fashions att our country weddinges":

Usually the younge mans father, or hee himselfe, writes to the father of the maid, to knowe if hee shall bee welcome to the howse, if hee shall have his furtherance if hee come in such a way, or howe hee liketh of the notion; then if hee pretend any excuse, onely thankinge him for his good will, then that is as good as a denyall. If the motion bee thought well of, and imbraced, then the younge man goeth perhapps twice, to see howe the mayd standeth affeckted; then if hee see that shee bee tractable, and that her inclination is towards him, then the third time that hee visiteth, hee perhapps giveth her a tenne shillinge peece of gold, or a ringe of that price; or perhapps a twenty shillinge peece, or a ringe of that price; then the next time, or next after that, a payre of gloves of 6s. 8d. or 10s. a payre; and after that, each other time, some conceited toy or novelty of less value. They visite usually every three weekes or a moneth, and are usually halfe a yeare, or very neare, from the first goinge to the conclusion. Soe soone as the younge folkes are agreed and contracted, then the father of the mayd carryeth her over to the younge mans howse to see howe they like of all, and there doth the younge mans father meete them to treate of a dower, and likewise of a joynture or feoffment for the woman; and then doe they allsoe appointe and sette downe the day of marriage, which may perhapps bee aboute a fortnight or three weekes after, and in that time doe they gette made the weddinge cloathes, and make provision against the weddinge dinner, which is usually att the mayds fathers. Theyre use is to buy gloves to give to each of theire freinds a payre on that day; the man should bee att the cost for them; but sometimes the man gives gloves to the men, and the woman to the women, or else hee to her friends and shee to his; they give them that morninge when they are allmost ready to goe to church to be marryed. Then soe soone as the bride is tyred, and that they are ready to goe forth, the bridegroome comes, and takes her by the hand, and sayth, "*Mistris, I hope you are willinge,*" or else kisseth her before them, and then followeth her father out of the doores; then one of the bridegroome his men ushereth the bride, and goes foremost; and the rest of the younge men usher each of them a mayd to church. The bridegroome and the brides brothers or freinds tende att dinner; hee perhapps fetcheth her hoame to his howse aboute a moneth after, and the portion is paide that morninge that she goes away. When the younge man comes to fetch away his bride, some of his best freinds, and younge men his neighbours, come alonge with him, and others perhapps meete them in the way, and then is there the same jollity att his howse, for they perhapps have love[?] wine ready to give to the company when they light, then a dinner, supper, and breakfast next day.[60]

By any standards, this is an elaborate ritual. Peter Laslett's comment is to the point: "It sounds rather like the marriage rites which anthropologists record of alien societies . . ."[61] The ritual may have been less elaborate elsewhere, and the details no doubt varied according to local custom, but there is no evidence to show that Yorkshire fashions were themselves alien to the English of the late sixteenth and early seventeenth century. If such behavior was pervasive, it is easy to see how a ritual pattern might be absorbed into Shakespeare's comedies of courtship.

Like most anthropological accounts, Henry Best's raises as many questions as it answers. The most glaring omission, from my point of view, is of any reference to the emotions of the protagonists. What did these couples say to each other during their ritual visits? What did they feel? Did these "gloves of 6s. 8d. or 10s. a payre" represent merely the coarse values of the market-place, as the careful noting of prices implies, or is it possible that they were love tokens as well, expressive of increasing affection?

What is the connection between prescribed ritual and personal feeling? Or, to extend the question, could arranged marriages accommodate romantic love? These questions have no easy answers, and this study will be much concerned with them. We know what courting couples might have said and felt, for the plays and poems of the period articulate the emotions of courtship with wonderful clarity and variety, but what they *did* say and feel survives only in tantalizing fragments. One wonders whether the young men of Henry Best's village wrote sonnets. But even that convention carries no guarantee of genuine feeling.

The most recent study of love and marriage in the period is that of Lawrence Stone, *The Family, Sex and Marriage in England, 1500–1800*. In Stone's view there is virtually no connection in Elizabethan England between literature and life, ritual and emotion, and love and marriage:

Until romanticism temporarily triumphed in the late eighteenth century, there was thus a clear conflict of values between the idealization of love by some poets, playwrights and the authors of romances on the one hand, and its rejection as a form of imprudent folly and even madness by all theologians, moralists, authors of manuals of conduct, and parents and adults in general. Everyone knew about it, some experienced it, but only a minority of young courtiers made it a way of life, and even they did not necessarily regard it as a suitable basis for life-long marriage.[62]

While there is a good deal of truth in this generalization, and in Stone's view generally, it is open to several objections. If by "love" Stone means sexual passion, it would be hard to find poets and playwrights who idealized it or, presumably, young people who did not experience it; both poets and moralists, on the other hand, idealized affection as the basis of marriage. That many men and women were afflicted by the symptoms of romantic love is clear from Richard Napier's descriptions of his troubled patients; their tales, according to Michael MacDonald, "make nonsense of historians' confident assertions that romantic love was rare in seventeenth-century England or that it was unimportant in choosing marital partners."[63] While it is true that many marriages were not based on love of any kind, it is important to recognize that arranged marriages do not necessarily preclude love, either before or after marriage. Implicit throughout Stone's survey, moreover, is the assumption that the rites of courtship and marriage, which center on professions of love, are devoid of emotions, except perhaps those aroused by prospects of status or wealth; in the course of his study, Stone never analyzes a single wedding. Finally, Stone's divorce between literature and life – in the present case, between a popular drama and its audience – is difficult to sustain. Admittedly, the relations are oblique and complex, but they must be acknowledged.

Although central to this study, Elizabethan rites of courtship and marriage are not my only concern; adolescent customs and conventions are also important. The details of these adolescent patterns will emerge later, but it may be useful at the outset to sketch their outlines. We will explore a wide range of ritualistic behavior in the lives of young Elizabethans from roughly the ages of twelve to twenty-six. This is the period of Elizabethan adolescence, and of adolescent love.

For the majority of Elizabethan boys and girls of all social classes, a dramatic separation occurred between the ages of twelve and fourteen, when they were sent away from their families to school, university, apprenticeship, domestic service, or training of various kinds in other households.[64] With the exception of periodic visits, this exile, if we can call it that, never ended, for its culmination was adulthood – marked in most cases by marriage and the formation of an independent household. As Keith Thomas observes, "marriage was the surest test of adult status and on it hinged crucial differences in wages, dress, and economic independence."[65]

Although no formal rites other than marriage conferred adulthood in Elizabethan society, adolescence was characterized by a variety of ritualistic practices. Both schooling and apprenticeship had many of the traditional features of initiation rites: hazing, special codes of dress and behavior, tests to determine admission to full status in the society, which for apprentices could not occur before the age of twenty-four. An ordinance of the Salters' Company of London in 1560–61 suggests the extent to which apprenticeship fulfilled the conditions of a liminal experience. Although all members of the craft were subjected to similar regulations, those directed at apprentices were the most severe. Masters were forbidden to "suffer their apprentices to swear or blaspheme the name of God, to haunt evil women, schools of fence or dancing, carding, bowling, tennis play or other unlawful games, to resort to taverns or alehouses (except about their masters' business) to wear any ruffs on their shirts, nor in their hosen any other colour cloth than white, russet, watchet, or blue, and to be made plain without any welts, guards, or cuts, and to have no manner of silk in or upon their hosen. The apprentice who obstinately offends to be scourged in our Hall."[66] The ritual function of the apprentice's costume is suggested by Edmund Bolton's description in the *Cities Advocate*. The apprentice, says Bolton, wears a "flat round cap, hair close-cut, narrow falling band, coarse side coat, close hose, cloth stockings, and the rest of that severe habit [which] was in antiquity, not more for thrift and usefulness, than for distinction and grace, and were originally arguments or tokens of vocation or calling."[67] Plays like *The Shoemaker's Holiday*, with its celebration of the special language, customs and camaraderie of a proud London company, suggest something of the liminal quality of an apprentice's life.

Scholars have approached both Elizabethan schooling and apprenticeship as initiatory phenomena from a variety of perspectives. Steven R. Smith has examined London apprenticeship as an adolescent fraternity.[68] Bernard Capp has argued for the existence of loosely organized youth groups.[69] Keith Thomas has analyzed rites of misrule in schools.[70] Walter J. Ong has suggested that the study of Latin fulfilled all of the requirements of a traditional male initiation rite.[71] For my purposes, the most important adolescent custom will be one of the subtlest and most pervasive: the practice of imitation, which affected all behavior, from the learning of Latin to pursuit of war. It is in this context, I hope to show, that we can best appreciate the initiatory "role-playing" of Shakespeare's adolescent lovers.

Adolescence was governed by Venus, according to Elizabethans, and customs of initiation and courtship overlapped. The conventional behavior of young men, as we shall see – the writing of sonnets, wearing of love-locks, posturing in romantic attitudes – fulfills many of the conditions of a liminal experience, both in Elizabethan society and in the comedies. The same is true of the conventional courting behavior of young women. To be "coy," as was expected of a young woman, was in many ways to play a role like that of Shakespeare's disguised heroines. The culmination of this phase of adolescent and romantic misrule, in society as in the comedies, was a rite of incorporation – marriage.

In devising his comedies, Shakespeare did not imitate a particular rite or even a prescribed pattern of adolescent or romantic behavior. The most meaningful social contexts for his comic structure are diverse and wide-ranging. Yet within this diversity a ritual pattern is discernible. The society as a whole was profoundly ritualistic; some of its most prominent ceremonies were rites of passage; courtship and marriage were conducted with especially elaborate rituals; and many of the customs and conventions of adolescent life fulfilled the conditions of rites of separation and transition. If behind these cultural phenomena we can perceive the shadow of a rite of passage, it was Shakespeare who gave it substance as a comic form. In responding to tendencies within his culture, and within the comic conventions he inherited, Shakespeare created a pattern distinctively his own, but one in which his age could recognize a displaced and refined image of itself. Such an art combines the mirror and the lamp.

In considering Shakespeare's relation to his society, it is important to remember that art not only draws upon social patterns but helps create them; life, as the inverted cliché goes, imitates art. In *The Family, Sex and Marriage*, Lawrence Stone suggests that the experience of romantic love was rare in the early sixteenth century and that marriages were generally impersonal affairs, arranged by kin and determined by the motives of the market-place. By the end of the seventeenth century, he argues, love became increasingly important as a basis for marriage and the right of choice of a partner increasingly available. If a general shift of this kind took place during the seventeenth century, as seems likely, it is reasonable to assume that the poets and dramatists who celebrated a romantic conception of marriage were at least partly responsible.[72] When Edmund Spenser concluded his sonnet sequence with an epithalamium, he gave unique poetic expression to what later became social convention. No other Elizabethan sonnet sequence depicts the confusions, exhilarations, and torments of romantic love as a stage en route to a happy marriage. Spenser, one might say, although no adolescent, saw in his own love affair a comic rite of passage.

It was Shakespeare, however, more than any other writer, who developed the myth of romantic marriage that has survived, though today in fragments, since the seventeenth century. And he achieved this by depicting courtship as a period of disorientation similar to a rite of transition – a nerve-racking, potentially dangerous, chaotic, but ultimately re-creative time out of which may emerge the form and meaning of marriage. In doing so, Shakespeare drew upon a ritual pattern not only implicit in Elizabethan culture but explicit in cultures of which he was not aware. To apprehend this pattern is not to comprehend Shakespearean comedy; the form is too rich and varied, fortunately, to be schematized successfully. To explore the plays in relation to rites of passage, however, may make us more sensitive to their dominant rhythms and to the paradoxical combination of uniqueness and universality in Shakespeare's art. Perhaps it may even enrich our laughter.

2

Separations

"And what should I do in Illyria?"

(*TN* I.ii.3)

Viola's first words in *Twelfth Night* are "What country, friends, is this?" When the sea captain replies that she is in Illyria, she asks, "And what should I do in Illyria?/ My brother he is in Elysium" (I.ii.1–4). Shipwrecked, separated from her brother, confronted with an unfamiliar landscape, Viola feels exposed, vulnerable, and, although among friends, alone. The pathos in her predicament is only lightly touched, for there is good hope of Sebastian's return, but her sense of loss and alienation casts a momentary shadow upon the play, deepening and enriching its comic tone. Not all of Shakespeare's comic protagonists are cast upon strange shores. Yet something like Viola's experience is common. Moments of intense estrangement – sometimes lyrical, sometimes farcical – provide some of the comedies' most haunting images: of Antipholus of Syracuse entering Ephesus; of Rosalind or Orlando entering Arden; of Julia leaving Verona in pursuit of Proteus; of Kate being snatched away from her own wedding; of Benedick losing himself while in a garden, alone. The first stage of the comic experience for Shakespeare's protagonists is often a state of mind akin to that induced in traditional rites of separation – of disruption and disorientation.

This kind of estrangement is of course not unique to Shakespearean comedy; separations are the stock in trade of romance. Nor can we say that Elizabethans were uniquely susceptible to their appeal, for the popularity of romance spans continents and centuries. If the motif is not unique to Shakespeare, however, it is at least distinctive, for no other comic dramatist turns to it so consistently or achieves through it such rich psychological effects. And although not uniquely Elizabethan, the romantic appeal of separations may have been accentuated by certain characteristically Elizabethan social customs, to which Shakespeare seems to have been peculiarly responsive.

33

The physical reality underlying all rites of separation, van Gennep argues, is a literal movement from one place to another.[1] Spatial dislocation may be cause or effect or symbol of psychic dislocation. To leave one's home is to lose oneself; to enter a secluded hut, a sacred place in the forest, or even the home of one's prospective in-laws is to be temporarily estranged. The experience of disorientation is familiar and universal; rites of passage give it shape and coherence, making it part of a dynamic social process. In their least traumatic form, as in the ceremonial visits of courtship, rites of separation announce a change of status; in their most, as in the circumcisions or symbolic deaths of initiation, they dramatize an irreparable break with the past. In *Twelfth Night*, Viola does not die but fears she has lost her twin.

It is not difficult to discover in Elizabethan conventions of adolescence and courtship resemblances to rites of separation, as we have seen in Chapter 1. Boys who became apprentices not only signed contracts for seven years and left their families but endured stringent restrictions on dress and behavior; to become an apprentice, after all, was to enter a "mystery." The young men of Henry Best's Yorkshire village courted by visiting their young women "every three weekes or a moneth" for the six months or so "from the first goinge to the conclusion."[2] These visits, like those to fairs or festivals that also provided settings for love, occurred in a time and place set apart.

As a context for Shakespeare's comedies, however, the most important separations in Elizabethan society are the most inclusive and perhaps least ritualistic – the actual departures from home that marked the entry into adolescence. One of the most striking features of Elizabethan domestic life, and one with profound but uncertain implications for the entire social structure, was the custom of sending out young boys and girls at about the age of puberty. The evidence for this practice, though fragmentary, is not in doubt, and it suggests that for the roughly twelve years of adolescence about two-thirds of Elizabethan boys and three-quarters of the girls, of all social classes, lived away from home. Since the end of adolescence was usually marked by marriage, at which point the couples established their own households, this meant that most young people left their homes early in their teens and, except for visits, never returned. For boys, the most common options, depending on social rank, included apprenticeship, school or university, the inns of court, travel, or service abroad; for girls, domestic service at various social levels and, occasionally, further education.[3] This custom stretched back into the middle ages and attracted considerable attention during the sixteenth century. The shock expressed by an Italian visitor to England in about 1500 suggests that such treatment of adolescents was not common in Europe at the time:

The want of affection in the English is strongly manifested towards their children; for after having kept them at home till they arrive at the age of 7 or 9 years at the utmost, they put them out, both males and females, to hard service in the houses of other people, binding them generally for another 7 or 9 years. And these are called apprentices, and during that time they perform all the most menial offices; and few are born who are exempted from this fate, for every one, however rich he may be, sends away his children into the houses of others, whilst he, in return, receives those of strangers into his own. And on inquiring their reason for this severity, they answered that they did it in order that their children might learn better manners. But I, for my part, believe that they do it because they like to enjoy all their comforts themselves, and that they are better served by strangers than they would be by their own children.[4]

If the English and Italians treated their adolescents as differently as this reaction suggests, it may help explain the virulence of English protests against their youths travelling in Italy. Underlying the expressed fears of lechery, idolatry, and machiavellism – epitomized in Ascham's discourse on the proverb, "an Englishman Italianate is the devil incarnate"[5] – may have been more general anxieties concerning an Italian permissiveness in the treatment of youth.

In the seventeenth century the practice of sending out adolescents seems equally widespread. Ralph Josselin's diary provides an instructive account of how it affected a single family. A Puritan clergyman who eventually became a man of some substance, Josselin had seven children who survived into their teens – two boys and five girls. The family lived in Earls Colne, a town in Essex, northwest of Colchester. The two boys were both bound apprentice in London at the age of fifteen. Of the girls, three were sent off to further their education – in Colchester, White Colne, and Bury St Edmunds respectively; two were ten years old when they left, the other thirteen. The remaining two girls were bound as servants in London – one at thirteen, the other at fourteen. Although they visited their parents frequently after leaving home, none of the children returned to stay. The absence from home naturally affected marriage arrangements, for although Josselin believed firmly in exercising parental authority in the choice of a spouse, in practice he had little more than veto power, if that; each of the girls initiated her own marriage, securing parental approval through betrothal visits at home. The two boys altered the pattern: when Thomas was twenty-three, his father "made mocons [motions] in a match for him," whether independently or at his request is unclear; and John married without even his father's knowledge.[6]

The scarcity of autobiographical accounts in the period makes it difficult to feel one's way inside this custom, to translate it from a statistical into an experiential reality, but a few case histories may be helpful. Simon Forman, for example, had a remarkably unsettled, but not untypical, childhood. At eight he was boarded out for his education at Wilton, not far from his home. At nine he was transferred to the free school in the Close at Salisbury, where he spent two years, boarding with a Mr Hawknight. While Simon was at home for the Christmas holidays in 1563, at the age of eleven, his father died. Convinced that his mother disliked him, Simon apprenticed himself at fourteen to Matthew Commin of Salisbury, signing for ten years instead of the usual seven on the condition that three be spent at the local grammar school. Although he learned several trades of Commin, who was generally a sympathetic master, Simon never attended the grammar school. Because of this breach of their agreement, and because of an altercation with Mrs Commin, Simon left after only six and a half years, moving on to become a schoolmaster and, at twenty-one, a poor scholar at Oxford.

Forman's journal, in which he refers to himself by name, records a fascinating account of a flirtation with a neighborhood girl while he was serving as Commin's apprentice:

There was a man of good reputation and wealth that dwelt not far from Simon's master, that had a proper fine maiden to his only daughter: which, being younger than Simon, loved Simon wonderful well and would surely see him once a day, or else she would be sick. Often she would come to Simon's master and entreat him very kindly on holy days that she might see him or speak with him, and sometimes to go to pastimes with her. She loved him so well that, if forty youth were at play before the door, in a spacious place that there was, if Simon were not among them she would not be there. But, if he were there, none could keep her from thence. If Simon stood by his master or

mistress at the door, she would come and stand by him, and would not go
from him till necessity did compel.

Simon's master, well perceiving the great affection of the gentlewoman
towards Simon, would often say unto her, "Mistress Anne, ye love my boy
well, methinks." And she would answer, "Yea, forsooth. If it will please you
to give him leave to go run with us, we shall give you thanks, sir." Whereupon
oftentimes he would give him leave. As for Simon, he loved her not but in
kindness. But because she was so kind to Simon, he would do anything he
could do for her. And this love on her side lasted long, as hereafter shall be
showed.[7]

The mixing of social classes, the openness of the young girl, the
relative freedom of the pair under the sympathetic eye of the
master, the opportunities for pastimes and play, all convey an
impression of Elizabethan adolescence at odds with modern
stereotypes. It must be admitted, however, that the young girl's
aggressiveness finally undid her, for as an adult in London she
entered into less innocent relations with her childhood
apprentice.

Thomas Whythorne grew up a generation earlier than Forman,
but his adolescence followed a similar pattern. Born in 1528,
Whythorne left home at the age of ten to live with an uncle in
Oxford who promised to treat him as his own son. At Oxford
Whythorne studied music for six years in Magdalen School,
entering the College at the age of sixteen in 1544. Shortly before
the end of the year, however, his uncle died, and Thomas set off
for London, where he was engaged as servant and scholar to John
Heywood. After serving Heywood for about three years, he took
a chamber in London and determined to "live of my self by
teaching in such sort as I had learned of him."[8] During this period,
as Whythorne relates in his autobiography, he struggled valiantly
to keep his mind off women, but with little success. Like Forman,
he had his adolescent flirtations. The first of many girls to thrust
herself upon him was a servant in a household where he gave
music lessons. Smitten by Whythorne's charms, she hid a love
poem in his gittern. The romance was short-lived, however, for the
unfortunate girl was discovered by her master and mistress and
promptly discharged. We shall return to some of Whythorne's
other amorous adventures in a later chapter. In the case of both
Forman and Whythorne, we can perceive a similar pattern: early
separation from home and family, complicated by the death of a
parent or protector, and an adolescence characterized by a

mixture of servitude and sturdy independence, with occasional interludes of amorous intrigue. That both men encountered aggressive girls may tell us something about Elizabethan sexual relations (and Shakespeare's comic heroines), or merely about the vanity of autobiographers, or both.

Although commonplace, these separations of adolescents from their families seem to have carried considerable emotional weight. In his diary, for example, Ralph Josselin charts anxiously the early days of his son Tom's apprenticeship. On May 25, 1659, father and son departed together for London:

I and my sonne being Wednesday in Whitsonweeke sett forward for London[.] wee had sweet shoures before and so coole but dry riding all the way wee came safe to London 26. on Thursday that afternoone Tom at Mr Jo. Cresseners putt on his blew apron . . . . my son is to serve 8. yeares his time will expire. May. 1: 1667. In a good time I hope the lord sparing his life, lord make him like Joseph a blessing to his Master and bee thou his blessing and portion.

The special notice of the "blew apron" and the solemn blessing suggest the extent to which this journey from Earls Colne to London took on for father and son the significance of a rite of passage. Tom returned to his father after two weeks, with smallpox, but with signs of other troubles as well. On June 10 Josselin notes that he is "amazed in spirit about Thomas not liking at London," and on June 16 he records his reaction to stories of Tom's behavior there: "Heard so much of Toms foolishness at London, that cutt my heart, Lord for, through Christ lay in principles into his spirit, let his life bee a mercy not a crosse to us."[9] Although he did not return to London until November, Tom apparently served out the remainder of his apprenticeship without major crises; he continues to be mentioned in the diary but never again with the same anxiety.

Less direct but equally powerful evidence for the emotional effects of such separations occurs in literary sources. In *The Truth of Our Times* (1638), Henry Peacham laments the plight of the numerous orphans of the time, who are commonly sent away from their native villages to

populous Citties, and publicke places, whither they are constrayned at fourteene or fifteene yeeres of age to come up with a silly Countrey-carrier, and some small summe of money (the benevolence of friends) to beare their charges, to seeke services and meanes of living; where they know no body, neither are they knowne of any; being left as poore chickens having lost their

Mother Hen, and defender, unable to protect themselves, to the mercilesse mercy of a most cruell and pittilesse Age: wherein besides they are in danger, through want and necessity to be seduced to lewd and ill courses, and as the Wise man saith, *To seeke death in the errour of their lives.*[10]

The connection between literal and metaphoric wandering, between erring and error, as we shall see later, is implicit in many of the comedies. A much earlier source, Vives' *The Office and Duetie of an Husband* (c.1553), captures the effect of adolescent separations on whole families with a single poignant observation. Arguing that relations between husbands and wives are closer than any others in a family, Vives describes the disruption caused by sending out children: "The father dothe labour and taketh paine for his children, but sildome the children for theyr fathers, and often tymes thei are sent to inhabite and dwel in other mens houses wherby in a maner it appeareth that their strayte and faste societe doth dissolve and break."[11]

Although evidence is sparse, it seems likely, given the high degree of ritualism in Elizabethan society, that the dissolving and breaking of these familial bonds would have been marked by ceremonies – by rites of separation. Shakespeare's depictions of formal leave-takings depend upon an audience appreciative of the conventional behavior dictated by such occasions. In *Hamlet*, Polonius attempts to compress a lifetime of maxims into the few moments of his farewell to Laertes, while Laertes follows suit in his warnings to Ophelia. In *Two Gentlemen of Verona* Launce mimics his own ceremonious departure from his family, acting it out with shoes, staff, hat, and his dog, Crab, as props:

Now come I to my father: 'Father, your blessing.' Now should not the shoe speak a word for weeping; now should I kiss my father; well, he weeps on. Now come I to my mother. O that she could speak now like a wood woman! Well, I kiss her; why, there 'tis; here's my mother's breath up and down. Now come I to my sister; mark the moan she makes. Now the dog all this while sheds not a tear, nor speaks a word; but see how I lay the dust with my tears. (II.iii.23–32)

Launce's mixture of rigidly conventional behavior, great personal emotion, and comic incongruity captures wonderfully the emotional complexity of such ceremonial occasions. Only his dog is so inhuman as to be immune to ceremony; like Proteus, who leaves Julia vowing to remain true but later betrays her, Crab is "the unkindest tied that ever any man tied" (line 38).

The reasons for the English custom of sending out adolescents have prompted considerable speculation from at least the time of the Italian visitor in 1500, but they remain obscure. In some cases the motive may have been economic, but money alone cannot explain the system. Sixteenth-century comments, like that recorded by the Italian visitor, suggest that the custom fulfilled the desire of parents to provide more discipline for their children than they would get at home. The harassed father of the prodigal son in a mid-century morality play, *The Disobedient Child*, vows in frustration that never again will he allow children of his "at home with me to tarry;/ They should not be kept thus under my wing,/ And have all that which they desire . . ."[12] In *A Mirrhor mete for all Mothers* (1579), Thomas Salter makes the same point: parents should not educate their children at home, for they are too often "blynded by affection."[13] In his study of Puritan New England, *The Puritan Family*, Edmund S. Morgan takes these contemporary explanations at face value: "Puritan parents did not trust themselves with their own children . . . they were afraid of spoiling them by too great affection."[14] In a more recent study, *The Puritan Way of Death*, David E. Stannard locates a deeper source of parental anxiety in the pervasive threat of childhood death. This anxiety, Stannard argues, complicated by the Puritan belief in the innate depravity of the child, may have made adolescent separation emotionally beneficial to Puritan parents, if not to their children.[15] Although stressed by the Puritans, however, the custom was by no means unique to them.

Lawrence Stone refuses to speculate upon the origins of the practice or the motives behind it, but he develops briefly four likely consequences: a reduction in oedipal tensions; a lessening of the danger of incest; a distance in relations between parents and children; and a "strong contemporary consciousness of adolescence . . . as a distinct stage of life."[16] One might add to this list, I suspect, a fascination with the period's most popular literary structure, that of romance, for one of the most persistent conventions of the genre is the division and reunion of families. Although admittedly few Elizabethan youths had to prove themselves in love or war after being shipwrecked upon strange shores, they did confront the perils of adolescence apart from their families and in unfamiliar surroundings. If modern psychologists agree that a "dread of separation seems to be basic" in all children, as David E.

Stannard observes,[17] it is not unlikely that Elizabethans would have felt keenly the appeal of romance, with its separations, wanderings, and miraculous reunions.

However this may be, Shakespeare exploits more consistently than any other comic dramatist the very romance conventions that mimic rites of separation. Most of his protagonists are cut off from their families, often traumatically, through shipwreck, exile, or flight. Thrust upon their own defenses, they confront strange and mysterious landscapes – Ephesus, the forest of Arden, Illyria, the wood outside Athens, Petruchio's country house. Viola, as we have seen, enters Illyria with quizzical pathos: "And what should I do in Illyria?" (*TN* I.ii.3). Rosalind enters the forest of Arden with comic understatement: "Well, this is the forest of Arden" (*AYL* II.iv.15). Although their emotions differ radically, both characters feel the need to mark the moment at which they encounter a new world. To enter these strange realms is to experience something of the disorientation an orphaned apprentice might have felt entering London or a tribal novice entering the sacred wood.

Even in the comedies that do not depend upon romance conventions, Shakespeare often creates analogous experiences of separation. When the courtiers in *Love's Labor's Lost* walk from the court of Navarre into the park outside, the journey, though short, reverses the direction of their lives. In *Much Ado About Nothing* both Claudio and Benedick are foreigners not only to love – they are fresh from the wars – but to Messina; and their estrangement, though understated, figures in the several intrigues of the play. In *The Taming of the Shrew*, perhaps the least romantic of the comedies, Lucentio and Petruchio enter Padua, hardly an enchanted or sacred place, with the familiar bourgeois motives for travel – studying and seeking a rich wife. Yet the language of their first appearances colors the bourgeois setting with romance. Lucentio's exhilaration upon arriving in Padua is expressed as a kind of bourgeois parody of the romantic excitement of loss at sea:

> I have Pisa left
> And am to Padua come, as he that leaves
> A shallow plash to plunge him in the deep,
> And with sacietyseeks to quench his thirst.   (I.i.21–24)

Lucentio promptly loses himself in the deep, if we may continue his metaphor, for his first glimpse of Bianca overwhelms him. His servant Tranio must "stir him from his trance" (line 177), which has in a few seconds cut him off from his home, his duties to his father, and his own wits. Although immune to this kind of enchantment, even Petruchio senses mystery in his journey:

> Antonio, my father, is deceas'd,
> And I have thrust myself into this maze,
> Happily to wive and thrive as best I may.   (I.ii.54–56)

Padua is no Ephesus, but a substantial, mercantile world. Yet to enter that world is to venture into the deep, to become entranced, to wander in a maze.

While the recurrence of separation in the comedies may suggest an oblique indebtedness to the custom of sending out adolescents, Shakespeare's ultimate concern is with separation as a state of mind. Throughout the plays the interactions between mind and place, between mental and physical journeys, are subtle and elusive. Travel may cause estrangement, as in the case of Viola's shipwreck, but it may also be a symptom of estrangement, as when Hermia and Demetrius flee into the wood outside Athens. With the sudden onset of love, moreover, a character – Olivia, for example – may be estranged at home. Although the literal separations of the plays are traumatic, they are ultimately less disruptive than the metaphoric. Shipwrecks are less unsettling than love.

The mental journeys of the plays do not always begin with love, however; sometimes they begin as self-imposed states of exile, withdrawals from society and from love itself. Several plays depict double gestures of separation – one marking a denial of love, the other a capitulation. In the first scene of *Love's Labor's Lost*, the young men sign an oath to retreat from the world into their "little academe" for three years, banning all contact with women. In *Twelfth Night* Olivia and Orsino both divorce themselves from society – Orsino losing himself in reveries of love, Olivia withdrawing into seven years' mourning for her dead brother. Both withdrawals highlight Viola's rather more sane desire to withhold herself from the world and are linked metaphorically to her shipwreck: Orsino imagines the "spirit of love" as a "sea" (I.i.8–11), while Olivia "seasons" her brother's dead love with "eye-offending brine" (line 29). Kate's shrewish "humor" in *The Taming of the Shrew* is a psychological retreat of this sort, as are the more complicated anti-social and anti-romantic roles of Beatrice and Benedick in *Much Ado About Nothing*. Self-imposed separations of this kind are typical of what

Sherman Hawkins calls the "closed world" comedies, in which "the heroes and heroines themselves sometimes resemble humor characters, imprisoned in their inhibitions and aggressions, isolated by fear or repugnance from the general life, cut off not merely from others whom they ought to love but even from themselves."[18] The second withdrawal for such characters is often an equally absurd retreat into a "closed world" of love. Both gestures – the attempt to escape love and escape into it – are familiar adolescent phenomena.

In *The Taming of the Shrew* Shakespeare executes this double pattern by converting a traditional rite of incorporation, a wedding, into a symbolic act of separation. Kate's initial withdrawal into her shrewish "humor" alienates her from her sister, father, and potential suitors. By refusing to acknowledge her shrewishness and outdoing her at it, Petruchio so unnerves Kate that she agrees to marry. Having decided to rejoin society as a bride, however, Kate discovers that her wedding forces her farther outside it. By overturning every part of the ceremony, Petruchio cuts off Kate from her social milieu. He arrives late and grotesquely appareled; shouts "Ay, by gogs-wouns" as his marriage vow; cuffs the priest; throws the sops of the wedding toast "all in the sexton's face"; and kisses the bride "with such a clamorous smack/ That at the parting all the church did echo." Even Gremio, a mere onlooker, slinks away from the celebration "for very shame" (III.ii.157–82). There is no wedding feast either, at least for Kate, for Petruchio draws his sword against any guests bold enough to detain them and abducts her. The feast goes on without them, with Bianca and Lucentio standing in as bride and bridegroom. Kate's wedding day continues with a perilous journey, climaxed by a dunking in mud, and concludes with dinner thrown away and a lecture on continency delivered by her husband in the bridal chamber. An inversion of a religious ceremony, an abduction, a substitution for the bride and bridegroom, a perilous journey, an immersion in mud, dietary and sexual taboos – these resemble rites of separation, not incorporation. They are Petruchio's means to break Kate's dependence on social convention, the first stage in an initiation that culminates in a kiss in broad daylight in the city streets.

A far more complicated version of this design occurs in *Much Ado About Nothing*, in the broken wedding ceremony staged by

Claudio to denounce Hero and break his engagement. The scene begins uneasily, with Leonato unceremoniously urging upon the Friar a perfunctory celebration of the rite: "Come, Friar Francis, be brief – only to the plain form of marriage, and you shall recount their particular duties afterwards" (IV.i.1–3). Claudio needs nothing so much as a recounting of his particular duties, which in the Anglican ceremony center upon the Pauline injunction that husbands must love their wives "even as Christ loved the Church."[19] Hero's wedding culminates not in a ceremonial kiss but in an event common in rites of separation – a mock-death. The interrupted ceremony is also a symbolic act of separation for Claudio, divorcing him not only from Hero but from his former sentimental romanticism. Henceforth he will retreat into the cynical stance typical of the early Benedick:

> But fare thee well, most foul, most fair! Farewell,
> Thou pure impiety and impious purity!
> For thee I'll lock up all the gates of love,
> And on my eyelids shall conjecture hang,
> To turn all beauty into thoughts of harm,
> And never shall it more be gracious.   (lines 103–08)

The scene's final twist comes when Beatrice and Benedick, alone together for the first time after realizing their love for each other, unite in a vow to avenge the shame of Hero. While Claudio becomes the cynic, Benedick becomes the romantic. As in *The Taming of the Shrew*, when Bianca and Lucentio stand in at the wedding feast for Kate and Petruchio, a rite of incorporation joins the wrong couple. Those it should have bound are divided by it.

In the comedies as a whole, of course, gestures that cut people off from love are far less common than those that cut off the world for love – as in the case of Lucentio's trance. The mock-deaths of most comic separations are caused not by public humiliation but by Cupid's arrows. While Cupid ultimately brings lovers into society, he often begins by forcing them outside. In *The Two Gentlemen of Verona* Julia leaves Verona in pursuit of Proteus, abandoning "my goods, my lands, my reputation" (II.vii.87). In *A Midsummer Night's Dream* Hermia flees from an Athens which before her love to Lysander seemed a "paradise" but is now transformed from "a heaven unto a hell" (I.i.204–07). In *Love's Labor's Lost*, love destroys the young men's "little academe," separating them from their oaths, their companions, and themselves. As one society dissolves, however, another congeals. In the play's wonderful scene of discovery, each man comes to terms with his love alone; yet each perceives in turn that he is not alone, that they are all involved, and that the dissolution of one set of social bonds can bring forth another fellowship.

Love in the comedies creates not only social but familial estrangement. The formula derived from New Comedy, of course, almost necessarily involves parental opposition to love, usually because the match is socially inappropriate. When Shakespeare uses the formula – and he does so only incidentally – he characteristically develops its psychological and spiritual rather than social significance. In *A Midsummer Night's Dream* Egeus's opposition to the marriage of Hermia and Lysander is absolutely without motive: her two suitors are identical. The relationship between fathers and daughters in love is explored further in two plays that begin with tension and end in harmonious resolution. In *The Merchant of Venice* paternal control, while indirect, is absolute. Although Portia's father is dead, his will dictates, to her dismay, the choice of a husband: "I may neither choose who I would, nor refuse who I dislike; so is the will of a living daughter curb'd by the will of a dead father" (I.ii.23–25). In Venice the struggle between a father's will and his daughter's is played out in the flight of Jessica and the violent reproaches of Shylock. In Belmont, however, flight is unnecessary, for in yielding to her father's will Portia achieves her own: marriage to Bassanio. In Belmont the dictates of the law and of love are paradoxically the same.

A similar paradox is developed in greater psychological detail in *As You Like It*. Rosalind's first words in the play, in Act I, scene ii, express her melancholy for her banished father. Later, however, after she has fallen in love with Orlando, she admits to Celia that her melancholy is no longer solely for her banished father: "some of it is for my child's father" (I.iii.11). The witty reference to Orlando as a father underlines the competitive relationship both men are drawn into in Rosalind's uncertain mind. Although it is never mentioned in the play, one source of this tension is presumably social: Orlando is no match for the daughter of a Duke. Foremost in Rosalind's mind, however, is a tension between the competing obligations of love. During her exile in the forest of Arden, she withholds her identity from both Orlando and her father. Her playful testing of Orlando, it seems, teaches her enough about his love, and hers, to enable her to sort out this subtle conflict of allegiances and resolve it. Like Portia, Rosalind ultimately finds no conflict between her love of her father and of her suitor. When she reveals herself at the end of the play, she gives herself to both in exactly the same words: "To you I give myself, for I am yours" (V.iv.116). This bond of love, Hymen assures us, encompasses not only the whole of society but earth and heaven.

More often than it divides fathers and daughters, love comes between friends. While temporary, the separations are usually traumatic: Proteus betrays Valentine; Antonio broods inconsolably over Bassanio's departure; Benedick challenges Claudio to a duel. In *A Midsummer Night's Dream* Hermia and Helena are transformed from best friends to bitter enemies in the very wood where, as Hermia puts it, "you and I/ Upon faint primrose beds were wont to lie,/ Emptying our bosoms of their counsel sweet" (I.i.214–16). In the midst of their farcical confusion in the wood, Helena's lament for Hermia's betrayal creates a moment of delicate pathos:

> O, is all forgot?
> All school-days friendship, childhood innocence?
> We, Hermia, like two artificial gods,
> Have with our needles created both one flower,
> Both on one sampler, sitting on one cushion,
> Both warbling of one song, both in one key,
> As if our hands, our sides, voices, and minds
> Had been incorporate. (III.ii.201–08)

From this they move rapidly to insults and, if not blows, at least savage threats: "How low am I? I am not yet so low/ But that my nails can reach unto thine eyes" (lines 297–98). "Beating or insulting one's childhood companions," as van Gennep notes, is a traditional rite of courtship.[20] In *A Midsummer Night's Dream* the identities of the protagonists are gradually stripped away until – no longer Athenians, lovers, or friends – they slump exhausted to the ground in utter isolation, experiencing a private despair that only the audience can perceive is communal. Although the comedies always end with friends reunited, the price, as in a rite of initiation, is a loss of innocence.

The ultimate separation, and that which for Shakespeare lies at the center of the experience of love, is separation from self. Cupid's arrows pierce the heart, shattering in an instant all sense of identity and of relation to the outside world. Lucentio, as we have seen, is entranced. Antipholus of Syracuse asks Luciana not only to teach him "how to think and speak" but to transform him, to create him anew (*Err* III.ii.33–39). Proteus is "metamorphis'd" by Julia (*TGV* I.i.66). Rosalind and Orlando are "overthrown" by love, a wrestler more dangerous than Charles (*AYL* I.ii.254). Benedick sighs, shaves, and tries his hand at sonnets. Don Armado, in love with the fair Jaquenetta, creates his own ceremony of separation, bidding farewell to the emblems of his former identity as a soldier and invoking those that will make him a lover:

Adieu, valor, rust, rapier, be still, drum, for your manager is in love; yea, he loveth. Assist me, some extemporal god of rhyme, for I am sure I shall turn sonnet. Devise, wit, write, pen, for I am for whole volumes in folio.

(*LLL* I.ii.181–85)

The syntactical balance of this extemporaneous little rite dramatizes the symmetry of the reversal: Venus has conquered Mars.

Although we shall explore the symptoms of love-melancholy as part of the liminal experience in the comedies, their onset resembles a rite of separation. Whether conscious or unconscious, the postures adopted by the novice in love announce that he is a being set apart from mundane reality. In *The Two Gentlemen of Verona* Speed recognizes that Valentine, his master, is in love simply by observing "these special marks":

first, you have learn'd, like Sir Proteus, to wreathe your arms, like a malcontent; to relish a love-song, like a robin-redbreast; to walk alone, like one that had the pestilence; to sigh, like a schoolboy that had lost his A B C; to weep, like a young wench that had buried her grandam; to fast, like one that takes diet; to watch, like one that fears robbing; to speak puling, like a beggar at Hallowmas.

Speed throws the transformation into sharp relief by recalling Valentine's former behavior:

You were wont, when you laugh'd, to crow like a cock; when you walk'd, to walk like one of the lions; when you fasted, it was presently after dinner; when you look'd sadly, it was for want of money: and now you are metamorphis'd with a mistress, that when I look on you, I can hardly think you my master. (II.i.18–32)

The reversal that Speed describes might well be compared to a rite of separation: Valentine no longer looks the same, eats the same, or talks the same; his former identity has been obliterated. And, like a novice in a rite of initiation, he walks alone, inhabiting his own private space. His new posture as a lover can hardly be called an identity, moreover, because, as Speed makes clear, his every symptom makes him "like Sir Proteus." This dissolution of personal identity is common to the liminal experience.

The "special marks" of the lover that Speed so precisely catalogues are not unique to Valentine and Proteus but are familiar Elizabethan conventions, both literary and visual. A woodcut in Samuel Rowlands' *The Melancholy Knight* (1615) depicts a brooding lover, his arms "wreathed" like Valentine's and his hat "penthouse-like o'er the shop of his eyes," in the fashion that Moth recommends to the infatuated Don Armado in *Love's Labor's Lost* (III.i.17–18). Hilliard's "Young Man amongst Roses" portrays an elegant young courtier in another amatory pose: a melancholy expression on his face, he leans against a tree, his right leg carelessly slung across his left, his hand upon his heart; eglantine surrounds him. Another of Hilliard's lovers, set off against a background of flames, gazes piercingly at the viewer, his left hand holding a locket to his heart.[21] The existence of such poses in portraits suggests a close connection between life and art; surely these courtiers played out the roles they were painted in, giving to their own love affairs the shape and passion of high drama.

The importance of separation in the comedies is suggested by the fact that the closest thing to a paradigm of the whole experience occurs in what is probably Shakespeare's earliest comedy, *The Comedy of Errors*. When Antipholus of Syracuse enters the hostile and alien realm of Ephesus, searching for his lost mother and brother, he reflects upon his melancholy condition:

> I to the world am like a drop of water,
> That in the ocean seeks another drop,
> Who, falling there to find his fellow forth
> (Unseen, inquisitive), confounds himself.
> So I, to find a mother and a brother,
> In quest of them (unhappy), ah, lose myself. (I.ii.35–40)

The lyricism of the comedies, as we have seen, often finds expression at moments like this, when the entry into an alien landscape becomes a figure for a deeper alienation – an estrangement from family or friend or lover which "confounds" the self. Thus "confounded," it seems, the individual is all the more vulnerable to love. Having lost himself in the ocean through love of his mother and brother, Antipholus later offers to "drown" for his love of Luciana: "Sing, siren, for thyself, and I will dote" (III.ii.47). Throughout the comedies the experience of love often begins with a profound sense of loss – of self, family, community.

Shakespeare's rites of separation, then, translate into comic terms many of the traditional motifs of rites of passage. And they may reflect, or re-create in oblique forms, the actual experiences of separation that were so prominent a part of Elizabethan adolescence. To be cast upon a strange shore, to lose one's family, to be estranged from one's friends, to withdraw into a fantasy of love or of life without love – all of these comic separations cut the individual loose from his social moorings and his past, "confounding" his identity. In their explorations of the self, the comedies are in some ways not unlike the tragedies, for in both genres Shakespeare consistently maneuvers his central characters into positions of psychological isolation, leaving them exposed and vulnerable both within and without. While this kind of isolation is conventional in tragedy, in comedy it is unique to Shakespeare. In both genres, too, identity is re-created only after having been destroyed – fragmented, sometimes, to the point at which the "confounded" self seems little more than chaos. But this experience – of madness in the tragedies and folly in the comedies – is matter for the liminal phase.

3
Natural Transitions

"We that are true lovers run into strange capers; but as all is mortal in
nature, so is all nature in love mortal in folly"

(*AYL* II.iv.54–56)

In *A Nest of Ninnies*, Robert Armin, the actor in Shakespeare's
company who specialized in the role of the witty fool, draws a
distinction between the two kinds of fools familiar to Elizabethans not only on stage but in noble households. The one, the
"natural" fool, is mentally deficient; the other, the "artificial"
fool, is a professional entertainer:

> Naturall Fooles, are prone to selfe conceipt:
> Fooles artificiall, with their wits lay wayte
> To make themselves Fooles, liking their disguise,
> To feede their owne mindes, and the gazers eyes.[1]

The distinction holds for Shakespeare's lovers as well. All are
capable of "admirable fooling," but some, like Sir Andrew in
Twelfth Night, "do it more natural" (II.iii.80–83). Often the
distinction is sexual: the male lovers, the Orsinos and Orlandos,
tend to act out their follies straightforwardly, without self awareness; the female lovers, especially those who take on disguise,
enjoy their folly, feeding their own minds and the gazers' eyes. In
the next chapter we will consider some "artificial" lovers; in this,
we are concerned only with the "naturals." The differences,
although important, should not obscure the similarities. Much of
the fun of Elizabethan fooling – and of Shakespearean loving –
lies in its ambiguity: "artificials" are capable of natural folly, and
"naturals" of accidental art.

"We that are true lovers," says Touchstone, "run into strange
capers; but as all is mortal in nature, so is all nature in love mortal
in folly." Touchstone's play on the word "mortal" links Shakespeare's comic pattern to the death–rebirth pattern of rites of
passage. When Shakespeare's lovers "die" for love, they encounter a special form of their mortality – their susceptibility to the

"strange capers" of "true lovers." Like novices in rites of initiation, the lovers are estranged from their familiar world, tested,
educated, and confused. Caught between childhood and adulthood, infatuation and married love, they "waver between two
worlds."[2] Divorced by love not only from society but from
themselves, they plunge into psychological states that, at their
most extreme, verge on chaos. The process is both destructive and
creative, for as one identity dies another is born.

Although Elizabethans had no formal rites of initiation to mark
the passage from childhood to adulthood, the separations that
occurred in early youth gave them, as Lawrence Stone remarks, a
"strong ... consciousness of adolescence ... as a distinct stage of
life."[3] This consciousness is expressed, moreover, in ways that
make adolescence, and adolescent love, resemble the liminal
phase of rites of passage. The Elizabethan stereotype of the
adolescent is that of a liminal creature – uncertain of his identity,
unstable, neither here nor there. The ambiguity of adolescence is
captured succinctly in Malvolio's description of the disguised
Viola in *Twelfth Night*:

Not yet old enough for a man, nor young enough for a boy; as a squash is
before 'tis a peascod, or a codling when 'tis almost an apple. 'Tis with him in
standing water, between boy and man.   (I.v.156–59)

Although Malvolio points out the difficulty of defining an adolescent, who is neither boy nor man, he himself is unaware of a
further, sexual ambiguity: this adolescent is named Viola. And yet
she is loved by both Orsino and Olivia as Cesario. To carry the
ambiguity one step farther, one might say that it is the liminality
of adolescence that enables a boy actor to play convincingly the
role of a girl disguised as a boy.

Malvolio sees no more than the physical, but Viola's psychological identity is similarly ambiguous. The metaphors in Malvolio's description – of vegetable, fruit, and the turning of the tide
– are implicit in Viola's uncertainty of her state at the beginning of
the play. In response to the possibility of her brother's death, she
desires not to be "delivered to the world" until she has made her
"own occasion mellow" what her "estate" is (I.ii.42–44). Viola
not only "mellows" in the course of the play; she attends quite
literally, in waiting for her brother, the passing of the tides.
Committing herself to time, she stands poised between two modes
of being. Although general and conventional, Nicholas Breton's

portrait of "A Young Man" captures something of this adolescent indeterminacy:

> His wit is in making or marring, his wealth in gaining or losing, his honour in advancing or declining, and his life in abridging or increasing. He is a bloome that either is blasted in the bud, or growes to a good fruit, or a bird that dies in the nest, or lives to make use of her wings.[4]

The shift in sexual identity that occurs in the course of the second sentence is no doubt unintentional, but the introduction of yet another ambiguous potentiality is appropriate.

In action, the ambiguity of youth becomes (for adults) a comical and maddening instability. *The Zodiake of Life* (1560) states the conventional view succinctly: youth is "amorous, brain-sick, and brawling."[5] In his character of "A Youngman," John Earle describes this peculiar brainsickness:

> He conceives his Youth as the season of his Lust, and the Houre wherein hee ought to bee bad: and because he would not lose his time, spends it. . . . Hee loves and hates with the same inflammation: and when the heate is over, is coole alike to friends and enemies. His friendship is seldome so stedfast, but that lust, drinke, or anger may overturne it. He offers you his blood to day in kindnesse, and is readie to take yours to morrow. He do's seldome any thing which hee wishes not to doe againe, and is onely wise after a misfortune. Hee suffers much for his knowledge, and a great deale of folly it is makes him a wise man. . . . Hee is a Shippe without Pilot or Tackling, and only good fortune may steere him. If hee scape this age, hee ha's scap't a Tempest, and may live to be a Man.[6]

In the comedies, these tempests – the metaphor comes naturally to both Earle and Shakespeare – prove kind. In *The Winter's Tale*, it is in the middle of a tempest that the old shepherd speaks his mind about youth: "I would there were no age between ten and three-and-twenty, or that youth would sleep out the rest; for there is nothing in the between but getting wenches with child, wronging the ancientry, stealing, fighting – ." At least he speaks part of his mind, for he is interrupted in mid-thought by some "boil'd-brains of nineteen and two-and-twenty" out hunting (III.iii.59–64).

As the old shepherd well knows, youth is a time of love. Venus is the planet of adolescence. "Venus," says Henry Cuffe in *The Differences of the Ages of Mans Life*, "guides our blossomming lustfull age."[7] In Jaques' version of the ages of man, it is the lover, "sighing like a furnace," who comes between the "whining schoolboy" and the soldier (*AYL* II.vii.145–49). Although the conventional association of youth and love hardly needs to be demonstrated, Thomas Whythorne's account of his own adolescence illuminates its experiential reality. Whythorne's description provides, to my knowledge, a unique opportunity to observe an Elizabethan not only conscious of the sexual tensions of adolescence but attempting to cope with them:

Here must I speak somewhat again of the foresaid age named adolescency, which is the first part of the young man's age: because I understand and perceive also that in this age Cupid and Venus were and would be very busy to trouble the quiet minds of young folk. Therefore, having passed nigh about the one half of this age, in the which time I had been sometimes dribbed at with Cupid's golden shafts, and yet more by good hap than by cunning I did put them by, and would not suffer them to pierce me, for the which I suffered some displeasures of some Venerian sort; I, for all that, fearing still to be stricken and wounded with the blind boy's arrows, sought and enquired ways how to be free from them ...

Whythorne attempted to escape Cupid's shafts by reading poetry and philosophy, by studying and practicing his music, and by sometimes "ranging" and "wandering" in the "pleasant woods and groves," the haunts of "Diana, the goddess of chastity."[8] He also fueled his resolve with anti-feminist anecdotes, which he took great delight in at the time, and later too, for they fill eight pages of the autobiography. Although Whythorne was able to restrain himself, he could not control his destiny: "For alack! that which one feareth most, and would not have it happen unto him, it is often seen that he escapeth the same very narrowly or never a whit at all. //And so chanced it with me also at this present. For I being now in place where were divers young women ..."[9] At this point the young woman we have already encountered (p.37) slipped a love poem into his gittern and his romantic adventures resumed, to be discontinued, if at all, only with his marriage at the age of forty-nine.

While Whythorne struggled to avoid Cupid's snares, many, apparently, sought them out, for the role of the lover is one of the most prominent stereotypes of the age. Since most of the conventions of this role are familiar from the poetry and drama of the period, extensive documentation is unnecessary. Thomas Overbury's "An Amorist," however, illustrates its liminal character:

[An amorist] Is a certaine blasted or planet-stroken, and is the Dog that leades blinde *Cupid*; when hee is at the best, his fashion exceedes the worth of his weight. He is never without verses, and muske confects; and sighs to the hazard of his buttons; his eyes are all white, either to weare the livery of his Mistris complexion, or to keepe *Cupid* from hitting the blacke. Hee fights with passion, and looseth much of his blood by his weapon; dreames, thence his palenesse. His armes are carelessly used, as if their best use were nothing but embracements. He is untrust, unbuttoned, and ungartered, not out of carelessnesse, but care; his farthest end being but going to bed. Sometimes he wraps his petition in neatnesse, but it goeth not alone; for then he makes some other quality moralize his affection, and his trimnesse is the grace of that grace. Her favor lifts him up, as the Sun moisture; when he disfavours, unable to hold that happinesse, it falls downe in teares; his fingers are his Orators, and hee expresseth much of himselfe upon some instrument. He answeres not, or not to the purpose; and no marvell, for he is not at home. He scotcheth time with dancing with his Mistris, taking up of her glove, and wearing her feather; hee is confinde to her colour, and dares not passe out of the circuit of her memory. His imagination is a foole, and it goeth in a pide-coat of red and white; shortly, he is translated out of a man into folly; his imagination is the glasse of lust, and himself the traitour to his own discretion.[10]

The verses, sighs, dreams, "arms carelessly used," trim or carefully disordered apparel, moodiness, abstraction, paleness – these are the stock in trade not only of Overbury's amorist but of Shakespeare's. The Elizabethen stereotype is of a liminal figure, confused, disoriented, paradoxical. Overbury's climactic image is that of the fool, whose motley is the emblem of his disordered mind. Like Valentine in *Two Gentlemen of Verona*, who is "metamorphis'd with a mistress" (II.i.30–31), the amorist is a man "translated."

In the comedies the experience of love varies from character to character, but certain symptoms recur, all signs of liminal confusion. The conventional signs of love are themselves emblems of derangement. Lovers weep and smile simultaneously, gaze distractedly, dress carefully and carelessly, cross their arms, learn the secret and nonsensical language of the sonnet – in a word, reverse their normal behavior with the alacrity of Malvolio, who adorns himself for his love with yellow cross garters and a smile. There are other symptoms as well, subtler and more profound, which are often developed in the interactions of plot, theme, and metaphor. Plays as dissimilar as *The Taming of the Shrew* and *A Midsummer Night's Dream* are drawn together by common metaphors of liminality. The most important are those of wandering, dreaming, going mad, becoming bewitched, undergoing metamorphosis, and taking on disguise. It is through these interrelated motifs that Shakespeare defines the disordered psychology of love.

The wandering of lovers is often literal but always metaphoric. To lose one's way in the comedies is always to lose one's self. The play that exploits most consistently the motif of wandering is, as the name implies, *The Comedy of Errors*. What the Abbess calls a "sympathiz'd one day's error" (V.i.398) begins with Antipholus of Syracuse deciding to "wander up and down to view the city" (I.ii.31). In the course of the play characters "err" in all senses of the word, particularly Antipholus of Syracuse, who loses himself not only in his love for his missing family but for Luciana: "Against my soul's pure truth why labor you,/ To make it wander in an unknown field?" (III.ii.37–38). Antipholus's brother is also errant – wandering around the city when he should be home for dinner. In *A Midsummer Night's Dream* all the young lovers eventually lose their way in the wood outside Athens, with consequences that lend unconscious irony to Lysander's naive apology to Hermia: "Fair love, you faint with wand'ring in the wood;/ And to speak troth I have forgot our way" (II.ii.35–36). Lysander does not discover his way until Oberon's magic herb takes "from thence all error with his might" and makes "his eyeballs roll with wonted sight" (III.ii.368–69). In *Twelfth Night* Orsino never leaves Illyria, and only once his own palace, yet he too is a wanderer in love, as much at the mercy of the wind and waves as Viola and Sebastian. "I would have men of such constancy put to sea," observes Feste, "that their business might be every thing and their intent every where, for that's it that always makes a good voyage of nothing" (II.iv.75–78). In *Twelfth Night* to love is to be lost at sea.

Like that of erring, the motif of dreaming appears in a title. In *A Midsummer Night's Dream* the wandering of the lovers occurs in the "fierce vexation of a dream" (IV.i.69). In *Twelfth Night* Sebastian's dream is less vexing. "If it be thus to dream," he muses as he follows Olivia to her house, "still let me sleep" (IV.i.63). In *The Taming of the Shrew* good and bad, true and false dreams are played off against one another with multiple ironies. Christopher Sly's transformation from beggar to nobleman is a "flattering dream" (Ind.i.44), so flattering that he easily overcomes his skepticism. Kate's wedding night is also a dream, but a nightmare. Petruchio afflicts her with a "sermon of continency,"

> And rails, and swears, and rates, that she, poor soul,
> Knows not which way to stand, to look, to speak,
> And sits as one new risen from a dream.   (IV.i.184–86)

The characteristic dream state in the comedies has the ambiguity of liminal experience. To perceive reality as a dream, or a dream as reality, is to "waver between two worlds."

Metaphors of dreaming slide easily into metaphors of madness, for both states are ambiguous, irrational, and disorienting. In *Twelfth Night* Sebastian's mysterious encounter with Olivia makes him wonder whether "I am mad, or else this is a dream" (IV.i.61). Love and madness appear so often together as to be nearly synonymous: "Love is merely a madness," says Rosalind in *As You Like It* (III.ii.400). The link is forged punningly in *The Comedy of Errors*. Antipholus of Syracuse protests to Luciana that he is "not mad, but mated" (III.ii.54). The Duke's response to the chaos at the end of the play, however, implies that madness, amazement, and mating are all one: "I think you are all mated, or stark mad" (V.i.282). The pun recurs in *The Taming of the Shrew*: Kate, "being mad herself," is "madly mated" (III.ii.244). In *Twelfth Night* "a most extracting frenzy of mine own" (V.i.281) causes Olivia to forget the "mad" and "madly-us'd Malvolio" (line 311). "Lovers and madmen," says Theseus in *A Midsummer Night's Dream*, "have such seething brains,/ Such shaping fantasies, that apprehend/ More than cool reason ever comprehends" (V.i.4–6).

In *The Comedy of Errors*, when Adriana concludes that her husband has gone mad, she calls for the exorcist, Dr Pinch. Ephesus is a land full of witchcraft, as Antipholus of Syracuse discovers when he is exposed to Luciana's "mermaid's song" (III.ii.164) and Dromio's account of the terrors of Nell, the "drudge or diviner" (line 140) who claims to possess him. Love at first sight is a kind of enchantment. Lucentio in *The Taming of the Shrew*, Navarre in *Love's Labor's Lost*, and both Orlando and Rosalind in *As You Like It* are entranced by the first sight of their lovers.[11] The sure sign of Navarre's love, Boyet tells the French princess, is that "all eyes saw his eyes enchanted with gazes" (II.i.247). Love also works by magic in the night-time wood of *A Midsummer Night's Dream* and, less directly, in the "circle of this forest" in *As You Like It* (V.iv.34). When the Duke of *The Comedy of Errors* accuses the bewildered throng of drinking of "Circe's cup" (V.i.271), he joins witchcraft and metamorphosis. Earlier in the same play Antipholus of Syracuse asks Luciana to transform him, to "create" him "new" (III.ii.39–40), a request that is parodied in Dromio's fear that he has been transformed into an ass (II.ii.195). In *A Midsummer Night's Dream* Bottom's "translation" (III.i.119) results in a literal asininity, with Bottom the prince consort acting out Helena's observation that "things base and vile, holding no quantity,/ Love can transpose to form and dignity" (I.i.232–33). In *Much Ado About Nothing* Benedick anticipates his metamorphosis into a foolish lover as he soliloquizes in the garden, the site of his undoing: "I will not be sworn but love may transform me to an oyster, but I'll take my oath on it, till he have made an oyster of me, he shall never make me such a fool" (II.iii.23–26). In this play the language of love is intertwined with that of fashion, which also transforms, or deforms. We learn from the Watch that fashion is a "deformed thief" who "giddily ... turns about all the hot-bloods" and goes dressed as a lover: "I know him," says the second Watch, "'a wears a lock" (III.iii.126,131,170). The motif figures in *Love's Labor's Lost* as well. "Your beauty, ladies," says Berowne as he struggles to excuse the follies of all the young men, "Hath much deformed us, fashioning our humors/ Even to the opposed end of our intents" (V.ii.756–58). For such characters the experience of love is comically Ovidean.

Disguising might be considered a variation on the theme of metamorphosis. Almost all disguising in the comedies, even that of the romantic heroines, as we shall see, both creates and reflects psychological confusion. In *The Comedy of Errors* Antipholus of Syracuse fears that he may be "to myself disguis'd" (II.ii.214), and the threat underlies even the literal disguisings of characters like Viola and Rosalind. In *The Taming of the Shrew* all the disguises are "supposes," hypothetical identities that mask a wide variety of confusions, ranging from Sly's pose as a nobleman to Kate's "humor" as a shrew. The masked ball in Act II scene i of *Much Ado About Nothing* epitomizes this motif, for every gesture precipitates misunderstanding, the maskers recognizing neither each other nor themselves. That disguise mirrors confusion is suggested by the behavior of the young men in *Love's Labor's Lost*, who court their ladies while wearing the "shapeless gear" (V.ii.303) of Russians.

All of these modes of disorientation – error, dream, madness, witchcraft, metamorphosis, disguise – center on the experience of love but also extend beyond it. The power they represent, in Elizabethan psychology, is that of the fancy, or imagination. "The lunatic, the lover, and the poet," as Theseus observes, "are of imagination all compact" (*MND* V.i.7–8). Both dreams and madness are symptoms of a disordered imagination. The power of magic, as is clear in the figure of Prospero, is fundamentally an imaginative power. And the transformations and disguisings make lovers akin to actors, who imagine themselves in another identity. The word "fancy" itself, as is evident in *A Midsummer Night's Dream*, can mean both "love" and "imagination." The imagination, moreover, is in Elizabethan psychology a "transitional" faculty of mind. As the intermediary between the faculties of sense and reason, it plays a crucial role in all mental transformations, and its power is disturbingly ambiguous: it can work towards the disintegration of lunacy or the integration of poetry. As one might expect, Elizabethan psychology makes of adolescence the period of most vigorous imaginative activity. Given these automatic links between love and poetry, the comedies cannot escape self-reflexiveness. The comic experience, for characters, actors, and audience, is fundamentally imaginative.[12]

Elizabethan adolescents were not only imaginative by psychological convention; they were trained to use their imagination as a means of becoming an adult. The subtlest and most pervasive mode of transition in the period is to be found in the psychology of imitation, through which adolescents defined their identity by imagining themselves in another role. W. B. Yeats preferred Renaissance to modern culture because it was based not on self-knowledge "but on knowledge of some other self, Christ or Caesar, not on delicate sincerity but on imitative energy." "Saint Francis and Caesar Borgia," according to Yeats, "made themselves over-mastering, creative persons by turning from the mirror to meditation upon a mask."[13] Yeats offers a profound insight into Elizabethan culture. His opposition between self-knowledge and knowledge of some other self is misleading, however, for the idea of imitation was to make knowledge of another a means of self-knowledge; meditation upon a mask was a mode of self-reflection and self-creation. Although the art of imitation affected the whole of a person's life, it was especially significant in adolescence, for it was through imitation that adolescents became adults. The loss of identity characteristic of this phase was not merely accepted as a symptom; it was encouraged as the first stage in an initiatory process. To understand how the process worked, and to probe its implications for Shakespeare's amorists, it will be necessary to detour briefly into the Elizabethan educational system. Exhortations to imitate came from every authority, but they were most insistent and most rigorous in the daily life of the school. Although the literary consequences of the doctrine of imitation have been thoroughly studied, its psychological consequences, less open to demonstration, have been generally ignored.

Although he does not mention the practice of imitation, Walter J. Ong has stressed the significance of the Renaissance educational system in defining adult identity. For Ong, Renaissance schooling was essentially a male puberty rite: learning took place in a world set apart from women; involved severe physical trials (the infamous flogging) and occasional bouts of lawlessness; provided the initiated with a "secret" language, Latin; and gave access to the specialized and esoteric lore of the society. The status of Latin, in particular, according to Ong, "encouraged in a special way the development of a puberty rite setting."[14] When one adds to Ong's account the way in which Latin was learned, it becomes even more convincing, for the initiate acquired his "secret" language and defined his identity by first losing himself, as in a rite of transition.

Renaissance education developed the natural tendency towards imitation in children. "In this respect," says Vives, "boys are naturally apes; they imitate everything and always, especially those whom they consider worthy of imitation on account of their authority, or because of the faith they place in them, such as parents, nurses, masters, and schoolfellows."[15] Not all theorists were as sanguine as Vives about these natural imitative tendencies. Erasmus, for example, fears the susceptibility of youth to bad models: "Nature has made the first years of our life prone to imitation – though perhaps it is easier to that age to copy evil than good."[16] It is this concern with imitation as the basis not only of literary style but of behavior, that prompts Roger Ascham's long lament in *The Scholemaster* that there are so few "faire examples" at Court for young gentlemen to follow.[17]

The reasons for this anxiety about imitation become clear if we examine the process as it applied to the earliest stages of learning Latin. Although the ultimate destination was originality, the road was long and laborious; one began by copying. In *The Scholemaster*, for example, Ascham recommends his method of double translation. His pupils first parse a Latin passage thoroughly, then translate it into English, and finally back into Latin. They then compare their final version to the original. Ascham praises the child who does well, "either in chosing, or true placing of Tullies wordes."[18] The aim is thus replication: the ideal student is the one who so assimilates Cicero's style that his own translation reproduces it. It is no accident that the model is Cicero, for it is vital that the child be exposed only to the best. Underlying the entire process is the assumption that imitation is partly unconscious and therefore dangerous. "The pure cleane witte of a sweete yong babe," says Ascham, "is like the newest wax";[19] it will take the form of whatever impresses it. Similar assumptions are implicit in Erasmus's impatience with the rote learning of rules. We learn not by rules, he argues, but by "copious reading of the best authors." Because this is in part an unconscious, assimilative process, teachers must "choose such works as are not only sound models of style but are instructive by reason of their subject-matter."[20] At the earliest stages, then, imitation effaces identity, sometimes with unconscious effect.

Anxieties about the consequences of imitation surface in Elizabethan attitudes towards acting. Although schoolboys were encouraged to act out dialogues and whole plays to sharpen both their Latin and their rhetorical skills, the imaginative adoption of a dramatic role was viewed as potentially dangerous. The plays of Terence, for example, which were often acted, were models of chaste Latin but unchaste behavior. Quintilian, whose *Institutio Oratoria* was highly influential, warns against allowing schoolboys to act undesirable roles: "For I do not of course wish the boy ... to talk with the shrillness of a woman or in the tremulous accents of old age. Nor for that matter must he ape the vices of the drunkard, or copy the cringing manners of a slave, or learn to express the emotions of love, avarice, or fear. Such accomplishments are not necessary to an orator and corrupt the mind, especially while it is still pliable and unformed. For repeated imitation passes into habit." Quintilian even warns against students imitating themselves. They should not commit their own compositions to memory, he says, but only those of the best models, for they will "unconsciously reproduce the style of the speech which has been impressed upon the memory."[21] The Puritan hostility towards acting reflects the same assumptions. In Th'overthrow of Stage-Playes (1599), John Rainolds points out the terrible effects that immoral roles have upon those who act them on stage: "the care of making a shew to doe such feates, and to doe them as lively as the beasts themselves in whom the vices raigne, worketh in the actors a marvellous impression of being like the persons whose qualities they expresse and imitate: chiefly when earnest and much meditation of sundry dayes and weekes, by often repetition and representation of the partes, shall as it were engrave the things in their minde with a penne of iron, or with the point of a diamond."[22] The positive side of this coin, which Rainolds does not acknowledge, is that the habitual imitation of good models can make one a good man. In either case one becomes what one plays. In this sense, conventional roles create the self.

Despite the dangers, Elizabethan schoolboys and university students acted regularly, even the roles of lovers and tyrants. As they matured, the dangers of imitation lessened, for the process became more conscious and more creative. Ascham, for example, encourages the advanced student to choose, within limits, his own model or models, selecting or adapting them for his own purposes. Ascham recommends that students learn to imitate as Vergil followed Homer, treating dissimilar material with a similar style or similar material with a dissimilar style. To learn this method, he suggests comparing parallel passages of Homer and Vergil or Demosthenes and Cicero. In the case of the latter pair, the student would make a list:

1 *Tullie* reteyneth thus moch of the matter, thies sentences, thies wordes:
2 This and that he leaveth out, which he doth wittelie to this end and purpose.
3 This he addeth here.
4 This he diminisheth there.
5 This he ordereth thus, with placing that here, not there.

6 This he altereth and changeth, either, in propertie of wordes, in forme of
sentence, in substance of the matter, or in one, or other convenient
circumstance of the authors present purpose.[23]

Having practised this method, the student could apply it to his
own compositions. Although the process is still rather mechanical
– the creativity consists in selecting and arranging a set body of
themes and styles – it is less so than copying. The student is
beginning to choose an identity rather than have it impressed
upon him.

The final, truly creative stages of imitation are more relevant to
the "artificial" lovers of the comedies, whose disguises are
deliberate, than to the "naturals," whose deformities are largely
unconscious. Since the process is continuous, however, it would
be awkward to defer its end to the next chapter; and even the early
stages become clearer if their goal is kept in mind. Perhaps the best
contemporary description of creative imitation is that of Ben
Jonson. The passage is not only about imitation but itself imitative, for its style and dominant image are classical:

The third requisite in our poet, or maker, is imitation: to be able to convert the
substance or riches of another poet to his own use: to make choice of one
excellent man above the rest, and so to follow him till he grow very he, or so
like him as the copy may be mistaken for the principal – not as a creature that
swallows what it takes in crude, raw, or undigested, but that feeds with an
appetite, and hath a stomach to concoct, divide, and turn all into nourishment; not to imitate servilely, as Horace saith, and catch at vices for virtue,
but to draw forth out of the best and choicest flowers with the bee, and turn
all into honey, work it into one relish and savour, make our imitation sweet,
observe how the best writers have imitated, and follow them: how Virgil and
Statius have imitated Homer; how Horace, Archilocus; how Alcaeus and the
other lyrics; and so of all the rest.[24]

The image of the bee making honey, which appears in Seneca and
other classical authors, conveys more precisely than any other the
extent to which mature imitation was considered a free and
creative act. Although it originates in the flowers of the ancients,
the honey that comes forth is truly the poet's: it is he who chooses
the flowers, gathers the pollen, and transforms it, turning "all into
nourishment." Unlike the schoolboy copyist, who passively
becomes his model, taking its impress like sealing wax, the mature
poet devours it, converting the "substance or riches of another
poet to his own use." The latter metaphor reveals the competitive
and even aggressive tendencies, by no means uniquely Jonsonian,

that characterize the advanced stages of a process that begins with abject self-effacement.

These aggressive tendencies were encouraged in the schools in the form of emulation. Erasmus, for example, urges teachers to arouse "the spirit of emulation in the class,"[25] inciting boys to imitate and finally surpass the efforts of their peers. As the child matured, he gradually directed his emulation to higher models, aspiring not only to copy Cicero but to outdo him. "If you take all of Cicero and him alone for your model," says Erasmus's spokesman in *Ciceronianus*, "you should not only reproduce him, but also defeat him. He must not be just passed by, but rather left behind."[26] It is not hard to find in the psychology of this process signs of the puberty rite that Ong describes. Bearing the impress of Cicero upon his mind and, through the strokes of the master, upon his back, the student could eventually avenge himself by devouring and converting to his own nourishment the source of both his pain and aspirations. Having thus defined and asserted his identity, the student, as Vives makes clear, would become a man:

That a boy should imitate is honourable and praiseworthy; that an old man should do so, is servile and disgraceful. It is meet that a boy should have a master and guide, whom he should follow; but not so, an old man. For this reason when you have had sufficient exercise on the racecourse (so to speak) of this imitation, begin to emulate, and to compare yourself with your guide, to see where you can approach nearer to him, and how far you are left in his rear.... Try to attain to his great beauties, and afterwards even to excel them.[27]

Vives does not mention the moral and spiritual dangers that surround this notion of emulation. They figure prominently in the poetry of George Herbert, however, as part of the predicament of celebrating God's Word with words of one's own. In "The Thanksgiving," the poet asks of God, "But how then shall I imitate thee, and/ Copie thy fair, though bloudie hand?" The problem posed is one for both life and art: the "bloudie hand" is that which not only suffered nailing to the cross but composed the Bible. The poet's immediate response is emulative: "Surely I will revenge me on thy love,/ And trie who shall victorious prove." And for forty lines he shows that for each gesture of Christ's love he will counter with one of his own. Until he comes to the Passion. At that point he confesses, "I will do for that – / Alas, my God, I know not what." In the final stanza of "Jordan (II)" the poet suffers a similar collapse of his emulative pretensions. Writing beautiful verse, the poet finds, is vanity, in both senses of the word:

> As flames do work and winde, when they ascend,
> So did I weave my self into the sense.
> But while I bustled, I might heare a friend
> Whisper, *How wide is all this long pretence!*
> *There is in love a sweetnesse readie penn'd:*
> *Copie out onely that, and save expense.*

The poet discovers that God is not the flower but the honey; the most the poet can do, reduced to the level of the schoolboy, is to "copie out" God's word. When one's father is God the Father, it is difficult to become a man.

The effects of this subtle and complex doctrine of imitation upon Elizabethan adolescent psychology are naturally difficult to demonstrate. Although it may have been more likely for imitative tendencies to develop among schoolboys than girls or apprentices, all youths were touched by the doctrine, if not at school then at home or in church. Elizabethan diaries and autobiographies, however, generally shun the more intimate psychological experiences, and almost never explore their causes. To unravel the influence of imitation from other, complementary influences, moreover, is itself a perplexing task. As Thomas van Laan has shown, the notion of offices, or duties, appropriate to each station in society gave to social life a theatrical dimension.[28] And one might turn as well to the contemporary faculty psychology, which allegorized individuals into fixed types or roles; the parts that Jaques assigns to his actors upon the stage of the world in *As You Like It* seem mainly unconscious and physiologically determined. Imitation is thus part of a complex set of cultural assumptions and practices. Most significant for my purposes is the broad pattern I have traced: the release of "imitative energy" in the loss and re-creation of the self. To catch a glimpse of at least some of the behavioral possibilities within this pattern, we might examine a few contemporary anecdotes.

In the early pages of his diary, the seventeenth-century Puritan clergyman, Ralph Josselin, recalls his imitative behavior as a child with a certain ambivalence. He recounts with pleasure the early signs of his calling as a minister: "I confesse my childhood was taken with ministers and I heard with delight and admiracion and desire to imitate them from my youth, and would be acting in corners." His youthful imagination took a distinctly Tamburlanean form at times, however, and for this he is somewhat ashamed: "I made it my aime to learne and lent my minde continually to reade historyes: and to shew my spirit lett mee remember with griefe that which I yett feele: when I was exceeding yong would I project the conquering of kingdoms and write historyes of such exploits."[29] Josselin was presumably distressed not because he imitated historical models, for that was one of the chief purposes of reading histories, but because he imitated the wrong ones. In his case, fortunately, living ministers made a stronger impression than dead conquerors.

Although Josselin does not mention it, another kind of emulation was urged upon children, that of imitating Christ. In 1616, for example, when Sir Thomas Browne entered Winchester school, the daily "morning prayer for a child" included the following: "Teach me, O Lord, the Scriptures of thy Childe; enlighten my understanding that I may readily conceive; confirme my memory, that I may faithfully retaine the knowledge and learning wherein I shall be instructed; that as young *Samuel*, I may profit both in virtue, and stature and favour, both with thee and Man. Give me grace to imitate the sacred childhood of my Saviour; and that I may grow up in vertue and knowledge, to my parents joy and glory."[30] Here the exhortation to imitate Christ is complicated by the introduction of Samuel, who is himself an imitation or, more precisely, a type of Christ. That some young men took this doctrine very seriously indeed is indicated by an anecdote in Father John Gerard's account of his work as a Jesuit in England. Gerard tells of the impression made by Thomas a Kempis upon Sir Oliver Manners, who was converted to Catholicism around 1604:

He read devotional books eagerly, and always carried one in his pocket. You might see him in the court or in the Presence Chamber, as it is called, when it was crowded with courtiers and famous ladies, turning aside to a window and reading a chapter of Thomas a Kempis's *Imitation of Christ*. He knew the book from cover to cover. And after reading a little he would turn to the company, but his mind was elsewhere. He stood absorbed in his thoughts. People imagined that he was admiring some beautiful lady, or wondering how to climb to a higher position.[31]

This wonderful example of the "folly" of imitating Christ in a court given over to worldliness is matter for Erasmus. Manners not only reads of imitating Christ and meditates upon it; in his otherworldliness, which those around him cannot fathom, he unconsciously puts his reading into practice.

Perhaps the most compelling example of the power of emulation in the period is that of Sir Philip Sidney's death, as described by his friend, Fulke Greville. Although there is some question of the authenticity of Greville's account, its ambiguous status as fact or fiction suits my purpose. As Sidney prepares for the battle of Zutphen, according to Greville, he remembers that "upon just grounds the ancient Sages describe the worthiest persons to be ever best armed"; he fits himself out appropriately. When he meets the marshall of the camp, however, he sees that he is "lightly armed." Sidney, in the "unspotted emulation of his heart, to venture without any inequalitie," casts off his thigh armor, "and so, by the secret influence of destinie ... [disarms] that part, where God (it seems) had resolved to strike him." Sidney is shot accidentally by his own men, in the thigh. His horse, "furiously cholleric," bears him off the field:

In which sad progress, passing along by the rest of the Army, where his Uncle the Generall was, and being thirstie with excess of bleeding, he called for drink, which was presently brought him; but as he was putting the bottle to his mouth, he saw a poor Souldier carryed along, who had eaten his last at the same Feast, gastly casting up his eyes at the bottle. Which Sir *Philip* perceiving, took it from his head, before he drank, and delivered it to the poor man, with these words, *Thy necessity is yet greater than mine.* And when he had pledged this poor souldier, he was presently carried to *Arnheim.*[32]

This entire performance, including Greville's, might be called a sustained act of imitation, both direct and indirect. Sidney first looks to the ancients for his model, then to the marshall of the camp, then, in his courtesy to the common soldier, to Christ, or perhaps to the chivalric ideal which is itself an imitation of Christ. And Greville, who is careful to distinguish Sidney's "unspotted emulation" from envy or ambition – recall George Herbert's spiritual conundrums – constructs of the events of Sidney's death a model that, in the words of the *Defense of Poesy*, "inflames" the mind with the "desire to be worthy."[33] For Greville's purpose, whether the event is literally true is almost irrelevant: where does one find the true Sidney, if not in the ideal towards which he aspired? For my purpose, the ambiguity is revealing. In a culture based on "imitative energy," it is hard to tell where life ends and art begins – to tell, in another phrase from Yeats, "the dancer from the dance."

Although the evidence is fragmentary, there is enough to show that the role of the lover, like that of the soldier, was not restricted to the stage. With this role, in particular, one senses the ambiguous relation of art to life, of literary to social convention. In *The Anatomy of Melancholy* Robert Burton treats love melancholy as a real disease, an affliction of the liver; presumably he encountered live victims, despite the derivative nature of his evidence. In *Erotomania*, another treatise on love melancholy, James Ferrand not only discusses all the usual symptoms, which are hard to tell apart from the conventions of the amorist, but describes a case he treated in 1604.[34] The portraits of lovers in the period, cited earlier, memorialize roles that must surely have been acted out by the courtiers who posed for them. The character books themselves, moreover, offer sufficient evidence of stereotypical behavior, for they would have had little appeal if not anchored in contemporary reality.

Most of the biographical evidence for courtship behavior, as one might expect, comes from the gentry and aristocracy of the seventeenth century. Dorothy Osborne, for example, whose letters record her passionate courtship in great detail, occasionally lapses into behavior worthy of Overbury's amorist. When her beloved gives her a lock of his hair, she writes to him of her gratitude: "I am combing and Curling and kissing this Lock all day, and dreaming ont all night."[35] But there is earlier evidence as well, like the letter Sir Christopher Hatton wrote to Alice Fanshaw in the latter half of the sixteenth century. In it Hatton describes how his "youthfull fancies," freed by her beauty, "are flowne abroad and have burnte theire winges in affections flame, soe that I feare they will never flye whome againe,"[36] and much else; at the end of the letter he even turns poet. Still earlier, and this time among the bourgeoisie, we can see the effect of love upon John Johnson, the serious young apprentice to a London wool merchant. Not only did Johnson send numerous gifts to Sabine Saunders from Calais in 1538, such as sweet French cherries and neck-kerchiefs, but he decked himself in all the current fashions: "The accounts show him buying fine lawn shirts (three at a time) of Antwerp making; new shoes, new slops, new nether hose; doublets of striped satin and russet satin and bombasine; Spanish cloaks and surcoats enriched with parsemano work, or gold and silver lace. His best gown was sent for furring; he bought new gloves, and 'a hat dressed with laces' off one of his friends; even perfume to make him smell like the lily."[37] Whether John Johnson also wore a lock, like the fashionable Deformed of *Much Ado About Nothing* (III.iii.170), is uncertain; enough young men did in the early seventeenth century, however, to provoke William Prynne into writing *The Unloveliness of Love-Lockes*.

In 1644 a love affair began that illustrates in rich and perplexing detail the intermingling of literary convention and social behavior. In her autobiography, Anne Lady Halkett describes her long, complicated, and disastrous relation with a Mr H. Throughout their courtship, Anne's role is that of the "artificial" lover, torn between the conflicting obligations of daughter and beloved. The role of Mr H. is from beginning to end ambiguous; neither the reader nor Anne is able to tell this dancer from his dance. The narrative is long but illuminating.

The affair begins with Anne disobeying her mother and accepting, reluctantly, the addresses of Mr H., who is the brother of a good friend. He has tried for six months to smother his passion, he tells her, but to no avail, and unless she gives him some "hopes of favor" he will return to his native France and become a Capucin monk. She refuses this urgent request outright, but after he becomes so ill that "the howse took notice" she allows him to speak to her one day while strolling in the gallery: "What he saide was handsome and short, butt much disordered, for hee looked pale as death, and his hande trembled when he tooke mine to lead mee, and with a great sigh said, 'If I loved you lese I could say more.'" Reproaching him for his folly, she urges him to "consult with his owne reason."

After being shunned for some time, Mr H. speaks with Anne once again, telling her that he is leaving for France the next day and that his turning Capucin will be her responsibility. Distressed at this "hazard of his soule," Anne attempts to restrain him, promising never to marry until he does. He agrees joyfully to this bargain and says that he will be her husband. Later, when his sister is preparing to leave England, he urges Anne to marry him secretly, telling her that he has "a wedding ring and a minister to marry us." Anne, however, will not marry without "his father and my mother's consent," neither of which is forthcoming; his father, in fact, gives Mr H. the option of marrying a wealthy citizen's daughter he has selected for him or of leaving England. In this desperate plight the lovers meet one more time, chaperoned by Anne's sister. Mr H. swears he will never marry any but Anne; she forbids such an oath, but swears in turn that she will remain constant as long as he, "for though duty did oblieege mee nott to marry any withoutt my mother's consentt, yett itt would not tye mee to marry without my owne." At this point in the conversation Anne's sister threatens to leave because they are being so foolish. Overwhelmed at causing his beloved such suffering, Mr H. falls "downe in a chaire that was behind him, but as one without all sence." Anne is not unmoved. When he revives, she sits upon his knee and allows him to kiss her for the first time. He finally agrees to leave for France, but only if Anne will permit a farewell meeting.

Anne's mother, however, refuses a leave-taking unless she herself is present. Fearful that the lovers may do something rash, she has Anne guarded. Mr H. comes in secret, but through a series of misadventures too complicated to relate here, is mistaken for Anne's brother and knocked out by her brother's enemies. Impressed no doubt by his perseverance, Anne agrees to meet Mr H. secretly; she keeps the letter of her mother's edict by blindfolding herself. Mr H. renews all his old oaths and they part. Although they exchange gifts afterward, they never meet again. On the "last Tuesday in July 1646, a litle before super," Anne receives a letter telling that Mr H. has been privately married. She struggles for a while with the news, convinces herself finally that he is unworthy of her affection, and goes in to supper.[38]

Was Mr H. sincere in his oaths or not? Anne seems to have thought so, for no matter how extreme his behavior she never mentions doubts or suspicions; his betrayal comes as a complete surprise. Still, even if he meant every word, were not his gestures slightly theatrical? Did he really intend to become a monk? Were his illness, his disorder, his paleness, his trembling hand, his great sigh, his fainting all unconscious reflexes? Anne does not pursue these questions, nor can we, for they are unanswerable. They take on a special interest, however, because Mr H.'s behavior is so flagrantly conventional. He is either playing a role or a role is playing him. If the former, he is an "artificial" lover; if the latter, a "natural." Such ambiguities can occur in all societies, but they seem particularly inevitable in a culture of great "imitative energy." If Mr H. were a character in a play, we would explain his behavior as literary convention. It may be that Elizabethan drama is more "realistic" than we assume, and Elizabethan life more artificial.

Admittedly, Mr H. is an extreme case. His was a love affair, not an arranged marriage. More typical would be the courtships described in Henry Best's journal, cited earlier (p. 26). Unfortunately, although Best provides a glimpse of the elaborate ritual of courtship – the regular visits, the prescribed order of gifts – he tells nothing of the actual behavior or emotions of the couples involved. Such information is difficult to come by, at least in any detail. Perhaps one very brief example might at least raise some pertinent questions. In 1626, at the age of twenty-four, Sir Simonds D'Ewes and his father were casting about for a suitable match that would bring the son the genealogy he wanted and the father some ready money. They finally settled upon Anne Clopton and entered into lengthy negotiations with the family. Once these were concluded, Sir Simonds decided to survey his future bride, who was only thirteen years old. This meeting had two consequences: the marriage contract was signed, and Sir Simonds sent Anne a carcanet and a love letter. Even in this simple marriage of convenience, the conventions of courtship were rigorously observed. Presumably, D'Ewes's love letter was no more than a polite gesture and was accepted as such. Curiously, however, he developed real affection for the girl, to the dismay of her mother, who did not believe in romantic marriages, especially for a girl so young.[39] It may be that D'Ewes fell in love at first sight, but is it not also possible that his decision to become a lover, his choice of that role, helped create the affection he later felt? Certainly the popular seventeenth-century argument that love begins after marriage suggests something of this psychology. Playing a role may perhaps redefine the self, which is exactly why John Rainolds opposed acting and why Ben Jonson hoped his masques might better the court of King James.

Shakespeare's "natural" lovers are less calculating than D'Ewes and more comic. They do not choose their roles as often as they lapse into them. In this sense they become like Bergsonian automatons – predictable, mechanical, and therefore laughable. They lose themselves in their roles. The link between this loss of self and the imitation of the schoolboy is most direct in *A Midsummer Night's Dream*. In the course of a single night the lovers experience all of the confusions of the liminal phase: they wander, they dream, they act madly, they are bewitched, they are "translated"; their loss of self is its own disguise. This chaotic experience begins with the decision of Lysander and Hermia to flee the harsh Athenian law that prohibits their marriage. Their method of reaching this decision might almost be a schoolboy joke.

Lysander's first response to their predicament is to recall all the stories of tragical love he knows:

> Ay me! for aught that I could ever read,
> Could ever hear by tale or history,
> The course of true love never did run smooth... (I.i.132–34)

The misery in the litany of lovers' complaints that ensues – "O spite! too old to be engag'd to young" (line 138), etc. – mingles with exhilaration, for both characters are subtly attracted to these models, seeing themselves, like the famous lovers of antiquity, heroical victims of "an edict in destiny" (line 151). Their first impulse is thus imitative; they cast about for traditional roles that will enable them not only to vent but to heighten and elaborate their emotions. Hermia draws back from these tragical models, however, and, like a proper scholar, states their moral: "let us teach our trial patience" (line 152). Yet the models prove more compelling than the moral. Neither lover is capable of patience. In an instant, they have decided to run away from Athens. Only Hermia glimpses the irony in their action, for she swears to meet Lysander "by all the vows that ever men have broke" (line 175). Like the later, disguised heroines, she plays her role with a certain self-consciousness. Her wit does not protect her, however, for like the "Carthage queen" to whom she alludes, she commits herself to a "false Troyan" (lines 173–74) who will betray her. Shakespeare's irony encompasses the whole situation. The lovers have been thrust into "tragic" roles by the lunacy of their elders; their own lunacy makes the roles models rather than warnings. The plot works out the comic consequences.

In the very next scene of the play, the business of choosing the right role and playing it well is mimicked by the "hempen homespuns," who have gathered to rehearse their version of "the course of true love." Bottom attacks confidently the role of the lover: "I will move storms; I will condole in some measure" (I.ii.27–28). He plays it later, not only at Theseus's wedding but in Titania's bower, although in the latter case he is more interested in hay than amour. As is often the case in Shakespeare, the notion of role-playing leads to an infinite regress: Bottom both acts the part of a lover and becomes one; the acting takes place in a play within a play, the becoming in a play called a dream. Slightly more controllable ironies occur at the end of *A Midsummer Night's Dream*, when the "awakened" lovers witness the "tragical mirth" of "Pyramus and Thisbe," a mangled version of their own "dream." Having escaped their tragical destiny as lovers, not through patience but the magic of Oberon, the couples fail to notice that they are watching what might have been their own plot. Having lost themselves in their imaginations, they must also find themselves in their imaginations, in their capacity to "amend" the performance of the actors (V.i.212). We in the audience are given the same test. In *A Midsummer Night's Dream* art and life imitate each other.

While this loss of self in the comedies is always ultimately benign – the lovers lose themselves to find themselves – it can be comically terrifying. Imitation, as we have seen, can be dangerously self-effacing, not only if the models are bad but if they completely absorb the self. When Orsino postures as a love melancholiac in *Twelfth Night*, he withdraws from reality into a comical solipsism. Lurching from mood to mood and stimulus to stimulus at a frantic pace, he becomes, as Feste says, a very opal for changeability (II.iv.75). In love with a fantasy, he fictionalizes not only himself but Olivia, losing both in the chaos of his imagination: "So full of shapes is fancy," he says, "That it alone is high fantastical" (I.i.14–15).

In *As You Like It*, too, a "natural" lover nearly loses himself in his fiction. The conventional role of lover that Orlando plays with such abandon, despoiling the trees of Arden with his verses "deifying" Rosalind (III.ii.363), threatens to turn him into an allegory, as Rosalind herself perceives when she overhears the exchange of barbed compliments between Orlando and Jaques. The one is "Signior Love," the other "Monsieur Melancholy," and the titles suggest the extent to which both have been absorbed by their roles. Orlando's fiction includes Rosalind, for in "deifying" her he creates a part she herself cannot recognize and refuses to play. Orlando's willingness to woo Rosalind in game, rather than to search her out in reality, suggests a suspicious willingness to fictionalize the experience of love, to retreat, like Orsino, into the closed world of the imagination. Orlando finally becomes impatient with his fiction, but only after Rosalind has filled it with fact, and after he himself has been jolted by the refreshingly straightforward sexual energy of Oliver and Celia, who must marry quickly "or else be incontinent before marriage" (V.ii.39). At that point Orlando decides he can "no longer live by thinking" (line 50). The play tests not only Orlando's fictions against reality, and those of Silvius and Phebe, but those of the pastoral mode, in which such fictions are most at home.

In *The Comedy of Errors* the comic threat of extinction is played out in less conventional ways. Although all the major characters lose themselves in "errors" of various kinds, the wanderings of Adriana and Antipholus of Syracuse are developed with the greatest psychological depth. Adriana is a jealous wife, possessive to the point of absurdity. She loses herself not in a role but in a love for her husband so extreme that she attempts to become him, possessing him so completely as to extinguish both his individuality and her own. The outburst in which she accuses him of adultery suggests the extent of her confusion:

> I am possess'd by an adulterate blot;
> My blood is mingled with the crime of lust:
> For if we two be one, and thou play false,
> I do digest the poison of thy flesh,
> Being strumpeted by thy contagion.   (II.ii.140–44)

Adriana's "error" here provides subtle intellectual comedy on the one hand and farce on the other. Her conception of marital union derives from the wedding ceremony itself, which in turn follows St Paul's injunction that "a man leave father and mother, and ... cleave to his wife, and they twaine shalbe one flesh."[40] Although her emotion is genuine, the pathos in the scene is deflected into high comedy by her hyperboles, for she hysterically misapplies a carefully restricted mystical doctrine. The comedy is heightened by the incongruity between her literalism here and her earlier refusal even to consider the equally Pauline doctrine of wifely obedience urged upon her by Luciana (II.i.29). Adriana's psychological error is combined with perceptual error, the occasion of the scene's farcical humor, for the man who stands before her, who is so much herself that she is "strumpeted" by his adultery, is her husband's brother, the wrong man altogether. The anxiety about "possession" that runs throughout Ephesus is in Adriana's case not unwarranted; by seeking to "become" her husband, Adriana herself becomes "possessed" by the threat of adultery. Before she regains her husband, he must be "unpossessed," and not by Adriana's exorcist, Dr Pinch.

Adriana's plight is mirrored in that of Antipholus of Syracuse, whose loss of self we have already observed (p. 48). Antipholus loses his identity not only upon his entry into Ephesus, however, but upon his falling in love with Luciana. In the comic ecstasy of his passion, he expresses his willingness to die:

> Sing, siren, for thyself, and I will dote;
> Spread o'er the silver waves thy golden hairs,
> And as a bed I'll take them, and there lie,
> And in that glorious supposition think
> He gains by death that hath such means to die:
> Let Love, being light, be drowned if she sink! (III.ii.47–52)

The imagery of drowning, of following this mermaid into the sea, recalls Antipholus's earlier expression of love for his family, for whom he loses himself "like a drop of water/ That in the ocean seeks another drop" (I.ii.35–36). And both images recall the original and literal shipwreck in which the family was sundered. Like Adriana, Antipholus yearns to lose himself in those he loves. "Call thyself sister, sweet," he says to Luciana, "for I am thee" (III.ii.66). The ecstatic union embodied in the simple statement "I am thee" is instantly shattered, however, when Dromio rushes in to tell his master of the siren luring *him* to destruction. Once Antipholus learns of the awesome Nell, he determines to save himself. Luciana, he concludes,

> Hath almost made me traitor to myself;
> But lest myself be guilty to self-wrong,
> I'll stop mine ears against the mermaid's song. (III.ii.162–64)

The chanting of personal pronouns suggests Antipholus's state of mind. For the remainder of the play, with mixed results, he attempts to reassert his individuality, struggling against the witchcraft that threatens to confound him. The play as a whole, as Ruth Nevo observes, holds out "the dire personal threat of traumatic non-entity, or total chaotic non-being."[41]

The dissolution of self that characterizes the separal Adriana and Antipholus of Syracuse is reminiscent o description of what happens to personal identity in l normal ego, according to Freud, develops out of the fluic childhood, in which inside and outside worlds are confused, into the bounded state of adulthood, in which they are kept apart. "Towards the outside," says Freud, the mature ego "seems to maintain clear and sharp lines of demarcation." Love, however, "an unusual state, but not one that can be stigmatized as pathological," dissolves these boundaries: "At the height of being in love the boundary between ego and object threatens to melt away. Against all the evidence of his senses, a man who is in love declares that 'I' and 'you' are one, and is prepared to behave as if it were a fact."[42] In a recent book, *Shakespeare and the Experience of Love*, Arthur Kirsch has attempted to fuse Freud's conception of love with that of St Paul as a means of defining Shakespeare's. His argument bears particularly on the comedies: "Common to the psychogenesis of ... humor, of love, and of religious faith ... is a regaining of infantile feelings whose major effect is to dilate the ego. This dilation, which corresponds exactly to St. Paul's description of the spiritual union of man and wife, if not also of man and God, is the core experience of Shakespearean comedy, explicitly sexual in the romantic comedies; more transcendental ... in the final plays."[43] This view, while richly suggestive, needs considerable qualification. When such a "dilation" of the ego occurs in the comedies, as in the case of Antipholus or Adriana, it is romantic, certainly, but it is also comical, potentially dangerous, and temporary – a symptom of the generative confusion of self characteristic of the liminal phase. The mature, adult love celebrated at the end of the plays also represents a mystical union but of a different kind – a union of distinct individuals.

The difference between these two experiences of love becomes clear if we consider Shakespeare's treatment of twins, his most compelling symbols of the mystery of identity. In both of the plays in which twins appear, *The Comedy of Errors* and *Twelfth Night*, each twin "imitates" the other, either by design, in the case of Viola, or by accident, in all the others. The inevitable result of this union of identities, this becoming of the other, is liminal confusion – in varying degrees, the disintegration of the self. Clarification and fulfillment in love are achieved only at the moment when each twin, in discovering the other, discovers himself. At this point, one might say, the ego dilates and contracts simultaneously. Viola's reunion with Sebastian frees her own identity. The Syracusan Antipholus and Dromio unite themselves joyfully to their twins at the end of *The Comedy of Errors*, but they discover themselves with equal joy: Antipholus does not belong to Adriana, nor Dromio to Nell. The twins both are and are not each other, just as Adriana is and is not her husband.

Shakespeare's paradoxes of identity are in some ways reminiscent of popular neoplatonism, with its emphasis on love as a union of souls. Shakespeare, however, stresses the autonomy of the individual soul in mature love as well as its union with another. The distinction is fine but important. In Bembo's famous speech in *The Courtier*, for example, the union of lovers in a kiss is so complete that they lose all individuality, becoming a "single soul" that "rules as it were over two bodies."[44] Shakespeare's twins, on the other hand, are unique not because they are one, but because they are both one and two; unlike Bembo, Shakespeare underlines both sides of the paradox. The notion is worked out most explicitly in the elaborate oxymorons of "The Phoenix and the Turtle":

> So they loved as love in twain
> Had the essence but in one,
> Two distincts, division none:
> Number there in love was slain.   (lines 25–28)

To emphasize the idea of union is to lose the paradox. The phoenix and the turtle are both double and single: "Two distincts, division none." We will return to this pattern in a later chapter, for it bears directly upon Shakespeare's comic rites of incorporation.

The most common threat to identity in the transitional phase of the comedies is not the loss of the self in another but, paradoxically, the loss of the self in the self – a contraction of the ego, to adapt Freud's terminology, to the vanishing point. This is the ultimate psychological consequence of the lover's proverbial inconstancy. Both the sonnets and comedies explore the psychology of fickleness with remarkable frequency – the sonnets with irony and pessimism, the plays with a qualified comic optimism. In the comedies, fickleness is an exclusively male affliction. Like Hermia in *A Midsummer Night's Dream*, the romantic heroines play the role of the "Carthage queen" while their lovers betray them like "false Troyans." In keeping with the optimistic tone of the comedies, however, only once, in *The Two Gentlemen of Verona*, is betrayal for another woman literal; the uniqueness of this event may help explain some of the traditional dissatisfaction with the play's ending. In the other comedies, betrayals occur obliquely, in a ritualistic or symbolic mode. Their natural habitat is the liminal realm of imagination. They occur in dream (*A Midsummer Night's Dream*), in "error" (*The Comedy of Errors*), in play (*As You Like It*). In these cases, and others, Shakespeare explores the effects of inconstancy not only upon the constant heroines but upon their "natural" lovers.

As his name implies, Proteus in *The Two Gentlemen of Verona* personifies this kind of folly. In the course of the play he betrays three people he loves: his betrothed, Julia; his friend, Valentine; and finally, as a would-be rapist, Valentine's beloved, Silvia. Proteus comes to his senses at the end of the play, fortunately, regains the love of all three, and points the moral to his own story:

> O heaven, were man
> But constant, he were perfect; that one error
> Fills him with faults; makes him run through all th'sins:
> Inconstancy falls off ere it begins.   (V.iv.110–13)

The final line is echoed in *The Merchant of Venice*; as Bassanio muses over the caskets, he listens to a song that locates the source of inconstancy in "fancy," which "dies/ In the cradle where it lies" (III.ii.68–69). In quite different but equally paradoxical ways, both plays test the value of constancy not only in romantic love but in friendship.

Proteus's inconstancy begins with a dilemma, which he wrestles with at length. If he leaves Julia for Silvia, he betrays not only Julia, to whom he has sworn his love, but Valentine, his sworn friend. To be true to them, however, is to be untrue to himself:

> Julia I lose, and Valentine I lose:
> If I keep them, I needs must lose myself;
> If I lose them, thus find I by their loss –
> For Valentine, myself; for Julia, Silvia.
> I to myself am dearer than a friend …   (II.vi.19–23)

Proteus's inconstancy begins, in this rationalization, as a quest to find himself. In his betrayals, he remains constant to himself alone: "I cannot now prove constant to myself,/ Without some treachery us'd to Valentine" (lines 31–32). The irony in this narcissism is that it ends in self-destruction, for as Proteus lurches from betrayal to betrayal he becomes more and more the embodiment of his own name, a shape-shifter whose very identity threatens to dissolve. In some ways his role is a romantic and comic version of that of Richard III, who declares "I am myself alone" (*3H6* V.vi.83); changes "shapes with Proteus for advantages" (III.ii.192); and awakens the night before the battle of Bosworth to discover that he has no self left.

An oblique version of this pattern occurs in *Love's Labor's Lost*. The young men first prove inconstant not to women but to their little academe, where they have sworn to live secluded for three years. Berowne's wonderfully sophistical excuse for their perjury, which runs to eighty convoluted lines, recalls Proteus's excuse for his, although it adds a note of religious hypocrisy that will return to haunt the men at the end of the play:

> Let us once lose our oaths to find ourselves,
> Or else we lose ourselves to keep our oaths.
> It is religion to be thus forsworn:
> For charity itself fulfills the law,
> And who can sever love from charity? (IV.iii.358–62)

As in the case of Proteus, the decision to find oneself by losing one's oath proves self-defeating, for the lovers are tricked into betraying still other oaths, those sworn mistakenly to the wrong ladies. When these oaths are sworn, both men and ladies are in disguise – the men, with perhaps a subtle echo of Proteus, in the "shapeless gear" of Russians (V.ii.303).

In its most extreme forms, then, the loss of self in the role of the lover may lead to the Scylla of self-absorption or the Charybdis of absorption into another. In either case, the self becomes a kind of chaos, and the transitional experience – of wandering, dreaming, madness, enchantment, metamorphosis, disguise – a regression into a formless state of being. Such a regression, as we have seen, is common to the liminal phase of rites of passage. In some initiation rites, as Mircea Eliade has shown, this pattern operates not only psychologically but mythically, re-creating not only the individual but the world. The sacred ground of the *bora* rites of the Kamilaroi in Australia, for example, is understood to be their god's first campsite, and the ritual itself, as Eliade describes it, is a "reactualization" of the god's "creative work, and hence a regeneration of the world." On the basis of such practices, Eliade interprets all initiatory "death" as a "temporary return to Chaos" – not an annihilation of self, as moderns understand death, but a "regression to a preformal state, to a latent mode of being" that contains a "new life in the course of preparation."[45]

In Elizabethan culture, a similar myth of creation is associated with the experience of love.[46] In "An Hymne in Honour of Love," for example, Spenser, drawing upon Hesiod and Ficino, depicts Cupid creating the universe out of chaos:

> Then through the world his way he gan to take,
> The world that was not till he did it make;
> Whose sundrie parts he from them selves did sever,
> The which before had lyen confused ever.　　　　(lines 74–77)

In Shakespeare, the paradox of love is that it both deforms and reforms. His archetype, in a sense, is Proteus, to whom he turns so early in his career. A sea-god, whose natural element is flux, Proteus is a notorious shape-shifter, capable of assuming any identity, even that of a bear, a dragon, or the sea itself. He is thus an emblem of the confusion and dislocation of self that characterizes the transitional phase.

But Proteus can be persuaded to re-form. He changes shape only to frighten away his visitors, who come to him for his prophetic knowledge. If they are not intimidated by his metamorphoses and hold him fast, he will eventually return to his true shape and give them their desires. In the comedies, those who will protean lovers into submission are women whose love, like that celebrated in Sonnet 116, refuses to alter "when it alteration finds" or to bend "with the remover to remove." The Proteus of *The Two Gentlemen of Verona* resumes his true shape because Julia loses her shape, and her self, in pursuit of him:

> I am my master's true confirmed love;
> But cannot be true servant to my master,
> Unless I prove false traitor to myself.
> Yet will I woo for him, but yet so coldly
> As, heaven it knows, I would not have him speed. (IV.iv.103–07)

Julia's choice is the opposite of her lover's, and her fate reverses the paradox of his: by betraying herself she finds not only herself but him. There are limits to her betrayal, however, as the final two lines make clear: she will woo for him, but coldly. Like Valentine, who gives away Silvia to his friend, Julia sacrifices herself for love; like Proteus, she pursues her own self-interest. She avoids both men's absurdities by becoming, in the paradox of mature love, both her lover and herself. "In Julia," as Ruth Nevo observes, "craft and constancy, spontaneity and morality, are no longer irremediably sundered as they have been for the two gentlemen, nor self and other doomed to a polarity of identity or non-entity."[47] Shakespeare's "artificial" lovers, like Julia, are both protean and constant; they choose their shapes, like the god himself, and experience consciously the chaos of love.

4
Artificial Transitions

"This fellow is wise enough to play the fool"
(*TN* III.i.60)

Although the subtlest and most elusive of Shakespeare's comic conventions, female disguise is from one perspective easy to explain. If laughter is at the heart of comedy, and incongruity at the heart of laughter, any disguise offers a simple and satisfying formula for both. Complications in disguise can lead to increasingly sophisticated effects. To dress a man in woman's clothes heightens incongruity because it creates not only a double identity but a sexual reversal. To dress a woman in man's clothes is even more incongruous, for it places the woman in a position of superior awareness and, sometimes, power – a position that is especially incongruous in a society dominated by males. Because his disguised heroines spend so much time in masculine company, particularly that of their lovers, Shakespeare's comedies exploit consistently this kind of incongruity.

As the latter case implies, laughter at disguise may spring not only from incongruity but superiority. Much of our delight in Shakespeare's disguised heroines arises from, in Hobbe's phrase, the "sudden glory" we experience as we share vicariously their gleeful manipulations of their helpless victims. Bassanio, Orlando, Orsino, and Proteus all prove fools under the watchful eyes of women they will marry but do not know. The audience's delight is not always the heroine's, however, for disguise may bring not only power but acute discomfort. When that happens, as in the duel between Viola and Sir Andrew, the feeling of "sudden glory" belongs to the audience alone.

When Shakespeare began writing comedy, the convention of the disguised heroine, or "female page," was already well established. Like many of the comic conventions of the period, it originated not in classical comedy – Terence and Plautus use only male disguise, and that sparingly – but in medieval romance.

81

From this source it followed a circuitous route to Shakespeare, through Italian novellas and plays and their Elizabethan translations and imitations. The convention touched Shakespeare most directly through contemporary prose romances, such as Montemayor's *Diana*, Lodge's *Rosalynde*, and Sidney's *Arcadia*, and through romantic drama, such as the anonymous *Sir Clyomon and Sir Clamydes*, Greene's *James IV*, and Lyly's *Gallathea*. Although the device had only the most oblique connection to actuality, it obviously possessed not only comic but imaginative appeal. Sir James Melville reports that when Queen Elizabeth expressed a desire to see Mary, Queen of Scots, he offered to take her "secretly to Scotland by post, clothed like a page, disguised, that she might see the queen ..." Although Elizabeth did not pursue the plan, she was sorely tempted: "She appeared to like that kind of language, and said, 'Alas, if I might do it.'"[1]

Both Greene and Lyly exploit female disguise in ways that anticipate Shakespeare. In Greene's *James IV* the heroine, Dorothea, disguises herself as a man in order to protect herself from her husband, James IV, who plans to kill her so that he can pursue Lady Ida, with whom he is infatuated. Wounded by her husband's accomplice, who sees through her disguise, Dorothea is nursed back to health by Lady Anderson, who does not, and who falls hopelessly in love with her. The situation, in short, is akin to that of Olivia and Viola in *Twelfth Night*. While Greene provides some incidental humor in Dorothea's awkwardness and discomfort as a man, he uses the device ineptly and to little dramatic effect. There are no wooing scenes between the two women, and no complications develop. The episode serves only a thematic function, as Norman Sanders remarks, Lady Anderson's "insatiate lust" for Dorothea parodying that of James IV for Lady Ida.[2] Shakespeare too provides such thematic parallels, and more skillfully.

It is to Lyly that we must turn for the characteristically Shakespearean use of the convention as a means of exploring the psychology of love. In *Gallathea* the two heroines, Phyllida and Gallathea, both disguise themselves as boys, then meet and fall in love with each other. In dialogues of delicate emotional tension and ironic innuendo, each girl probes the other's identity, fearing that her beloved may also be in disguise. Two brief exchanges, one from *Gallathea* and one from *Twelfth Night*, may illustrate the affinity of the two dramatists:

Phyllida. Have you ever a sister?
Gallathea. If I had but one, my brother must needs have two.
But, I pray, have you ever a one?
Phyllida. My father had but one daughter, and therefore I
could have no sister.[3]

Duke. But died thy sister of her love, my boy?
Viola. I am all the daughters of my father's house,
And all the brothers too – and yet I know not. (II.iv.119–21)

While the psychology of each situation is not identical – Lyly's is
in some ways more complicated, since both characters are disguised – it is remarkably close; both dramatists create a sophisticated comedy of emotions, in which role and feeling are at odds
and imperfect perception is a symptom of the folly of love.

Despite their similarities, Lyly and Shakespeare develop the
convention of female disguise in quite different directions. While
Lyly accentuates its artificiality, Shakespeare anchors it in human
psychology. Lyly's heroines take on disguise for fantastic reasons
– to avoid becoming sacrificial victims; Viola wears her brother's
clothes, imitating him as a gesture of love. Lyly, more importantly, not only provides *two* heroines in disguise but puts them in
a dilemma that can only be resolved by a change in sexual identity
for one or the other, which Venus promises at the end of the play.
Which one changes does not matter. When Viola unmasks, on the
contrary, her identity is fulfilled. Whereas Lyly complicates the
convention as convention, Shakespeare complicates it as a projec-
tion of human psychology.

Although further comparison of Shakespeare with his contemporaries would highlight his mastery of this comic medium, the
point hardly needs demonstration. More significant is what a
review of his contemporary dramatists tells us about Shakespeare's distinctive concerns. Most striking, although in some
ways least explicable, is the fact that no other Elizabethan dramatist exploits the convention of female disguise so consistently; to
think of Shakespearean comedy is to think of Julia, Rosalind,
Viola, and Portia in disguise. It is also remarkable that other
dramatists are more inventive than Shakespeare in using the
device to complicate their plots. This is true not only of Lyly, but
of Jonson and Heywood, both of whom create effects that
Shakespeare never attempts – Jonson, in *Epicoene*, using disguise
to fool his audience; and Heywood, in *Wise Woman of Hogsdon*,
using disguise within disguise. In contrast to such elaborations, as

Victor O. Freeburg observes, Shakespeare's use of the device is simple and formulaic: he focuses attention on a single, dominant personality, who puts on disguise with the full knowledge of the audience, lives within it for a time, and removes it at the end of the play.[4] Shakespeare's aim is not maximum complication of plot, or startling theatrical effects, but the complication and development of character.

The notion of role-playing, developed in many modern studies of the comedies, offers a fruitful approach to female disguise because it enables us to see the convention as part of a continuum. The disguised heroines are set apart in the plays not because they alone are playing roles, but because their roles are consciously assumed and, more than those of others, at least, under control. While Rosalind plays the role of Ganymede, Orlando and Jaques allow their roles to play them – as Signior Love and Monsieur Melancholy. One problem of this approach, however, also common to more traditional approaches, is that it results often in mere celebrations of the heroines as static ideals. In *Role-playing in Shakespeare*, for example, Thomas van Laan's Rosalind is little different from that of the critical tradition we have reviewed in an earlier chapter (above, p. 17). "Rosalind," he says, "emerges as the pageant of love's ideal figure because she possesses the two attributes required for all successful role-playing, both onstage and off: the insight to pick the right role and the ability to play it with creative detachment."[5] Because the heroines play their roles with such grace and sophistication, critics too often overlook the fact that disguise marks for them, as unconscious role-playing does for their lovers, a temporary loss or confusion of identity, a period of disorientation. The disguised heroines may be "artificial" fools, but they are fools nonetheless; their consciousness of their folly, and their helplessness before it, create much of our comic delight. Disguising, in other words, is a dynamic process. To put on a mask is to lose oneself; to take it off is to "discover" oneself – in both senses of the word.

What is distinctive about female disguise in Shakespeare's comedies, then, is that it occurs as a phase in a process of self-discovery and self-revelation. In this sense disguise functions very much like the face-painting, masking, or sex reversal characteristic of novices during the liminal period of rites of passage. Because the disguised heroines choose their liminal roles, however, unlike their male counterparts, who usually lapse into them, they become not only novices in the rites of love but teachers. If disguising can be considered a kind of imitation, then the disguised heroines are students in the upper forms, consciously crafting their identities, choosing personas that enable them to define and become themselves. As these rough analogies suggest, female disguise is the most complicated of Shakespeare's comic conventions. It can be best approached, I think, in two ways: as a courtship rite, marking the transition from a single to a married state, and as an initiation rite, marking the transition from childhood to maturity. The two naturally overlap.

Queen Elizabeth's daydreams notwithstanding, young Elizabethan women neither travelled nor courted disguised as pages. Nor, surprisingly, did they ritually unveil at their weddings. Their masks were subtler and more indirect, consisting of a set of conventions, still familiar, by means of which they were to conduct themselves and control their lovers. If being a lover imposed a role, so did being loved. Since there is very little biographical evidence for the intimate details of this role, and since it was not open to the same satiric treatment that immortalized the "amorists," we must reconstruct it in rather roundabout ways.

Perhaps the most important requirement of a woman during courtship, aside from all the obvious virtues, was that she be "coy." The slight jolt the word gives the modern reader suggests what it is to live in a culture based on sincerity instead of "imitative energy." Although "coyness" could mean "false modesty," and take on the negative connotations the word has today, it more often meant simply "modesty," or an innocent shyness. "There is no time that exacts more modesty of any woman," says Richard Brathwait, "than in her time of suiting; a shamefast red then best commends her, and the movingst Orator that speakes for her." Because even virtuous modesty was a role, or mask, the distinction between false and true was blurred, at least to the modern mind. Consider, for example, Brathwait's description of a pleasing feminine modesty in courtship:

There is a pretty pleasing kinde of wooing drawne from a conceived but concealed *Fancy*; which, in my opinion, suits well with these amorous younglings; they could wish with all their hearts to be ever in the presence of those they love, so they might not be seene by those they love. Might they chuse, they would converse with them freely, consort with them friendly, and impart their truest thoughts fully, yet would they not have their bashfull loves finde discovery. They would be seene, yet seeme obscured; love, but not disclose it; see whom they love, but not be eyed.[6]

Brathwait's manner of expression is as revealing as his matter, for he obscures the boundaries not only between role and reality but between feeling and action. This kind of wooing is on the one hand a calculated performance, an act of imagination, springing from a "conceived but concealed *Fancy*"; on the other, it expresses their "bashfull loves." It is an art of coyness. Such courtship, moreover, is at once a mode of action – a "kinde of wooing" – and a mode of thought, for Brathwait's description is almost entirely of wishes and desires. That such ambiguities are intentional is highly unlikely; probably, Brathwait merely expresses unconsciously ambiguities that were built into the Elizabethan conception of feminine modesty in courtship. Whatever the reason, the overall effect of the passage is clear and wonderfully apt, for it captures much of the psychology of Shakespeare's disguised heroines. A literal disguise affords them the protection that coyness affords Brathwait's "amorous younglins"; by taking on another identity, by acting out a "conceived but concealed *Fancy*," Shakespeare's heroines can "see whom they love, but not be eyed."

Although Brathwait focuses on the romantic appeal of coyness – his admiration seems more than academic – it had also a practical and moral function. Expected to play the passive role in courtship, women could find in coyness a shield behind which they could rally their forces and survey the foe. Like chivalric warfare, courtship was a game played in deadly earnest. With no possibility of divorce, the choice of a mate, as Lord Burghley advised his son, was "an action like a strategem in war where a man can err but once."[7] Nearly all the contemporary handbooks on marriage have similar, if less picturesque advice. Alexander Niccholes' version is typical: "Marriage of all the humane actions of a mans life, is one of the greatest weight and consequence, as thereon depending the future good, or evill, of a mans whole aftertime and dayes: that Gordian knot once fastened not to be unloosed but by death ..."[8] Although most of the handbooks are written from a masculine point of view, they almost invariably imply freedom of choice for women as well, and with it the awesome burden of making what the Princess in *Love's Labor's Lost* calls a "world-without-end bargain" (V.ii.789). The anxieties aroused by such a system, at least for those who sought marital peace as well as prosperity, may help to explain the popularity of books with advice on how to choose a spouse.

By convention, at least, women especially needed a protective shield during courtship because of their extreme susceptibility to romantic passion. Infatuation, which for moderns is usually interpreted as a healthy sign of adolescent development, the first step towards mature love, was more likely to be interpreted by Elizabethans as an unequivocal sign of danger. When Anne Clopton gave evidence of falling in love with her formal suitor, Sir Simonds D'Ewes, her grandmother used this as part of her argument against the marriage, fearing, as D'Ewes puts it, that "the very interest I had already gained in her grandchild's good will and affections was no solid or real love grounded on judgment, and might therefore alter and lessen again after marriage ..."[9] If marriage was to be based on rational choice, whatever affection arose during courtship was a potential source of anxiety as well as delight. Such tensions underlie much of the comedy of Shakespearean courtship.

Since the purpose of courtship was to increase the likelihood of rational choice, the handbooks stress the need to become a kind of moral detective. According to John Dod and Robert Cleve, a long betrothal is vital because the attributes of a spouse

are not spied at three or foure commings, and meetings of the parties for hypocrisie is spunne with a fine threed, and none are so often deceived as lovers. He therefore which will know all his wives qualities: or she that wil perceive her husbands dispositions, and inclinations, before either be married to the other, had need to see one the other eating, and walking, working, and playing, talking, and laughing, and chiding too: or else it may be, the one shall have with the other, lesse then he or shee looked for, or more then they wished for.[10]

In *A Preparative to Mariage* Henry Smith shows, with a wry humor that seems to be unconscious, just how far this kind of spying might extend: "To begin this concord well, it is necessarie to learne one anothers nature, and one anothers affections, and one anothers infirmities, because ye must be helpers, and ye cannot help, unlesse ye know the disease."[11] Shakespeare's disguised heroines, it is safe to say, enter marriage well aware of the disease.

Shakespeare's familiarity with the handbook approach to courtship is delightfully apparent in *The Two Gentlemen of Verona*, when Launce parcels out the qualities of his potential spouse. Too shrewd to be swayed by dangerous passions, Launce plays it safe with greed. He itemizes credits and debits with the nicety of a merchant. The business is weighty and trying, for his list tells him not only that his intended can milk, brew good ale, sew, knit, wash, and spin, but that she has bad breath when fasting, talks in her sleep, is slow in her words, proud, toothless, curst, and too liberal. Although it requires careful thought, the final item in the list tips the balance in her favor: "she hath more hair than wit, and more faults than hairs, and more wealth than faults" (III.i.353–54). Launce need not meet his intended; his shopping list tells him all he needs to know.

Launce satisfies, in a rather more practical manner than they recommend, the advice of the marriage handbooks to think carefully about the nature of one's prospective spouse. He ignores, however, their other conventional recommendation, that one know oneself. In one wedding sermon, printed in 1617 as *A Bride-Bush or A Wedding Sermon*, the preacher, probably William Whately, curtly asked his audience, "Wouldst thou be married? See what wisedome, what patience, what grace fit to governe or fit to obey thou findest in thy selfe."[12] The wedding apparently went forward anyway.

Whately is as unromantic about marriage as Brathwait is romantic. In another work, aptly entitled *A Care-Cloth, or the Cumbers and Troubles of Marriage*, he devotes more than twenty pages to the rigorous self-examination men and women should conduct before marrying. For a woman, he proposes questions such as, "What if mine husband should prove unkind, and disregardfull of me? What if hee should bee bitter and ragefull towards me? What if hee should rate me with words of disgrace, more than ever my Father or Master have done? What if hee should lay upon me with his unmanlike fist? and that when I seeke to give him all content?" Having run through enough troubles to make even the hardiest lover "forswear" the "full stream of the world" and "live in a nook merely monastic" (*AYL* III.ii.419–21), Whately concludes with this consolation: "Know you, that this which we have spoken, is but, as it were, a Map before your eyes, or as an imperfect narration, of a dangerous and troublesome voyage, which your experience will make you feele, to be ten times more troublesome, then any words can describe it."[13] This is the voyage Jaques sees Touchstone embarked upon at the end of *As You Like It*, and for only "two months victuall'd" (V.iv.192). Although violently anti-romantic, Whately does not oppose marriage; he merely urges men and women to enter the blessed state with eyes wide open – to each other and themselves. In a woman, coyness permits the detachment necessary for such insight.

The extent to which actual courtships consisted of the serious moral probing recommended by sermons and tracts is difficult to determine; some couples no doubt married with Whately's advice in mind, some with Launce's list. Although there is considerable evidence of the ritual of romance, as in the exchange of love tokens and the like, there is little of its dialogue, or of the progress of representative courtships over a sustained period. Two illustrations, however, might give some indication of the possibilities. One is literary, although not composed as art – Erasmus's colloquy, "Courtship"; the other is historical – an excerpt from Thomas Whythorne's autobiography. In different ways, each takes us more deeply into the woman's role in courtship.

Erasmus's colloquy is the kind of school-text he himself must have had in mind when urging schoolmasters to teach Latin through materials that were both entertaining and instructive. In a witty and sophisticated manner, the two lovers of the dialogue, Pamphilus and Maria, run through most of the conventional questions addressed in the marriage tracts and most of the clichés of Petrarchan poetry. The dialogue begins with Pamphilus uttering the usual Petrarchan and neoplatonic clichés – she is a murderess, she has robbed him of his soul; but these Maria debunks unmercifully. Threatened finally by the prospect of Cupid's revenge against her refusal to love, Maria playfully agrees to return Pamphilus's affection. He, however, demands a stronger commitment:

Pamphilus. But I crave that love at your hand, which should be perpetuall and to love me as your owne. I seeke a wife, not a friend.
Maria. I know that well inough, but that thing requireth long deliberation, and much advisement, which when it is done, cannot be undone againe.
Pamphilus. I have deliberated uppon it to long for my part.
Maria. Well ... take heede, least love who is not the best counsellor beguile you, for men say that love is blinde.

Pamphilus takes up the challenge and demonstrates the rationality of his love, listing all the conventional attributes that insure a successful marriage: good birth; good education; family ties; equality in age, wealth, reputation, and rank; long acquaintance; and compatible temperaments. Maria counters with doubts: her youth will wither; her virginity, once lost, can never be regained; the loss of children brings misery. Pamphilus answers each objection satisfactorily, but Maria refuses to commit herself until he has secured the approval of both parents and reflected further himself: "that which affection decerneth is liked for a ceason, but that which reason aviseth is never misliked." As if this were not enough, the poor man must leave without a kiss:

You saye that your soule is alreadie gone well neere altogither into my body, and a very small parte thereof taryeth behinde in your owne, so that I feare in time of a kisse, that which remayneth might happen to sterte out after it, and then were you altogither without a soule. Have you therefore my right hande in token of mutuall love, and so fare you well.[14]

Even in an unwieldy translation, the colloquy provides a lively psychological drama. Although Pamphilus is wittier than most of Shakespeare's male lovers, he is the "natural" of the pair — passionate, earnest, single-minded in his pursuit. Maria is all innocent artifice — in love but in control. She manipulates the situation coolly, playfully, coyly, testing Pamphilus's love and her own before fully committing herself. Her modesty is her mask. If the dialogue had any relation to actual Elizabethan courting behavior, it is as likely to have shaped as reflected it. Not only were the colloquies standard textbooks in schools throughout the sixteenth century, but they were taught through imitation. Students were encouraged to act the roles "as if they themselves were the persons which did speak in that dialogue."[15]

One of Thomas Whythorne's many amorous adventures shows that feminine coyness could be not only a defensive but an aggressive weapon. Like the courtship of Anne Halkett and Mr H., this episode reveals the tendency of such performances to blur distinctions between fact and fiction, self and role. At this time in his career, Whythorne was serving as music teacher in a family whose servants had friendly relations with the household next door. The master of this household, a widower, had a housekeeper, named Elsabeth, who was rumored to be both his bedfellow and heir. Although he scarcely knew the woman,

Whythorne was invited by a chaplain, a mutual friend, to have breakfast with her one day. During the meal the chaplain complimented Elsabeth on a special dish she had prepared, saying that if she had her own household she would take good care of it. "'Yea,' quod she," writes Whythorne, "'and if I had Mr Whythorne,' (naming me) 'to be my husband.'" Whythorne smiled at these words and parried them wittily, jesting that if she had a spouse with his income she would indeed be "'well husbanded.'" Nonetheless, he "mused a little at her words, imagining why she should say so much to me, I being of so small acquaintance with her as I then was." But he put away his suspicions, concluding that "she spake these words but in jest and pastime and by the way of merry talk."

When later in the meal he proposed a toast to her, however, the tantalizing innuendos resumed. "'Call ye me mistress Elsabeth?'" she asked, "'And why not wife? Will ye not be my husband?'" This time Whythorne was lured into the game and answered, "'I drink unto you, gentle wife, with all my heart,'" to which she replied, "'I pledge you, good husband.'" At this point the chaplain entered in. Asserting that he would "make" them "sure," he took Elsabeth by the hand and reached for Whythorne's. But Whythorne drew back:

"Nay, I will woo a little while before I be made sure. For we do see sometimes that they, who do wed and marry in haste, have time enough afterward for to repent them." "Nay," quoth he [the chaplain] then (and with that he did let go her hand), "I do mean but merrily." "It may be so," (quoth I). But for all that, I thought then that such a contract, made by a priest, and in such sort as it seemed that he would have done it, might have turned some one or both of us unto some disquietness in the end.

After this unusual breakfast, the game never again became quite so intense, but both Whythorne and Elsabeth continued to address each other as husband and wife, he "merrily" entreating his scholars and friends to "give my 'wife' friendly entertainment" when she visited. His friends protested against marriage with such a "withered scroil," but Whythorne assured them that there was nothing between the two but "pastime and mirth." A while later, however, the relationship suddenly changed, for she told him that he "should be but her day husband, and not her night husband"; and when he called, he often found her not at home. Perplexed by this behavior, Whythorne wondered whether it might have been provoked by the gossip about her in his household or her desire "to make me the more eager of love towards her." Relations having finally grown quite distant, Whythorne discovered that Elsabeth was seriously ill. Suspecting that her love for him was responsible, his friends urged him to visit her, hoping that this would cure the disease. Whythorne did so, although reluctantly, and was relieved to find that "I could not perceive by any words of hers that she was towards me as it was reported to me to be." He learned later that she showed some signs of improvement after his visit, but he never saw her again, for he fell out with the mistress of his household and left for London.[16]

It is fortunately unnecessary for us to interpret this remarkable affair; its significance lies in its very ambiguity. Whythorne himself remains perplexed. Several interpretations are possible. It may be that Elsabeth's role-playing was spontaneous and uncalculated, a mere diversion. At the other extreme, it may be that she and the priest were in collusion, hoping to trap Whythorne into an unintended oath; since betrothals were the legal equivalent of marriage, Whythorne's unwillingness to play the breakfast game to its conclusion is understandable. Or, more likely, and more to our purpose, it may be that Elsabeth was engaged in a kind of serious play, as Whythorne himself suspected – testing imaginatively his affection and hers, getting the "feel" of marriage without the full commitment. One wonders, too, whether there might not have been some unconscious magic on Elsabeth's part, an attempt to transform Whythorne and herself into husband and wife by playing the roles; never far beneath the surface in Elizabethan discussions of imitation, as we have seen, is the notion that one becomes what one plays. Whatever one's interpretation, the episode reveals dramatically how feminine coyness might become a sustained feat of imagination, a loss of self in a role of one's choosing. It is a surprisingly small step from Whythorne's actual experience to one of Shakespeare's most artificial scenes. In *As You Like It*, Rosalind, playing Ganymede playing Rosalind, also takes the initiative, marrying Orlando in sport before she marries him in earnest. "Come sister," she says to Celia, "you shall be the priest, and marry us. Give me your hand, Orlando" (IV.i.124–25). Unlike Whythorne, Orlando offers no resistance.

Rosalind's is the most aggressive coyness in the comedies, for she uses her disguise to test Orlando's love. She proposes her mock-courtship as a "cure" for Orlando's love-melancholy and applies many of the traditional medications, such as witty slanders of the beloved, and thoughts of the decay of the flesh and the horrors of marriage.[17] Although Rosalind's earlier patient was so successfully cured that he forswore "the full stream of the world" and retreated to "a nook merely monastic" (III.ii.419–21), she has no such designs upon Orlando. Instead, she uses her disguise to play out two pressing questions – whether Orlando's love is true, or merely a conventional pose; and if true, whether his idealism, his "deifying" of her, the source of Touchstone's mockery, is hopelessly naive or strong enough to withstand her mere humanity. In the game of courtship Orlando is no match for Rosalind's wit, but he outdoes her in tenacity, for no matter how many variations she invents upon the theme of woman's frailty, he refuses to be disillusioned: "Virtue is no horn-maker; and my Rosalind is virtuous" (IV.i.63–64).

Rosalind is not satisfied with words, however, but demands actions. In this she is radically different from her prototype, Lodge's Rosalynde, who accepts her lover after he has assuaged her doubts in romantic verse. As a test of his faith, Rosalind insists that Orlando, who has been late for their first appointment, come to their next on time: "Time is the old justice that examines all such offenders, and let Time try" (IV.i.199–200). In one sense Orlando fails this test, for all that appears at the next interview, late, is his "bloody napkin." In another sense, he succeeds beyond Rosalind's wildest expectations, for the act that delays him, the hazarding of his own life to save his brother's, is proof of the highest love, charity. And it is this love that joins not only Rosalind and Orlando at the end of the play but earth and heaven:

> Then is there mirth in heaven,
> When earthly things made even
> Atone together. (V.iv.108–10)

The "bloody napkin" that unmans Rosalind ends all her doubts about marriage.

In *The Merchant of Venice* Portia also uses disguise to test her lover, and with similar consequences. Portia's role-playing begins with another end in mind. Bassanio has already proved his love by choosing the right casket. Portia determines to play Balthazar not to test him but to save his friend. Antonio's fate, however, stands between the marriage of the lovers and its consummation. Before paying his "debt" to his wife, Bassanio must pay his debt to

Antonio, which raises, for all three characters, the question of where Bassanio's ultimate loyalties lie. Although it figures only tangentially in the great drama of the courtroom, the question surfaces when Bassanio offers impulsively to sacrifice himself, his wife, and "all the world" to save Antonio. At this Portia comments wryly, "Your wife would give you little thanks for that/ If she were by to hear you make the offer" (IV.i.288–89). The test of the ring is thus not merely a test of Bassanio's word in the abstract, but of whose love he values most. Bassanio is persuaded to yield the ring only when Antonio weighs his own love against Portia's: "Let his [Balthazar's] deservings and my love withal/ Be valued 'gainst your wive's commandment" (lines 450–51).

Like Antonio, Bassanio fails to keep his bond, and he too is put on trial, although at Belmont instead of Venice. And once again his access to Portia lies through Antonio, who hazards this time his very soul – "I dare be bound again" (V.i.251). Portia now holds the "surety" (line 254), not Shylock, and although her husband's guilt may be of some use to her in marriage, she is likely to be merciful, for she is well aware that "in the course of justice, none of us/ Should see salvation" (IV.i.199–200). This play, like As You Like It, ends by celebrating a union of romantic love and charity, making it possible for Bassanio to give all his love to Portia and Antonio simultaneously and for Antonio to keep Bassanio's friendship by giving it away.

Not all of the disguised heroines deliberately put their lovers to a test. Julia and Viola watch helplessly in disguise as their lovers play the fool unassisted. For these heroines courtship is less a game than an initiatory ordeal. Like the Patient Griseldas of popular tradition, they see, endure, and forgive all. Whatever their motives or predicaments, however, all the disguised heroines fulfill through disguise some of the psychological and social needs of Elizabethan courtship. Shielded against premature discovery and commitment, the heroines can probe themselves and their lovers with temporary immunity. "Artificials" rather than "naturals," they play two roles simultaneously, that of novice and teacher. For them, assuming another identity is a means of redefining the self.

Although Elizabethan courtship conventions illuminate certain features of female disguise in the comedies, they leave some in shadow. Viola's disguise as Cesario, for example, is initially

unrelated to courtship. Unlike that of the other heroines, moreover, her assumed identity is not fictitious; she plays her lost
brother, Sebastian. In that sense, hers is the most literal and
specific case of disguise as imitation:

> I my brother know
> Yet living in my glass; even such and so
> In favor was my brother, and he went
> Still in this fashion, color, ornament,
> For him I imitate.   (III.iv.379–83)

Viola also differs from the other heroines in having not even a
pretext for disguise: she needs no protection, for Illyria is a
friendly place and a trustworthy sea-captain accompanies her.

Viola's sole motive for disguise appears in her desire to withdraw from society in service to Olivia. She describes her wish for
seclusion in language that reminds one of transitional rites:

> O that I serv'd that lady,
> And might not be delivered to the world
> Till I had made mine own occasion mellow
> What my estate is!   (I.ii.41–44)

Viola compresses into a single clause the essential processes of
initiation – rebirth, ripening, aligning oneself with time (occasion), discovering and disclosing one's personal and social
identity. Her disguise has something in common with both rites of
initiation and death. By imitating her brother, she mimics the
mourning of Olivia for hers. Both characters are trying to keep
their brothers alive: Olivia, by "seasoning" her brother's "dead
love" so it will stay "fresh/ And lasting in her sad remembrance"
(I.i.29–31), and Viola by wearing Sebastian's clothes. The difference between the two approaches is that between "seasoning"
and "mellowing" – between a futile attempt to preserve what is
already dead and a patient trust in the benign processes of
maturing time. Although she too retreats from the world, Viola
waits, not in the death-like state of Olivia's seven-year mourning,
a self-destructive becoming of one's brother, but as a foetus,
growing towards delivery. Or so she plans to wait, for her retreat,
like Olivia's, is hardly tranquil.

Viola is the only heroine who imitates a "living" person. The
others take on identities that are both more playful and symbolic.
Portia's "Balthazar" links her indirectly to Daniel, the wise young

judge who name figures so prominently in the court scene.[18] Rosalind's "Ganymede" makes her "Jove's own page" (*AYL* I.iii.124), a figure of ambiguous sexual orientation. Julia's "Sebastian" suggests her own martyrdom for love. Viola, oddly, does not take her brother's name, Sebastian, although she too martyrs herself for love: "And I must jocund, apt, and willingly,/ To do you rest, a thousand deaths would die" (V.i.132–33). Instead of taking the name of Sebastian, she becomes Cesario, "the king," suggesting perhaps Christ himself, the figure whose "delivery" is celebrated by the feast of Twelfth Night; or, ironically, the "king" whom Orsino hopes will fill the "sovereign thrones" of Olivia's being when she falls in love (I.i.35–40); or the Caesar whose "thrasonical brag" of his swift conquest is mocked by Rosalind in *As You Like It* (V.i.31). Although the names cast symbolic auras around the heroines, they are loosely suggestive rather than allegorical and figure scarcely at all in the psychology of imitation: Julia does not play Sebastian consciously, as Viola plays her brother. What we are most conscious of in all of these roles, including even Viola's, is not the impersonation of a particular individual but of a man or, more precisely, a youth. What we are most conscious of, in short, is sex reversal, a confusion of identity less characteristic of courtship than of seasonal festivals and rites of initiation.

Before examining these liminal modes, however, it may be worth turning to a more general social context. Although the evidence is fragmentary and difficult to interpret, there are signs that late Elizabethan and Jacobean social fashions reflected considerable questioning of conventional sexual roles. There are complaints that men are imitating women, as when Barnaby Rich protests against "this wearing, and this imbrodering of long lockes, this curiositie that is used amongst men, in freziling and curling of their hayre, this gentlewoman-like starcht bands, so be edged, and be laced, fitter for *Mayd Marion* in a *Moris dance*, then for him that hath either that spirit or courage, that should be in a gentleman."[19] More common, however, are complaints against women for dressing as men. In *The Anatomie of Abuses* (1583), Stubbes reproaches contemporary women for wearing doublets and jerkins as men do, citing Deuteronomy 22, the customary biblical text, in his defense. "Our Apparell," says Stubbes, "was given us as a signe distinctive to discern betwixt sex and sex, and therefore one to weare the Apparel of another sex is to participate with the same, and to adulterate the veritie of his owne kinde. Wherefore these Women may not improperly be called *Hermaphroditi*, that is, Monsters of bothe kindes, half women, half men."[20] Stubbes's accusation that wearing men's apparel leads women to "participate" in masculine qualities, thus adulterating their own, recalls the doctrine of imitation, with its assumption that playing a role may transform the self. Since women cannot become men, such role-playing can only result in monstrosity; they become "Monsters of bothe kindes, half women, half men."

In his *Description of England* (1587), William Harrison extends Stubbes's protest to women's fashions, which have become indistinguishable from men's. Attire that used to be seen only on "light" women, he says,

is now become an habit for chaste and sober matrons. What should I say of their doublets with pendant codpieces on the breast, full of jags and cuts, and sleeves of sundry colors? their galligaskins to bear out their bums and make their attire to fit plum-round (as they term it) about them? their farthingales and diversely colored netherstocks of silk, jersey, and suchlike, whereby their bodies are rather deformed than commended? I have met with some of these trulls in London so disguised that it hath passed my skill to discern whether they were men or women.[21]

In 1620, according to a letter of John Chamberlain, the abuse had become so widespread that the Bishop of London ordered it suppressed:

Yesterday the bishop of London called together all his clergie about this towne, and told them he had expresse commandment from the King to will them to inveigh vehemently against the insolencie of our women, and theyre wearing of brode brimed hats, pointed dublets, theyre hayre cut short or shorne, and some of them stilettoes or poniards, and such other trinckets of like moment; adding withall that if pulpit admonitions will not reforme them he wold proceed by another course; the truth is the world is very much out of order, but whether this will mende it God knowes.[22]

In the same year that the Bishop delivered his warning, the issues behind these fashions received a public airing in two pamphlets. The first, *Hic Mulier, or the Man-Woman*, attacks the "new Hermaphrodites." Although the anonymous author claims that women of all social classes are infected, he censures most strongly the great: "they swimme in the excesse of these vanities, and will bee man-like not onely from the head to the waste, but to the very foot, and in every condition: man in body by attyre, man

in behaviour by rude complement, man in nature by aptnesse to
anger, man in action by pursuing revenge, man in wearing
weapons, man in using weapons: And in briefe, so much men in
all things, that they are neither men, nor women, but just good for
nothing."[23] The shift from external appearance to inner nature
illustrates the extent to which the issue of fashion was essentially
an issue of sexual identity; hence the passions it aroused.

The second pamphlet, *Haec-Vir, or the Womanish-Man*, turns
the tables on the first. It begins with a meeting of the two
protagonists, neither of whom recognizes the other's sex. If
women have become masculine, men have become effeminate. In
the debate that ensues, the man-woman vigorously defends her
freedom to choose her fashions: "we are as free-borne as Men,
have as free election, and as free spirits, we are compounded of
like parts, and may with like liberty make benefit of our Cre-
ations."[24] She finally agrees to resume her proper role, however, if
the womanish-man will resume his. He agrees, and the debate
ends on a note of sexual decorum. Although the man-woman
presents a stirring argument for sexual equality, she never questions the fixity of sexual identity.

This entire phenomenon raises many questions, the answers to
which would require further study. How widespread were these
practices? Were they a London or national fashion? Were they as
typical of men as women, who can be presumed to have aroused
the most indignation? Were they really characteristic of all social
classes, as *Hic-Mulier* asserts? Were they the same in 1583 as in
1620? Were they trivial, or were they symptoms of genuine social
protest? If the latter, is it fair to call such a protest feminist, and in
what sense? Or, since men are also implicated, does the protest
reflect more pervasive ambivalences concerning sexual identity?
In her provocative study, *Shakespeare and the Nature of Women*,
Juliet Dusinberre interprets the phenomenon as a "symptom of
Jacobean feminism,"[25] the chief outlet for which was the drama
of the period, particularly Shakespeare's. Although insightful,
Dusinberre's argument oversimplifies the issues, converting a
complicated set of social gestures into a coherent feminist
program that often sounds more modern than Jacobean. At the
very least, however, we can say that the contemporary unrest in
sexual fashion provides a rich context for Shakespeare's disguised
heroines. From this perspective a device that is often accepted as

mere dramatic convention takes on a complicated and potentially controversial social meaning. The author of *Hic-Mulier* even accuses the offending men-women of the day of believing they can act like heroines in a romance.[26] A more familiar social context for the device of female disguise is provided by C. L. Barber in *Shakespeare's Festive Comedy*. Barber links our delight in Shakespeare's disguised heroines, and their delight in their roles, to "the festive pleasure in transvestism" characteristic of seasonal holidays.[27] Most of the transvestism in such festivities seems to have been male: the May Day ceremonies, Mummers' plays, and morris dances all included men dressed in women's clothes, with the inevitable bawdy behavior. Women got their turn on Hock Tuesday, not by dressing but by acting like men – blocking the roads with ropes and demanding money from travellers for charitable purposes. When the Queen visited Kenilworth in 1575, the men of Coventry performed their traditional Hock-tide pageant, which dramatized the supposed origin of this custom, the defeat of the Danes by English women on November 13, 1002.[28] In a stimulating essay, Natalie Zemon Davis surveys not only the rituals of sex reversal common to women of the period but the conventional images, in literature and art.[29]

In anthropological studies such reversals, along with others characteristic of liminal experience, are often explained as safety-valves which re-confirm the traditional social order by allowing the periodic release of accumulated social tensions. The seasonal sex reversals of Zulu women, according to Max Gluckman, re-enforce their normal social roles by allowing them "to behave in normally prohibited ways."[30] In 1444, some French clerics defended the misrule of the Feast of Fools with the same argument: "We do these things in jest and not in earnest, as the ancient custom is, so that once a year the foolishness innate in us can come out and evaporate. Don't wine skins and barrels burst very often if the air-hole ... is not opened from time to time? We too are old barrels."[31] The social conservatism of such customs is illustrated by the clerics' view that the "foolishness" vented annually is "innate"; the process is as natural and cyclical as the making of wine. The views of participants are not always correct, however; in her study of female sex reversal, Natalie Zemon Davis argues convincingly that the phenomenon was both conservative and innovative. It confirmed the subjection of women, she observes, but also encouraged resistance: the motif of the woman on top "renewed old systems, but also helped to change them into something different."[32] Given the affinities between seasonal rites and rites of passage, it is not surprising to find similar sex reversals in the initiations of boys and girls. In such cases the pressures that are released and the changes that are encouraged are more directly individual than social. When Bemba girls reach the end of their combined initiation and marriage ceremonies, they are visited by mock-bridegrooms – the sisters of the real bridegrooms, mimicking their behavior. At the ceremony Audrey I. Richards witnessed, the mock-bridegrooms were greeted with the cry, "'Here come the bridegrooms,'" and "shrieks of delighted laughter." The disguised women "imitated the swaggering gait of young gallants, and pretended to speak in bass voices. They carried male symbols – the bow and arrow, the red cam-wood powder of the successful warrior and lion-killer, and the salt, which the husband had to fetch for the household in the old days."[33] The emotional release is clear from the "shrieks of delighted laughter." And perhaps the release itself helps the brides master psychologically the world of men.

In Elizabethan society, sex reversal was closely associated with courtship, if not in ritual at least in convention, for the Petrarchan rhetoric of love assigned "female" attitudes to lovers and "male" qualities to their ladies. In Spenser's "Amoretti," for example, the lady is proud, cruel, cold, hard, and unyielding and plays, at various times, the role of god, tyrant, warrior, murderer and lion; her poet-lover is humble, submissive, a suppliant, a victim of conflicting passions – and plays a thrall, a defenseless prey, a corpse. She is the idol, he the worshipper; she the master, he the servant. The mind of the "amorist," indeed, described earlier, is a repository of feminine stereotypes: fickleness, inconstancy, narcissism, emotional volatility. In *The Merry Wives of Windsor*, Falstaff tells Mrs Ford that he cannot court in the fashion of conventional lovers, "these lisping hawthorn buds, that come like women in men's apparel" (III.iii.71–72). In Sidney's *Arcadia*, Musidorus is even more contemptuous. "This effeminate love of a woman," he says, "doth so womanish a man that (if he yeeld to it) it will not onely make him an *Amazon*; but a launder, a distaff-spinner; or what so ever other vile occupation their idle heads can imagin, and their weake hands performe."[34] Musidorus's tone recalls that of the moralists who attacked women for wearing masculine attire.

Sidney's attitude towards Pyrocles's transvestism, however, is complicated enough to have occasioned scholarly debate over its significance – whether it symbolizes a heroic synthesis of both feminine and masculine qualities or immoral subjection to passionate love.[35] If regarded as a liminal phenomenon, both attitudes can be suspended in paradox. Perhaps the appropriate response is ambivalence.

Certainly ambivalence characterizes the Renaissance development of one basic symbol of sexual disorientation, that of the hermaphrodite. The word is used as a simple pejorative by Stubbes, as we have seen, yet the literary tradition is complex. For neoplatonists, the symbol of the hermaphrodite generally represents the spiritual union of true lovers, a meaning based upon Ovid. In *The Metamorphoses*, Salmacis joins bodies with Hermaphroditus and fulfills her strongest desire: eternal union with her beloved. But Ovid's story has other implications, if seen from Hermaphroditus's perspective. When he sees what has happened to him, Hermaphroditus petitions Mercury and Venus "that whoso commes within this Well may so bee weakened there,/ That of a man but halfe a man he may fro thence retire."[36] As Donald Cheney has shown, this reaction, although underplayed by neoplatonists, also affected the development of the symbol: "the body of literary and philosophical treatment of the Hermaphrodite, in antiquity as in the Renaissance, hovers between two attitudes: on the one hand, an emphasis on the perfection, the union of contraries, represented either statically in the single figure or dynamically in the coupling of the wedded pair; and on the other hand, an awareness that such union occurs in a watery context of dissolution where rational and moral distinctions are no longer operative ..."[37] This "watery context of dissolution," in which "rational and moral distinctions are no longer operative," aptly characterizes the liminal phase of courtship. If such "dissolution" of sexual identity occurs temporarily, and within a comic context, it need not be viewed as either heroic or immoral – merely as a natural, if potentially dangerous, stage in the development of romantic infatuation into married and mature love.

In *Symbolic Wounds* Bruno Bettelheim offers a provocative approach to initiatory sex reversal, which may help to explain its presence in Elizabethan courtship metaphors as well as in primitive rites of passage. Reduced to its essentials, Bettelheim's argument is that the custom reflects a desire on the part of both society and the young "to resolve the great antitheses between child and adult and between male and female; in short, between childish desires and the role ascribed to each sex according to biology and the mores of society." Since childhood is characterized by sexual polyvalence, an uninhibited exploration of both sexual roles, sex reversal at initiation is partly regressive – an attempt to play out a childish completeness of identity one last time before it is lost. But since the playful indulgence in this fantasy leads to an acceptance of an adult sexual role, the process is also progressive, enabling an "actual or symbolic understanding of the functions of the other sex and a psychological mastery of the emotions they arouse."[38] For Bettelheim, the tension between the loss of sexual identity and sexual fulfillment, which Ovid fixes for eternity in the static union of Hermaphroditus and Salmacis, forms part of a dynamic process – a rite of passage.

Bettelheim's approach to sex reversal provides an illuminating context for female disguise in Shakespeare's comedies. Although his heroines do not put on men's clothes for the purpose of achieving masculine power, the prospect is liberating. As they don their disguises, the heroines experience the exhilarating release characteristic of seasonal festivals. They mock the very masculinity they adopt. Julia's waiting-woman, Lucetta, dismisses codpieces as things "to stick pins on" (*TGV* II.vii.56). Portia looks forward to her new role with the same satiric glee she lavished earlier on her suitors:

> I have within my mind
> A thousand raw tricks of these bragging Jacks,
> Which I will practice.   (*MV* III.iv.76–78)

Rosalind, picturing herself with a "gallant curtle-axe" upon her thigh and a "boar-spear" in her hand, tells Celia,

> We'll have a swashing and a martial outside,
> As many other mannish cowards have
> That do outface it with their semblances.   (*AYL* III.ii.120–22)

The perception that masculinity is often no more than a pose is a mark of liberation in a society dominated by males. Like the girls in the Bemba marriage ceremonies, who laughed gleefully at the "swaggering" of their mock-bridegrooms, Shakespeare's heroines free themselves temporarily from such subordination and revel in their freedom. The mockery of men is not merely general, for the superiority that disguise confers is specifically a superiority over future husbands, whom the women will eventually promise, in the order of *The Book of Common Prayer*, to obey, serve, love, honor, and keep.[39] When Rosalind plays "the saucy lackey" with Orlando, or Portia taunts Bassanio for his faithlessness, or Viola stands up for feminine love against Orsino, the comedy takes its edge from a loving aggressiveness that can only be expressed in disguise. Although the mask that Rosaline wears in *Love's Labor's Lost* is not masculine, she uses it to vent emotions one senses in all the heroines:

> That same Berowne I'll torture ere I go.
> O that I knew he were but in by th'week!
> How I would make him fawn, and beg, and seek,
> And wait the season, and observe the times,
> And spend his prodigal wits in bootless rhymes,
> And shape his service wholly to my device,
> And make him proud to make me proud that jests!
> So pair-taunt-like would I o'ersway his state
> That he should be my fool and I his fate.   (V.ii.60–68)

What Rosaline desires, as her language makes clear, is the role of Petrarchan mistress, with all its masculine power. Her rueful admission that she would only so indulge herself if she were sure of Berowne's absolute devotion, however, illustrates the continuing tension in all the heroines between "artificial" and "natural" folly. Their disguises enable them to play "fate" to their foolish lovers; the folly of their own love subjects them. Even their disguises subject them, however, for while their masculine roles are liberating, allowing them the power and freedom denied by society, they are also constricting, forcing upon them the realization that these roles do not square with life. The fantasies that at first offer freedom create comic predicaments for which the heroines are ill-prepared. When Valentine offers Proteus his interest in Silvia at the end of *The Two Gentlemen of Verona*, Julia faints right out of her masculine role, as does Rosalind in *As You Like It*, when Oliver shows her Orlando's "bloody napkin." Rosalind's masculinity hangs by a witticism: "Ah, sirrah, a body would think this was well counterfeited!"

(IV.iii.165–66). Viola, in disguise, must not only endure the infatuation of Olivia but the prospect of a duel with the jealous Sir Andrew, hardly more man than she, although she does not know it. "Pray God defend me," she cries, "A little thing would make me tell them how much I lack of a man" (*TN* III.iv.302–03). The quibble on "thing" reduces the comic predicament of a woman in man's clothes to its essentials; the satiric "little," however, speaks well of Viola's self-possession.

While the disguised heroines discover at moments of crisis that they are "o'erparted" as men, they discover as well that their assumed identities make it impossible to fulfill themselves as women. Not only do their disguises forestall their marriages, but they inhibit the expression of their love; this limitation is particularly ironic in the case of Julia, who puts on her disguise as a gesture of love. If disguise releases some emotions, it forces others to remain uncomfortably bottled up. Left alone with Celia after playing the "saucy lackey" with Orlando, Rosalind simply explodes:

> O coz, coz, coz, my pretty little coz, that thou didst know how many fathom deep I am in love! But it cannot be sounded; my affection hath an unknown bottom, like the bay of Portugal.   (*AYL* IV.i.205–08)

A good deal of the comedy of disguise arises from the heroic efforts of passionate women to keep their masks on. When their romantic passion does break through, it often recoils upon them in unexpected ways. In *Twelfth Night*, for example, Viola's efforts at wooing Olivia for Orsino are comically ineffectual (and therefore in her own interest) until Olivia asks her how she would court were she the one in love. Viola responds with an extended rhapsody of building a willow cabin at the beloved's gate and hallowing her name "to the reverberate hills" (I.v.272). The sentimental fantasy is playful, but it is partly prompted by Viola's suppressed love for Orsino, which is genuine. And its emotional truth makes it efficacious: to Viola's dismay, Olivia falls in love with her. What captures Olivia, although she does not know it, is less masculine disguise than feminine truth.

The very weapon that offers the women freedom and power, then, at moments of crisis recoils against them; like the Elizabethan pistol, disguise proves difficult to aim and likely to blow up in one's face. Given this state of affairs, it is not surprising that, with the exception of Portia, whose steady self-control is unique, all of the disguised heroines find themselves reinventing female roles in order to release feelings that could otherwise have no outlet. While disguised as men, they re-create themselves as women. Rosalind plays not only Ganymede but Ganymede playing Rosalind, and although the caricature she invents does not enable her to express her love to Orlando, it calls forth from him the expressions of love she wants to hear: "Virtue is no horn-maker; and my Rosalind is virtuous." "And I am your Rosalind," she replies (*AYL* IV.i.63–65). At times of extreme feeling both Julia and Viola also invent feminine roles, only momentarily, but with wonderfully subtle comic effect.

When Julia, in disguise, is sent by Proteus to woo Silvia, she determines to court "so coldly/ As, heaven it knows, I would not have him speed" (*TGV* IV.iv.106–07). Moved by Silvia's unexpected sympathy for Julia's betrayal, however, she improvises, with considerable emotion, a story in which she works herself back into her own character. The indirection is dizzying. Speaking to Silvia in her role as Sebastian, she tells how she once wore Julia's clothes to play the part of Ariadne. Her acting, she says, was so successful that it brought Julia, who was in the audience, to tears:

> And at that time I made her weep agood,
> For I did play a lamentable part.
> Madame, 'twas Ariadne passioning
> For Theseus' perjury and unjust flight;
> Which I so lively acted with my tears
> That my poor mistress, moved therewithal,
> Wept bitterly; and would I might be dead
> If I in thought felt not her very sorrow.   (lines 165–72)

This is Shakespeare's version of disguise within disguise, and it occurs not as a device of plot but of character. It is hard to imagine a more complicated act of imitation. Julia plays Sebastian, who tells a story of himself playing Ariadne, in Julia's clothes and before her eyes; and the drama he recounts re-enacts the very moment of the telling, for Julia is Ariadne in this play of "perjury and unjust flight" and Silvia her sympathetic audience. Through this labyrinth of disguises Julia is able to vent her grief without losing self-control. By fictionalizing herself, she becomes herself and, indirectly, furthers her own ends. By disclosing herself in the truth of fiction, she increases Silvia's sympathy for her plight and her aversion to Proteus. By venting her passion, paradoxically, she woos "so coldly" that Proteus does not "speed."

In *Twelfth Night,* in a passage which Francis Berry rightly calls the "most poignant in the play,"[40] the disguised Viola also reinvents herself as a woman. After singing his melancholy song of the death of a true lover, Feste exits, leaving Orsino and Viola alone on stage. Frustrated by Orsino's sentimental posturing, which at this moment takes the form of a claim that no woman can love as profoundly as he, and distressed by her own inability to make her love known, Viola tells a story of her father's daughter, who "lov'd a man/ As it might be perhaps, were I a woman,/ I should love your lordship" (II.iv.107–09). When Orsino asks to hear more about this sister, Viola replies that her history is,

> A blank, my lord; she never told her love,
> But let concealment like a worm i' th'bud
> Feed on her damask cheek; she pin'd in thought,
> And with a green and yellow melancholy
> She sate like Patience on a monument,
> Smiling at grief.   (lines 110–15)

Like Julia, Viola re-creates herself not only as a woman but as a work of art, a statue of Patience, "smiling at grief." Both characters discover themselves in a labyrinth of imitations.

Viola's story, moreover, affects Orsino as Julia's does Silvia. Moved by Viola's emotion, Orsino is drawn out of his narcissism. The shock of his sympathetic interest brings Viola perilously close to self-revelation:

> *Duke.* But died thy sister of her love, my boy?
> *Viola.* I am all the daughters of my father's house
> And all the brothers too – and yet I know not.
> Sir, shall I to this lady?   (lines 119–22)

Viola averts disclosure by withdrawing into another disguise, that of the artificial fool, the "corrupter of words" (III.i.36). And she also quickly changes the subject. Although ripening, the time to declare her "estate" is not yet "mellow" (I.ii.42–43). By losing herself in a series of fictions, however, Viola not only re-creates herself as a woman, but teaches Orsino how to love. Her fancy tames his.

The sex reversal of the disguised heroine, then, functions in two, contradictory ways – as a completion of the self, a liberating assertion of masculine power, and as a constriction of the self, a restraint that can only be overcome by reinventing the feminine? This liminal paradox corresponds to that described by Bettelheim, in which temporary sex reversal, if successful, results in a heightened understanding of both sexual roles and a mature acceptance of one's own. In *Shakespeare and the Nature of Women*, Juliet Dusinberre errs, it seems to me, by responding to only one side of the paradox. For her, the Saturnalian release of the disguised heroines simply completes them, making them whole human beings, both masculine and feminine. Because of this, she argues, we regret their return to female roles, especially since their husbands are so uninspiring. "Rosalind is a perfect woman when a man," observes Dusinberre, "as a woman she needs more of a man than Orlando." Viola too "is diminished by a return to a world where she must be Orsino's lady after the momentary freedom of a Twelfth Night masculinity which restored Nature's wholeness."[41] The feeling of regret is true enough, but not the whole truth; mingled with it is relief and delight. Neither Rosalind nor Viola is completely "free" in male apparel, even in fantasy, and the comedy depends on the fact. If we accept their love, even for husbands who are no match for them, then we must accept that marriage fulfills them and that their wit will keep them free.

The "artificial" folly of Shakespeare's disguised heroines, then, like the "natural" folly of their lovers, is a means of defining the self through imitation. In some ways it resembles the conventional coyness of the feminine role in courtship; in others, more subtly, it follows the initiatory pattern described by Bettelheim. Playing the role of men is both regressive and progressive. It frees the women to complete themselves in fantasies of masculinity, licensing them to mock and test the male world and their husbands before they become women and wives. Like the "artificial" fools of Armin's verse, and the Salmacis of Ovid's story, the heroines enjoy their disguise; it fulfills some of their desires. But not all. Playing the role of men is also constricting. Like Hermaphroditus, the heroines sometimes feel estranged and unsexed in their roles. As long as they remain in disguise, they cannot fulfill themselves, either sexually or emotionally. Hence they struggle, at moments of crisis, to reinvent themselves as women. The result is a comedy of wonderful psychological tension, in which the self threatens to dissolve. The very process that destroys the self, however, re-creates it. The "watery" dissolution that unnerves Hermaphroditus permits for Shakespeare's heroines a "sea-change/ Into something rich and strange" (*Tmp* I.ii.401–02). In the comedies, liminality is a dynamic process; Shakespeare's men-women are figures of creative confusion, wavering between two worlds.

5
Natural Philosophers

"Tush, I may as well say the fool's the fool"
(*Ado* III.iii.123)

The aptness of metaphors of folly to the conditions of romantic love helps explain Shakespeare's continuing fascination with literal fooling in the comedies. His clowns and fools come in many varieties and play many roles. They can be servants, solid citizens, or jesters. Like his lovers, they can be either "natural" or "artificial," and sometimes, tantalizingly, both. Yet whatever their specific nature or dramatic function, they all display the common marks of folly and touch an audience with a surprisingly common delight. The source of their distinctive appeal, it seems to me, lies in their remarkable affinity with the liminal world and with the mysterious energy that moves through it in rites of initiation and marriage. Folly is a liminal state, and the fool a liminal being.

In Act V of the anonymous play, *The Pilgrimage to Parnassus* (c. 1598), a clown is suddenly and inexplicably drawn on stage with a rope. "What now," he asks, "thrust a man into the common wealth, whether hee will or noe? What the devill should I doe here?" Dromo, the rope-bearer, replies:

Why, what an ass art thou? Dost thou not knowe a playe cannot be without a clowne? Clownes have bene thrust into playes by head and shoulders, ever since Kempe could make a scurvey face, and therfore reason thou shouldst be drawne in with a cart rope.

Left alone on stage, with no lines and no role in the play, the clown sizes up the audience – "Gentles, I dare saie youe looke for a fitt of mirthe" – and proceeds to entertain them with a bawdy love letter he has written, which he sings to the tune of "*Put on the smock a mundaye.*" No sooner does he settle into his routine, however, than Dromo returns with some characters who belong in the play and sends him packing. Although the clown exits promising to give his audience better sport next time, he never returns; the play resumes as if he had never been there at all.[1]

This brief episode tells a great deal about clowning on the Elizabethan stage. The problem of the clown or fool, from the point of view of the serious playwright, lay in his self-sufficiency. The theatrical fools of the end of the sixteenth century were only one manifestation of a long tradition of fooling, more or less continuous since at least the Middle Ages, which evolved alongside the theater but was by no means dependent upon it. Dromo's reference to Will Kemp suggests this independence. Tarlton, Kemp, and Armin, the most famous theatrical fools of the day, were entertainers both onstage and off. Singers, dancers, jugglers, comedians, writers – these men had less need of the stage than the stage of them.

It was the tradition of fooling that gave all three of these actors their status and to which they displayed conscious allegiance. Tarlton, who became the most famous actor of the Queen's Men during the 1580s, was already famous as a clown in the 1570s, before he took to the stage; according to Robert Weimann, he was "the first plebeian artist to achieve national recognition in England."[2] Kemp carried on Tarlton's tradition of clowning – he is described in 1590 as "Vice-gerent generall to the Ghost of Dicke Tarlton"[3] – and achieved at least as much notoriety for dancing the morris from London to Norwich as for any role in the theater. Armin's sense of tradition was more scholarly; in *Foole upon Foole* (1600), later revised as *A Nest of Ninnies* (1608), he collected anecdotes of "natural" court jesters, some of whom he had met himself. While playing Touchstone, Dogberry, and Feste, Armin was thus also engaged in research. Their independence from the theater gave all of these actors a status akin to that of modern "stars," with the familiar result that playwrights could live neither with nor without them.

One symptom of this frustration is the episode in *The Pilgrimage to Parnassus*, which mocks the intrusiveness of clowns. The joke is academic, for the episode literalizes Sidney's famous objection that playwrights "thrust in the clown by head and shoulders to play a part in majestical matters with neither decency nor discretion."[4] Hamlet's insistence that clowns should "speak no more than is set down for them" (*Ham* III.ii.39–40) shows that even when provided with fully integrated roles clowns were tempted to extemporize. Though in the play, the clown is often not truly of it; his reality lies elsewhere, in an independent tradition and personal relation to the audience. The attack upon clowning in *The Pilgrimage to Parnassus*, like Hamlet's remarks, satirizes the abuses of the role in hopes of reforming it. The dramatic effect of the scene in *The Pilgrimage*, however, is curiously double-edged. Whether the anonymous author was conscious of his duplicity is uncertain, but his mockery of clowning enables his audience to revel in the very abuses he mocks. From the resiliency of the clown, his immediate rapport with his audience, his inexhaustible supply of bawdy songs and jokes, one can see that this indecorous interruption might go on indefinitely, and to the audience's delight. If the fooling is good, no one needs the play. Whether consciously or inadvertently, the author of *The Pilgrimage* solves the problem of clowning in perhaps the only satisfactory way. He puts a rope around the clown, giving him a satiric or parodic function that serves the larger designs of the drama, and then leaves him to his devices. The trick is to make the clown serve the play while being himself.

This is the trick that Shakespeare brings off with such flair. Influenced by the "new criticism," most literary critics have been more impressed by the rope than by the free rein. Studies of clowning in the comedies almost always focus on its dramatic function, chiefly as parody or satire, conscious or unconscious, depending upon the clown in question – whether Feste, say, or Bottom. All of Shakespeare's clowns are fully integrated into their plays. In *The Two Gentlemen of Verona*, Speed describes at length the familiar posings of the amorist, mocking his master's love. In *As You Like It*, Touchstone matches Orlando's bad verses with a dogtrot of his own, and Orlando's love for Rosalind with his own for Audrey. Feste ministers in turn to all the fools of *Twelfth Night*. Both Bottom and Dromio of Syracuse stumble into romantic misadventures that burlesque those of their social superiors. The effect of these devices is not only to integrate clowning into the themes of the plays but to enrich their comic texture. The clowns add sex to romantic love and farce to sophisticated wit. And they increase not only the social but intellectual range of comic invention – as when Bottom's difficulties as an actor add to the confusions of fancy in *A Midsummer Night's Dream*, or when Dogberry's investigative methods extend the epistemological tangles of *Much Ado About Nothing*.

Shakespeare's art lies in the subtlety with which he brings his fools and clowns within the comic structure. Yet they remain traditional fools and clowns; their relation to the plays is symbiotic rather than dependent.[5] Much of their appeal derives from sources that, while not seeming extrinsic to the play, are not wholly contained by it. Some of the most haunting stage images in the comedies are provided by the clowns – as when Launce tells of the treachery of his dog; or when Dogberry defends himself against the charge that he is an ass; or when Feste, alone on stage, sings of the rain that rains every day. Though not extemporaneous performances, like that of the clown in *The Pilgrimage to Parnassus*, these moments have a similar appeal. What touches our imagination most directly is not their dramatic function, thematic or otherwise – though one can always be discovered – but some mysterious energy that is released by the role itself and by its characteristic rhythms of speech and action. This is a peculiarly liminal energy, it seems to me, closely allied to that which moves through rites of initiation and marriage. The affinity between comic and ritual vitality may be explained, in part, by Robert Weimann's demonstration that the Elizabethan clown "remains, more than any other figure in drama, closest to his early ritual heritage."[6]

To generalize about Shakespeare's fools and clowns, even within the sphere of the comedies, is necessarily to oversimplify. Each is a distinct individual, and as types they represent not one but several. Some are servants – either clownish, like the twin Dromios, or witty, like Tranio or Speed. Some are buffoons, usually with an air of rusticity, if not actually countrymen – such as Costard, Bottom, and Dogberry. Two, Touchstone and Feste, are court jesters. Even in single roles, moreover, Shakespeare assimilates diverse traditions of clowning, including those of the "wily servants" of Plautus and Terence and their neoclassical imitators; the *zanni* of Italian comedy; the Vice figures and clowns of the domestic drama; and the professional jesters of court life. Touching them all, in various ways, are the literary and philosophical traditions of folly epitomized in Erasmus's *Praise of Folly*.

This variety of types and traditions is further complicated by a development in Shakespeare's company, the replacement of Will Kemp by Robert Armin, sometime in 1599 or 1600.[7] With Armin's arrival, as is well known, Shakespeare turned away from the relatively coarse clowns of the early comedies, such as Bottom and Grumio, to witty and "artificial" fools such as Touchstone and Feste. In broad terms, then, Shakespeare's interests develop from farce to wit and from unconscious to conscious fooling. In what follows it will be important to remember such distinctions, but they represent differences of degree rather than kind. Nearly all the clowns and fools are servants, and those that are not, like Bottom and Dogberry, are in their own fashion servants of the state. Whether "natural" clowns or professional jesters, they all take stabs at wit; even Bottom can "gleek upon occasion" (*MND* III.i.146–47). All serve as entertainers, either to amuse their masters or play roles in performances at court. Whether consciously or unconsciously, all are parodists or satirists. And all exploit, to varying degrees, the traditional repertory of the clown – jesting, singing, dancing, and, especially, playing with words. Whether we call them fools or clowns (Elizabethans used the terms synonymously); whether they evoke laughter by accident or design; whether they earn their living through folly or merely the good graces of their superiors – these figures are undeniably kin. Dromio of Syracuse, probably Shakespeare's first clown, plays nearly all the roles that Shakespeare was to develop. Buffoon, servant, and jester, he is a "trusty villain," who "lightens" his master's humor "with his merry jests" (*Err* I.ii.19–21). Robert Armin, who played Feste, Shakespeare's wittiest and most sophisticated fool, did research on "naturals" and also played the roles of Dogberry, the buffoon, and Touchstone, the "clownish fool" (*AYL* I.iii.130).[8]

To appreciate the comic energy that propels these characters and connects them not only to each other but to the ancient traditions of fooling, it is useful to begin with Susanne Langer's interpretation of the buffoon. Citing Harlequin, Pierrot, the Elizabethan jester, the *Vidusaka* of Sanskrit drama, and the Punch of the puppet show, among others, Langer describes their common appeal:

These anciently popular personages show what the buffoon really is: the indomitable living creature fending for itself, tumbling and stumbling (as the clown physically illustrates) from one situation into another, getting into scrape after scrape and getting out again, with or without a thrashing. He is the personified *élan vital*; his chance adventures and misadventures, without much plot, though often with bizarre complications, his absurd expectations and disappointments, in fact his whole improvised existence has the rhythm of primitive, savage, if not animalian life, coping with a world that is forever taking new uncalculated turns, frustrating, but exciting. He is neither a good man nor a bad one, but is genuinely amoral, – now triumphant, now worsted and rueful, but in his ruefulness and dismay he is funny, because his energy is really unimpaired and each failure prepares the situation for a new fantastic move.[9]

Langer's description is wide-ranging enough to include both buffoons and jesters: unconscious and conscious wit, slapstick and repartee. And what she describes is not merely a mode of being but a pattern of action – an "improvised existence" of "getting into scrape after scrape and getting out again." This is the pattern of the brief scene in *The Pilgrimage to Parnassus*: thrust upon the stage, faced with an expectant audience and no lines to speak, the clown catches his balance, settles into his comic routine, only to be thrust away again; but even then, as Langer puts it, "his energy is really unimpaired," for he exits with promises of better fooling next time, preparing us for a "new fantastic move."

Behind Langer's description of the buffoon one can glimpse the outlines of an ancient archetype, that of the trickster, whose attributes and adventures represent the most primitive version of fooling we know. Appearing in a variety of guises in the mythology of many North American Indian tribes, the trickster, according to Paul Radin, is "a hero who is always wandering, who is always hungry, who is not guided by normal conceptions of good or evil, who is either playing tricks on people or having them played on him, and who is highly sexed."[10]

In the Wakdjunkaga cycle of the Winnebago, which Radin transcribes and analyzes at length, the trickster, like Langer's buffoon, stumbles from one escapade to the next, emerging sometimes victorious, sometimes defeated (even by himself), but always indestructible and on the move. His essence is self-contradiction: he can be both sly and foolish, self-aware and naive, egotistical and generous, man and woman, animal and demi-god. In what seem to be his most primitive manifestations, he is both physically and mentally inchoate: in one adventure, his right arm literally fights against his left; in another, he swims parallel to the shoreline in an attempt to reach land. In Jung's interpretation, the trickster is "a faithful reflection of an absolutely undifferentiated human consciousness, corresponding to a psyche that has hardly left the animal level."[11] For Radin, the many cultural layers of the composite Winnebago myth reveal the gradual differentiation and ordering of this primitive consciousness into a recognizably human form.

Whatever his origins and the ultimate significance of his myth, the trickster affords us a glimpse of clowning at its most elemental. And what the archetype embodies is a mode of being and a pattern of action that might be called liminal. Whether the trickster represents literally a transitional phase in the development of human consciousness, as Jung and Radin suggest, is at best highly uncertain. In his most elemental form, in any event, he is a liminal figure – a figure of ambiguity, paradox, and inversion, whose confusion mimics the chaos he inhabits and whose escapades, like those of Langer's buffoons, trace an endless but not hopeless circle of predicaments. His misadventures often burlesque or satirize conventional behavior or institutions, as Radin shows,[12] but the source of his unnerving appeal runs deeper, deriving, like that of Shakespeare's clowns, from the chaotic, inexhaustible, and mysterious vitality that Langer so persuasively describes.

Given the trickster's liminal nature, it is not surprising to find clowns active in seasonal rites and rites of passage. Among the Indians of the American Southwest, for example, ceremonial buffoons perform during religious rites of various kinds, including seasonal festivals. At the dances and processions of the Pueblo, clowns figure prominently – attending on dancers, dancing the mask dance, policing observers, doing manual labor for hosts or chiefs, engaging in burlesque behavior and personal satire, playing in and supervising ritual games, making rain, and controlling the Water Serpent. They are speechless when masked, use falsetto voices when unmasked, speak and act backwardly, and eat excrement. Their costumes include a variety of incongruous items, such as masks, feathers, face or body paint, shabby clothes or animal skins, leg and hand rattles, and berry necklaces. And they carry an assortment of implements ranging from painted sticks to dried mudhens. Figures of fear and farce, satire and burlesque, restraint and license, they embody some of the central paradoxes of the liminal experience.[13]

A European approximation of this festive liberation of the fool occurred in the medieval Feast of Fools, celebrated mainly in

France. This feast brought Saturnalia within the walls of the church itself. The customs varied from place to place, but all emphasized ritual inversion and festive misrule. Drinking bouts were held, doggerel verses sung, the liturgy parodied, asses led in procession – all under the direction of the inferior clergy, elevated temporarily above their masters. E. K. Chambers calls the feast "an ebullition of the natural lout beneath the casssock."[14] Although the feast was celebrated in medieval England, it apparently did not take root, for it was permanently suppressed at the end of the fourteenth century. Fools were important festive characters throughout fourteenth and fifteenth century England, however, particularly during the Christmas season,[15] and something of the spirit of the Feast of Fools was probably transmitted through them. In Elizabethan England, as C. L. Barber observes, the popular Christmas feast of the Lord of Misrule "seems to have been a secularized version of the Feast of Fools."[16]

Although misrule figures prominently in primitive initiation and marriage rites, as we have seen, the appearance of actual fools or clowns in these rites is infrequent. When Audrey I. Richards witnessed the Chisungu ceremony among the Bemba, however, a fool took part in a way that is particularly suggestive for both Elizabethan social practice and Shakespeare's comedies. At about midpoint in the combined initiation and marriage ceremony – the thirteenth of thirty-one days – Richards observed the women modelling the figure of "a squat, round, female form, highly stylized." As soon as it was completed, the figure evoked shrieks of laughter. It was the *cipuba*, or fool – a person "who is either naturally stupid, or else just obtuse, unconscious of the niceties of civilized life, and either unaware of her social obligations or just too lazy to bother to carry them out."

To the delighted women, according to Richards, the *cipuba* represented "both the uninitiated woman who has not been taught the patterns of female conduct, and the lazy wife who has forgotten the lessons she has learnt."[17] Physiologically a woman, yet psychologically and socially a child, the *cipuba* embodies the confusion of the liminal stage. Her presence serves as a reminder to both novices and initiates that one may remain fixed in liminal confusion or relapse. In the midst of a ceremony whose ends are progressive and integrative, the *cipuba* stands as an emblem of recalcitrant humanity. Whether the spontaneous laughter that greeted the figure's appearance was derisive or sympathetic is uncertain; it may have been both. At Elizabethan weddings fools may have served a similar function. As Charles R. Baskervill has shown, Elizabethan social pastimes of various kinds, particularly seasonal festivals and weddings, were accompanied by jigs, morris dances, and an assortment of informal games, songs, and dances. Many of the dances were pantomime wooing dances, like the bergomask that Bottom's fellows perform at the end of *A Midsummer Night's Dream*. Baskervill prints a typical wooing dance, "The Wooing of Nan," and its hero is the fool. The dance begins with two rival lovers asserting their claims to Nan. They agree to settle their difference by competing in dance, with Nan going to the winner. Before the victor is decided, however, a gentleman enters, woos Nan with gifts, and apparently wins the contest. At the moment of his success, the fool appears, stakes his claim to Nan, and wins her consent immediately. The dance ends with the fool showing off his skill, dancing to a livelier measure than the others, and with the gentleman flouted by Nan.[18] If performed at a wedding, this enactment of folly's success in love might provide not only a parodic but celebratory comment on the event.

At the local wedding observed by Queen Elizabeth during her visit to Kenilworth in 1576, as we have seen, the procession included morris dancers – a "lively morisdauns," as Robert Laneham described them, "according too the auncient manner, six daunserz, Mawdmarion, and the fool."[19] Exactly what kind of dancing, singing, and horseplay these figures provided Laneham does not say, but the general drift is not difficult to imagine. An allusion to morris dancing in *Pasquill and Marforius* (1589) has the fool dancing around a Maid Marion whose beard was muffled with a "diaper-napkin" and courting her "with a Leatherne pudding, and a wooden Ladle."[20] That these were phallic implements is clear from numerous contemporary references.[21] Although the evidence is sketchy, it thus suggests that the fool played at least an incidental role at weddings, and that he and his fellows kept alive in burlesque wooing dances the folly of courtship. During a rite of incorporation, as at Theseus's wedding in *A Midsummer Night's Dream*, re-enactments of liminal confusion are a potential source of joy.

Fooling was by no means restricted to seasonal festivals or

wedding celebrations in sixteenth-century England, but was institutionalized in the figure of the court fool, either "natural" or "artificial." Both idiots and professional entertainers were kept for amusement in noble and royal households. Henry VIII had a "natural" fool, Patch, and an "artificial" fool, Will Sommers. Thomas More's fool, Henry Patterson, was important enough to appear in Holbein's painting of the family. Queen Elizabeth's account books reveal tantalizing payments to an Italian named Monarcho, a "lyttle Blackamore," "Thomasina the Dwarf," "Ipolyta the Tartarian," and fools named Robert Greene, Jack Greene, Mr Shenstone, and Clod.[22] The social function of these figures was obviously complicated and has been variously explained. For our purposes, Victor Turner's interpretation is particularly suggestive. For Turner, Renaissance court jesters and their counterparts in primitive cultures institutionalize the social values of liminality: "representing the poor and deformed," these figures "symbolize the moral values of communitas as against the coercive power of supreme political rulers."[23] Although Turner's approach might be fruitfully applied to a play like *King Lear*, his emphasis upon the fool's political function is somewhat restrictive. Even the anecdotes in *Foole upon Foole* reveal that the liminal function of these figures was broader and more complicated than Turner implies. Whatever their role in aristocratic households, it was necessarily transmuted in the public theater. Our concern is more with the drama of the fool's liminality than its sociology.

Whether their origins are social, philosophical, or dramatic, Shakespeare's clowns tap the kind of energy embodied in figures as diverse as the Winnebago trickster, the Bemba *cipuba*, the morris fool, or the court jester. As a liminal creature, the clown has a special place in romantic comedy. If "all nature in love" is "mortal in folly," as Touchstone remarks (*AYL* II.iv.56), then loving and fooling are close kin. "If ye owe your lives to wedlocke, and wedlocke ye owe to my damoisell *Madnes*," says Folly in Erasmus's mock-encomium, "now ye maie soone gesse, what ye owe, and shoulde referre to me."[24] In a broad sense, the parodic and satiric roles of the clown depend upon this built-in mockery of love. As I have tried to suggest, however, clowning is also integrated into the plays at a deeper, less conscious level – a level at which the fool is able to play himself and in so doing body forth his archetype. Agents of ambiguity and paradox, Shakespeare's clowns remind us, in word and action, that our "natural" home is chaos.

Hints of perpetual confusion are conveyed even in the physical appearance of the clown, as William Willeford suggests.[25] Whether he is naturally deformed or deforms himself in one of the many guises of clown or jester, the fool betrays visually his affinity for chaos and disproportion. The Elizabethen court fool was conventionally bald or shorn like a monk and carried a marotte or bauble. He wore ass's ears and a monk's hood, tapered occasionally into a cockscomb; a long coat or a jerkin of motley, sometimes parti-colored; bells; and sometimes a fox tail.[26] Since the uniform of the fool varied a good deal both on and offstage, and since Shakespeare's fools range from simple weavers to court jesters, it is impossible to be precise about the dramatic effects of the fool's costume. Given the tendencies of the theater, however, it is likely that even the Dromio twins, who wear the attire of servants and not Touchstone's motley, may have conveyed hints of the grotesque. The stage is a visual medium, and qualities of mind usually make themselves felt in external form.

The hints of animality in the costume of the fool – the cockscomb, ass's ears, and fox tail – remind us of his close links to nature, which were probably forged in ancient ritual. Implicit in Shakespearean fooling are a series of unstable oppositions between "nature" and "grace," in several senses of both words. Although none of Shakespeare's clowns is a true "natural," an idiot, all are extensions, either by nature or art, of the notion that the idiot is a child of nature. The close kinship between folly and nature is traditional and, as Walter Kaiser has shown, figures as one of Erasmus's themes in his *Praise of Folly*.[27] To survey Elizabethan usage of the word "natural" in the *Oxford English Dictionary* is to review some of the most common attributes of Shakespeare's clowns. To be "natural" is to be "naturally deficient in intellect"; to be in "a state of nature, without spiritual enlightenment"; to conform with "the ordinary course of nature," as opposed to the "unusual, marvellous, or miraculous"; to be "free from affectation, artificiality, or constraint"; to have a "real or physical existence, as opposed to what is spiritual, intellectual, fictitious"; to be "the real thing" (or, one is tempted to add, a touchstone).

Among these attributes, broadly speaking, lie the clowns' most common satiric and parodic roles. They oppose "natural" to "courtly" behavior, physical to spiritual and intellectual man, gracelessness to grace. In place of high spiritual and intellectual aspirations, they offer bodily needs and comforts. In place of romantic love, they offer sex. In place of exaltation and transcendence, they offer common sense. In place of the extreme and extraordinary, they offer the everyday. It is within such a dialectic that the incongruities of fooling take effect. Whether consciously or unconsciously, artificially or naturally, the clown is, as Touchstone calls Corin, "a natural philosopher" (*AYL* III.ii.32). But the clown's alignment with nature is neither fixed nor simple. Although his naturalness gives his role a semblance of stability, it too generates ambiguity and paradox, especially in relation to sex, self-interest, and wit.

To be natural is to be sexual. The very first of Folly's many blessings, the goddess herself informs us in Erasmus's *Praise of Folly*, is the act of generation. We owe this, she says, not to the head, face, breast, hands, or ears, but to "that selie membre, so fonde, and foolisshe, as maie not without laughter be spoken of, whiche is the onely planter of mankynde."[28] The Elizabethan translator's choice of words – "selie," "fonde," and "foolisshe" – suggests the innocency and benignity of the clown's sexuality in the comedies. True vice, of the kind that might be called "folly" in the Bible, is "knavery." "I am but a fool," says Launce in response to Proteus's betrayal of Valentine and Julia, "and yet I have the wit to think my master is a kind of knave..." (*TGV* III.i.263–64). In his sexuality, the clown may be gross, but he is not a figure of unbridled lust; like that "membre" he sometimes carries in symbolic form, as bauble or bladder, he is "selie" – innocent, laughable, and endearing.

Although sexual creatures, Shakespeare's clowns are surprisingly chaste. In *The Merchant of Venice*, we learn that "the Moor is with child" by Launcelot Gobbo (III.v.39), but the character and deed scarcely register. In *Love's Labor's Lost*, Costard is caught following Jacquenetta into the park, "Such is the simplicity of man to hearken after the flesh" (I.i.217), but it is Don Armado who eventually gets her with child. Touchstone, who shares Costard's simple desires, complicates them with irony and cushions them with civilization, for he eventually takes his place among the rest of the "country copulatives" (*AYL* V.i.55–56) and gets married. Although Launce is a wooer, he shows little interest in sex; he marries because his wife has "more wealth than faults" (*TGV* III.i.354). Some of the clowns, such as Dogberry, Bottom, and Feste, reveal scarcely any interest in feminine charms. Most of the sexuality in the comedies bubbles through the language. In their bawdy, as in their ironic detachment, the clowns resemble the disguised heroines, whose wit often extends to a ribaldry outside the range of their sentimental and idealistic lovers. The Julia who is idolized by Proteus is to Speed a "lac'd mutton" (*TGV* I.i.97). Orlando's fair Rosalind is for Touchstone a "cat," who will "after kind" (*AYL* III.ii.103). Dromio's Luce is a whole world of flesh, with Ireland in her buttocks and Spain in her breath (*Err* III.ii.117,131). Sometimes the bawdy is conscious, sometimes unconscious. Sometimes one cannot tell, as when Touchstone says, "I remember when I was in love, I broke my sword upon a stone, and bid him take that for coming a-night to Jane Smile . . ." (*AYL* II.iv.46–48). Rosalind's comment after this equivocation is, "Thou speak'st wiser than thou art ware of" (line 57). Does she see the equivocation on "sword," "stone," and "coming," but not he? Or has her romantic passion blurred her vision so much that she cannot perceive his intentional word-play? Or is it possible that the full jest is caught only by the audience?

The clown's close but enigmatic relation to sexuality is epitomized in Bottom's encounter with Titania in *A Midsummer Night's Dream*. The relationship between the two characters resonates with sexual overtones of a grotesque but curiously innocent kind. Bottom is Pyramus, the lover, and he wears the head of an ass. Bottom's asininity is multi-faceted, but one conventional attribute of the ass is sexual prowess.[29] And Titania, as she entices Bottom into her bower, has only one thing in mind:

> Come wait upon him; lead him to my bower.
> The moon methinks looks with a wat'ry eye;
> And when she weeps, weeps every little flower,
> Lamenting some enforced chastity.
> Tie up my lover's tongue, bring him silently.
>
> (*MND* III.i.197–201)

The final line hints that Titania's desires are unlikely to be fulfilled. Bottom, ironically, the romantic lover transformed into lustful brute, is more enamored of ruling his new court than courting, and hungrier for a "bottle of hay" (IV.i.33) than for Titania's kisses. Of all the many incongruities in this episode, the subtlest, least expected, and most characteristically Shakespearean, is the bestial lover's lack of interest in sex. And this extends throughout the play. With the single exception of a quip on the cuckoo in the song he sings to cheer himself up (III.i.135), Bottom does not even indulge in bawdy jokes. The sexual potency of the ass expresses itself through Bottom, however, but unconsciously. His desire that his company should rehearse their play "most obscenely" (I.ii.108) is fulfilled without his awareness in the actual performance before the Duke. When Pyramus and Thisby whisper through the wall that divides them, their language muddies the high-flown romanticism of their sentiments, clogging the aspirations of the spirit with the grossness of mortal flesh. The wall is made of stones, knit up with lime and hair, which Thisby's "cherry lips have often kiss'd" (V.i.190), and it has within it a "crannied hole or chink" (line 158). Pyramus curses the wall's stones for deceiving him, and in the frenzy of his passion, cries out to Thisby, "O, kiss me through the hole of this vild wall!" In dismay, Thisby discovers that she has kissed "the wall's hole, not your lips at all" (lines 200–01). If Falstaff is a coward by instinct, Bottom, it seems, is by instinct a lover. His sexuality, like that of other clowns, is innocent because automatic and unconscious − "silly," in a word. Because his sexuality is natural, in this sense, the clown often seems paradoxically highly sexed and sexless. As such, he stands in contrast both to the male lovers who yield to lust, like Proteus, and to those who flee from it into fancy, like Orlando.

Some of this sexless sexuality of the clown may be attributed to the strength of other basic impulses. Langer calls the buffoon "the indomitable living creature fending for itself"; to accent the final word is to discover something essential to the role. Two of the conventional playthings of the jester, the mirror and phallic marotte, are self-reflexive; both give him back an image of himself. Bottom assures Titania that he is not really as wise as he is beautiful. Launcelot Gobbo leaves Shylock for a new master, who gives him better clothes, more food, and less work. Launce considers marriage a business venture, Touchstone an obstacle on the way to bed. And Dogberry, no ass, is "a wise fellow, and which is more, an officer, and which is more, a householder, and which is more, as pretty a piece of flesh as any is in Messina, and one that knows the law, go to, and a rich fellow enough, go to, and a fellow that hath had losses, and one that hath two gowns, and every thing handsome about him" (*Ado* IV.ii.80–86). The egotism of the clowns, though impressive, cannot be confused with the egomania of a character like Malvolio, who is "sick of self-love" (*TN* I.v.90). The self-love of the clowns is healthy, child-like, instinctual. Incapable of hypocrisy or scheming or heroic ambition, they settle for survival; their egotism is mainly a defensive rather than an aggressive weapon. There are no rogues in the romantic comedies like Autolycus in *The Winter's Tale*, and no servants as wily as those in Plautus and Terence. As Leo Salingar observes, Shakespeare's comic clowns are "commentators, not intriguers."[30]

The same clowns who are self-absorbed are also paradoxically selfless. Sometimes, as in the case of Bottom and Dogberry, their egotism is utterly oblivious and therefore without self-interest. But even the more conscious clowns show a fierce and tenacious loyalty. Touchstone lives up to Celia's expectations that "He'll go along o'er the wide world with me" (*AYL* I.iii.132), enduring with only minor complaints the hard life of Arden and the sad memory that when he was at home he was in a "better place" (II.iv.17). At the beginning of *The Comedy of Errors*, Antipholus of Syracuse entrusts his money to his servant, Dromio. Although the thought crosses Dromio's mind that some servants would seize such an opportunity and run away, he remains loyally in his master's service throughout the play, despite extraordinary provocations. Dromio's twin, equally loyal to *his* master and equally bruised, captures the resilient and dogged affection of the clown in a single phrase: "If I last in this service, you must case me in leather" (II.i.85). Escape, retaliation never enter his mind; to the end, he will care for his master's property, even if it happens to be himself. Such fidelity may have been a social convention of sorts. Several court fools were famous for astonishing acts of loyalty, among them Wolsey's fool, Patch, who required six yeoman to drag him away from his master when he had fallen into disgrace.[31]

Paradoxical connections between selfishness and selflessness are deeply embedded in the Elizabethan vocabulary of nature and the natural. In one sense, to be natural is to be selfish; it is a "law of nature," as Falstaff says, for the "old pike" to "snap" at the "young dace" (2HIV III.ii.330–32). In another sense, it is natural to show kindness and affection, the word "kind" itself meaning "nature." The paradox is sharpened further when the word "natural" is used of children, for it can mean both "legitimate" and "illegitimate." Hence a "natural" child may be kindly or unkindly, legitimate or illegitimate, in a variety of combinations – as is played out in the complicated patterns of *King Lear*. It is the fool in *King Lear* who stretches these paradoxes to the breaking point, thinking the part of a knave and acting the part of a fool:

> But I will tarry, the Fool will stay,
> And let the wise man fly.
> The knave turns fool that runs away,
> The Fool no knave, perdie. (II.iv.82–85)

In tragic fooling, it seems, the two competing value systems meet and expire; the fool does not live out the play. In comic fooling, there are glimmerings of paradoxical reconciliations.

Perhaps the most elaborate instance of this comic conjunction of self-interest and selflessness lies in Launce's relationship with his dog, Crab. When they first appear onstage, Launce is reproaching his "cruel-hearted cur" (*TGV* II.iii.9) for his refusal to weep at their departure; alone among the family, Crab "sheds not a tear, nor speaks a word" (line 31). Despite this outrageous behavior, Launce takes Crab abroad with him, maintaining his bond to what he calls, in a weak pun, "the unkindest tied that ever any man tied" (line 38). Later, however, we find that Launce has tried to give away his dog to Julia, to replace the one sent by Proteus, which was stolen; to serve his master, he will sacrifice his dog. Yet even as he tries to give Crab away he remains fiercely protective, so much so that when Crab pisses under the table, Launce takes the blame and is whipped out of the chamber. "How many masters would do this for his servant?" (IV.iv.29–30), he asks. This curious blend of love and loathing, self-sacrifice and self-interest provides one variation on the theme of bonding in the play, elaborated in greater earnest in Julia's relation with Proteus. Both Launce and Julia are betrayed, yet both remain loyal. And both mingle self-sacrifice and self-interest, Julia most subtly in her decision to woo Silvia for her master "so coldly/ As, heaven it knows, I would not have him speed" (IV.iv.105–07).

Julia plays "true servant" (IV.iv.104) to her master, and there is as much tension in her bond as in the rope that ties Launce to his dog. Relations between masters and servants invite such ambiguities and paradoxes, for they are relations in which self-interest and selflessness inevitably commingle. To serve one's master is to serve oneself. This is the paradox Dromio of Ephesus invokes when he suggests that his master case him in leather. In a spiritual sense, this is the paradox that Folly speaks of in Erasmus's *Praise of Folly* when she labels as the biggest fools those who serve Christ: "no maner fooles are in apparence more ideotelike, than suche as are totally ravisshed, and enflamed with the ardent zeale of *Christian charitee*."[32] These people are fools because they neglect their worldly interests, but they are also fools because they pursue them – true worldly interest being unworldliness. The motif of serving, which touches nearly all of Shakespeare's clowns, since nearly all are servants, provides fertile ground for such paradoxes. And it establishes yet another connection between folly and love, and clowns and disguised heroines.

Although the naturalness of the clown aligns him with the instinctual and irrational, it by no means precludes conscious wit. In practice, the distinction between "natural" and "artificial" fools is difficult to sustain. Court fools could be either, and as Robert Armin makes clear, even the "naturals" had their little store of practical jokes and wit. In *Foole upon Foole*, Armin tells how Jack Oates tried to atone for offending his master by telling a jest of "how a young man brake his Codpeece-point and let all bee seene that God sent him."[33] Nature and art, after all, lie on a continuum. A "natural" speaks nonsense, but by tradition he may also speak unconscious wisdom. An "artificial" fool speaks sense, but since he is human, he too may speak foolishly. Since the "artificial" fool imitates the "natural" fool, moreover, his role opens up endless ambiguities: he may speak wittily or foolishly by design or accident. Much of the fun of Elizabethan fooling, and much of its mystery, hinges upon the delightful conceptual difficulties it poses: it may convey folly or wisdom, natural or artificial, and the fool himself may not know the difference. This is as true for Feste, who lives by his wit, as for Bottom, who "gleeks" upon occasion.

In responding to the language of folly, as William Willeford observes, there is a common tendency to oversimplify it – to see it as mere nonsense or as hidden wisdom. Either extreme misses the actual experience of fooling, the unsettling delight of being caught in the middle, where sense and nonsense are on equal and unstable footing. The fool's "truth-telling," according to Willeford, "is more or less interchangeable with expressions of stupidity, madness, or freakishness. This amounts to a confusion between what has value (truth of whatever kind) and what has none (nonsense); it is this *confusion* that is central – the fact that diamonds and dull stones are treated as interchangeable, both of them either supremely valuable or worthless, depending upon the momentary state of the fool's mind."[34] The fool's mental universe, then, is a kind of no-man's land, a liminal landscape between sense and nonsense, where the boundaries are unstable and ill-defined. Feste calls himself Olivia's "corrupter of words" (*TN* III.i.36); once corrupted, words run out of control and may turn upon their masters.

Since this kind of verbal liminality is central to Shakespeare's comic fooling, it is worth exploring in some detail. The ambiguities, puns, and paradoxes that characterize the language of the clown have been often discussed. What I should like to focus on is one aspect of that liminal language – the mysterious prophetic energy that runs through it. To illustrate this phenomenon, we might examine a single pattern of word-play that recurs in most of the comedies and touches both clowns and jesters. The pattern is particularly striking in three plays, the clowns of which range from Shakespeare's least to his most sophisticated. Dromio of Syracuse, in *The Comedy of Errors*, though somewhat less than shrewd, is of the classical tradition of the wily servant; Grumio, in *The Taming of the Shrew*, has more of the buffoon about him; while Feste, in *Twelfth Night*, is the wittiest of Shakespeare's professional jesters. Bringing these diverse characters and plays together highlights the extent to which Shakespeare's imagination is drawn to a mode of verbal fooling that taps the liminal energy of the clown.

In *The Comedy of Errors*, Antipholus of Syracuse, mistaking his own Dromio for his brother's, angrily accuses him of carrying his joke about the missing gold too far:

> Because that I familiarly sometimes
> Do use you for my fool, and chat with you,
> Your sauciness will jest upon my love,
> And make a common of my serious hours.   (II.ii.26–29)

Antipholus urges Dromio to "fashion your demeanor to my looks" (line 33), to act, in other words, with the kind of decorum a master expects of a servant or jester. This is the ability that Viola praises in Feste in *Twelfth Night*: "He must observe their mood on whom he jests,/ The quality of persons, and the time ..." (III.i.62–63). Perceiving that his master's anger is beginning to cool, Dromio acts upon this very concept of decorum and seizes the opportunity for a quip. When Antipholus admonishes, "Well, sir, learn to jest in good time – there's a time for all things" (lines 64–65), Dromio objects, "There's no time for a man to recover his hair that grows bald by nature" (lines 72–73). By a long, circuitous route, this proposition leads finally to the explanation that "Time himself is bald, and therefore, to the world's end, will have bald followers" (lines 106–07). Dromio's jest, like Feste's to Olivia, restores him to his employer's good graces.

The dialogue between master and servant sets off a few puns, satiric thrusts, and some mild bawdy, but the wit is hardly memorable and is obscure enough to justify cutting in modern productions. The episode does provide some subtle revelations of character and psychology, for the relationship between master and servant is epitomized in their opposed views of time. In the conventional wisdom of the master – "there's a time for all things" – time is a benign ruler, to whose will man must necessarily conform. To the servant, who wrenches the proverb out of context, time is a tyrant; because he is bald, he demands bald followers. Dromio, ironically, postulates a Time who is a spiteful and destructive master; Antipholus, a Time who is benign and rational. The opposition thus reflects upon the tensions that provoked the exchange in the first place.

This playful opposition of views of time illuminates not only the characters of Dromio and Antipholus but one of the central themes of the play. Both views of time are collapsed in the unconscious pun in Dromio's "There's no time for a man to recover his hair that grows bald by nature." Dromio uses the pun on "hair" and "heir" intentionally at a later point, when he describes Luce's forehead as France, "arm'd and reverted, making war against her heir" (III.ii.123–24). Taken in one sense, Dromio's pun focuses on inevitable destruction and loss: one who grows bald by nature cannot recover his hair. Taken in another sense, however, the pun disproves this proposition, at least hypothetically, for a man who grows bald by nature may recover his lost heir. And it is this hypothesis that the play as a whole vindicates: Egeus, who himself views time as a destructive force, recovers his sons and his wife. In his case, time seems magically reversible, as in Dromio's later witticisms with Adriana about the striking of the clock: "It was two ere I left him, and now the clock strikes one" (IV.ii.54). The hours come back, Dromio explains, because "Time is a very bankrout and owes more than he's worth to season" (lines 57–58). This paradoxical reversibility of time reaches its climax in the "nativity" the Abbess describes at the end of the play:

> Thirty-three years have I but gone in travail
> Of you, my sons, and till this present hour
> My heavy burthen ne'er delivered.   (V.i.401–03)

In the overall design of the play, then, Dromio's jest with Antipholus turns against the jester: there *is* a time to recover one's heir. The pun, though not the punster, is prophetic. Although the recovery of heirs obliquely endorses the notion that there is a time for all things, as Antipholus says, this is not what he means by it; his concern with decorum is based on a rationalism that does not encompass the miraculous possibilities the plot unfolds. The clown is closer to these truths than his master, or at least his language is, the full implications of which escape him. The fool speaks one truth consciously, another unconsciously.[35]

Another version of this prophetic word-play occurs in Act I, scene ii of *The Taming of the Shrew*, when Petruchio asks his servant, Grumio, to knock on Hortensio's door. Whether Grumio misunderstands or merely pretends to misunderstand for the sake of the joke is uncertain, but he asks, "Knock, sir, whom should I knock? Is there any man has rebus'd your worship?" (lines 6–7). In his reply, Petruchio uses an ambiguous idiomatic expression that allows for further confusion: "Villain, I say, knock me here soundly" (line 8). Like Dromio in *The Comedy of Errors*, Grumio takes a conventional expression the wrong way: he refuses to knock his master and has his ears wrung for his insolence. The slapstick establishes for an audience the kind of relationship that this master and servant thrive upon, but the wit is undistinguished at best.

If one considers it, however, the misunderstanding provides a paradigm for a central theme of the play and a prophecy of its central action. Grumio's misunderstanding rests on his refusal or inability to take an idiomatic expression in its idiomatic meaning. Communication, however, indeed any ordered relationship between master and servant, depends upon the acceptance of certain conventions and a knowledge that these are conventions, artificial constructs imposed upon a complex and fluid reality. To view the episode from this angle is to perceive its relevance to Kate's conversion at the end of the play. In accepting the sun as the moon, or an old man as a young woman, Kate repudiates what her eyes tell her, just as Grumio must repudiate his ears; both must understand and accept their master's true meaning, although his words are open to more than one interpretation. Once she has accepted the meaning enfolded within Petruchio's metaphors, Kate can also accept her wifely role, knowing that both exist as conventions, figures of speech and conduct, within which more complicated and subtle relationships lie hidden. The frame story of the play, Sly's transformation from beggar to lord, itself demonstrates the advantages that can accrue from accepting conventions imposed from outside.

Later in the scene in which Grumio refuses to "knock" his master, he indulges in a bit of nonsense with Hortensio that also anticipates Kate's transformation. Speaking of Petruchio's ability to handle Kate's shrewish humor, Grumio says,

She may perhaps call him half a score knaves or so. Why, that's nothing; and he begin once, he'll rail in his rope-tricks. I'll tell you what, sir, and she stand him but a little, he will throw a figure in her face, and so disfigure her with it, that she shall have no more eyes to see withal than a cat. You know him not sir. (I.ii.110–16)

The point of this, if there is any conscious point other than confusion, slides over Hortensio, who continues his conversation with Petruchio. What the nonsense seems to mean (which is not to say what Grumio means by it) is that Petruchio will treat Kate just as he has treated Grumio. He will throw a figure (metaphor) in her face and disfigure her; Grumio, after all, has just had his ears wrung for failing to catch a double meaning. The main action of the play might be described in just such terms, as Petruchio throwing figures at Kate, railing in his "rope-tricks" of rhetoric. He pretends upon meeting her that she is "passing gentle" (II.i.242), a fiction he sustains despite her perversity, and later he demands that she accept the sun as the moon and an old man as a young virgin. Kate is disfigured by these figures – as well as by the more direct "rope-tricks" of starvation and sleeplessness – but in a sense opposite to that which Grumio apparently intends, for they transform her from a shrew into a human being. Grumio's reference to the eyes of the cat executes a double reverse on this theme. If Kate will see no better than a cat, she will see very clearly indeed, perhaps with the sharp eyes of insight, which will tell her that the sun is the moon when Petruchio says it is.

Both Dromio and Grumio are clownish servants who, in the episodes we have examined, take on the role of court fool – entertaining their masters, consciously or unconsciously, with word-play. What is striking about the game is the way in which the words turn about and play them, casting glimmers of prophetic illumination which the speakers themselves cannot see. In this, the clowns are reminiscent of genuine "naturals," whose nonsense contains occasional sense and whose dimness occasionally yields to insight. In *Foole upon Foole*, Robert Armin tells how the "natural" Jemy Camber prophesied his own death. Directed by the Chamberlain to come to the King, Jemy replied, "I will not ... I will goe make my grave." "See how things chaunced," notes Armin, "he spake truer then he was aware."[36] Jemy dug his grave in the churchyard, rode off to visit a gentleman of the town, and was dead within two hours; he never went to the King. Unlike Jemy Camber, Shakespeare's clowns speak comic prophecies, but they too speak truer than they are aware.

Feste, however, might seem a clown of another sort. An "artificial" fool, a professional entertainer, he is clear-headed, rational, apparently in complete control of his wit. The central paradox of his role lies in the fact that in the topsy-turvy world of Illyria the fool's is the only voice of reason. When he mocks Olivia for her excessive mourning, or Malvolio for his ignorance, or Orsino for his love-melancholy, Feste uses folly to speak for common sense. Yet even Feste's language gets away from him at times, turning reason against itself. Consider his ironical blessing of Orsino after the Duke, having listened to his sad song of love, abruptly dismisses him:

Now the melancholy god protect thee, and the tailor make thy doublet of changeable taffata, for thy mind is a very opal. I would have men of such constancy put to sea, that their business might be every thing and their

intent every where, for that's it that always make a good voyage of nothing.
                                                        (II.iv.73–78)
Although oblique, this blessing is easily rationalized. Melancholy,
taffeta, opals, are all associated with inconstancy or changeability, which Orsino has just demonstrated in his sudden shift in
mood. The second sentence is ironic: a man with no destination in
mind will return empty handed from his voyage. Like most of
Feste's satiric gibes, these depend upon underlying assumptions of
common sense: unless you know where you are going and keep
yourself on course, you will not get anywhere.

Yet Feste is Olivia's "corrupter of words," and his words
cannot be trusted. Like a "chevril glove" (III.i.12), the phrase
"makes a good voyage of nothing" can be turned inside out. In
one sense, as already indicated, it may mean "makes a potentially
good voyage into nothing"; in another, it may mean "makes out
of nothing a good voyage." The former interpretation is common-
sensical and satiric. The latter is nonsensical: how can one sail in
all directions at once and still get somewhere, or make something
out of nothing? Yet the plot of the play shapes this nonsense into
truth. The reunion of Sebastian and Viola, after they have been
lost at sea, converts their "nothing" into a "good voyage." And
Orsino, having been tossed in a "sea" of "love" (I.i.9–11)
throughout the play, claims at the end his "share in this most
happy wrack" (V.i.266) – Viola. Twelfth Night, like the holiday
to which it alludes, celebrates a mystery that transcends common
sense. From this perspective, Feste, the rationalist of the play, is as
much at sea as the others, for the common sense that he opposes to
their nonsense is ultimately folly. Feste, like Dromio and Grumio,
is a prophet of a truth he neither sees nor understands. His critique
of Orsino mixes wisdom and folly, affording, like the twins of the
play, a "natural perspective, that is and is not" (V.i.217).

One might pursue this phenomenon in other plays – in the
chaotic investigations of the watch in Much Ado About Nothing,
for example, which ultimately bring truth to light, or in Touchstone's demonstration of the virtue that lies in the word "if,"
which immediately precedes the appearance of a god on the stage.
The examples of Dromio, Grumio, and Feste, however, should be
enough to suggest the persistence of the pattern. In each case we
are taken through a labyrinth of equivocations. We begin with
nonsense – Dromio's denial of a proverb; Grumio's reference to

"rope-tricks"; Feste's rapid-fire metaphors. Then, as the riddle is unriddled or the joke made plain or the satiric jab hits home, we perceive the sense in the nonsense – usually, a sense based on common or "natural" reason. Yet the next step denies us sense again, as in Dromio's pun on "heir," or Grumio's quip about the eyes of a cat, or Feste's equivocation on "a good voyage of nothing." The final step yields more meaning, with the equivocations foreshadowing nonsensical, miraculous conclusions, in which Egeon's heirs are recovered, Kate becomes quick-eyed, and Orsino reaches his unknown destination. To unravel the mental tangles in this way is of course artificial and simplistic. For most audiences, I suspect, the delight lies in the dizziness – not the dizziness produced by no meaning at all, but by glimpses of meaning held tantalizingly before us. Stumbling from one confusion to the next, our minds mimic the actions of the clown.

This technique of fooling may originate in the traditional capacity of "naturals" to speak unconscious, cryptic, and prophetic truths, but its dramatic function, if we want to approach it from that perspective, is uncertain. What purpose does it serve? The clown is unconscious of the farthest reaches of his wit, since he cannot know the end of his own play, and the same is true of the characters to whom he speaks. No one onstage is capable of even suspecting prophetic truths. Glimmers of insight are possible in certain audiences, but only to those who know the play intimately or, conceivably, know the genre so well that they see the inevitability of the comic transformations in question. However we explain their presence – perhaps even as the playful "fooling" of the dramatist – these cryptic, riddling, prophetic mixtures of sense, nonsense, and transcendence epitomize the natural art of clowning. In her brief conversation with Feste, Viola remarks that "They that dally nicely with words may quickly make them wanton" (*TN* III.i.14–15). The clown's words are "wantons," untrustworthy but fertile, capable of yielding unexpected fruit. His riddles are the linguistic counterparts of the liminal experience – a generative chaos out of which a comic order mysteriously emerges. "Liminality," observes Victor Turner, "may perhaps be regarded as the Nay to all positive structural assertions, but as in some sense the source of them all, and, more than that, as a realm of pure possibility whence novel configurations of ideas and relations may arise."[37]

In Shakespeare's comedies, the nonsense of the clown mimics in words the creative confusion of love.

Although spontaneous and labyrinthine, the word games of the clown generally follow a well defined pattern. The familiar structure of witticisms, riddles, and jests is basically that of predicament and resolution. The games of wit between masters and servants – Antipholus–Dromio, Armado–Moth, Valentine–Speed – are potentially infinite, for each turn of phrase resolves one conundrum only to provide a springboard for the next. When the game becomes especially competitive, it offers players and spectators some of the pleasure of tennis, as is suggested by the Princess's remark to Katherine and Rosaline in *Love's Labor's Lost*: "Well bandied both, a set of wit well played" (V.ii.29). The sport can have two or more players, or one and an audience, as when Touchstone mocks Orlando's verses. In either case, a simple question drives it on: "How can I keep the ball moving to my advantage?" Such games threaten to go on for ever; they are usually brought to a close only by the entrance of new characters. "But soft, who wafts us yonder?" (*Err* II.ii.109) signals the end of the set between Antipholus and Dromio on recovering one's hair. For the clown, all punchlines are preparations for the next assault.

This predicament–resolution pattern structures not only the clown's spontaneous word-play but his whole random existence – his "tumbling and stumbling," as Langer puts it, "from one situation into another." It can frame a single episode, as when Feste, faced with Olivia's disfavor, wins back his position with some admirable fooling. It can shape a single scene, as when Dogberry salves the anxieties of his watch by instructing them in the full course of their duties. Or it can span an entire role, as in *The Taming of the Shrew*, when Tranio, disguised as his master, maneuvers from crisis to crisis – persuading Baptista he is a wealthy suitor, finding a surrogate father, fending off Lucentio's real father, and somehow avoiding the slit nose Vincentio promises him at the end of the play. Whether they end an episode, a scene, or a role, the resolutions in this pattern are always fragile – temporary respites in a life of turmoil. Predicament is the clown's natural condition.

Rapid alternations of predicaments and resolutions provide the comic drive in a scene that is a touchstone for Shakespearean comedy, that in which Bottom meets Titania. The scene begins with Quince assuring his dramatic company that everything is in order and that the wood provides a "marvail's convenient place for our rehearsal" (*MND* III.i.2–3). Immediately, Bottom poses a problem: "There are things in this comedy of Pyramus and Thisby that will never please" (lines 9–10). The ladies, he says, will not abide Pyramus drawing a sword to kill himself. This stymies Snout and Starveling, but Bottom, whose answer was prepared before his question, is undismayed: he will speak a prologue, informing the audience that Pyramus is not "kill'd indeed" (line 19), but is indeed Bottom the weaver. This pattern is repeated, with variations: the problem of a lion on the stage is raised and settled; of moonlight; of a wall. In each case Bottom resolves the difficulties, which would not have arisen, one suspects, without his initial example.

The next predicament, however, proves more serious: Bottom enters with his head transformed into that of an ass. This is too much for his fellows, who scatter, leaving Bottom offended, perplexed, and frightened. He does not yield to his fear, however, but masters it by singing: "I will walk up and down here, and I will sing, that they shall hear I am not afraid" (lines 122–24). Having resolved one problem through song, he thrusts himself immediately into another, for his song awakens Titania: "What angel wakes me from my flow'ry bed?" (line 129). Although her appearance does not pose a problem, exactly, it presents a challenge – how does one respond to the love of a goddess? Bottom resolves this predicament by not acknowledging it; he converses with Titania naturally and adapts to his new role with gracious ease. The scene ends in a state of harmony and contentment, with Bottom being escorted to Titania's bower.

To analyze the scene in this way is not to explain the sources of its laughter, for these lie in the multiple incongruities of situation, character, and language. It does suggest, however, at least one source of the scene's delight – the characteristic rhythm of clowning that Langer describes in physical terms as the "tumbling and stumbling . . . from one situation into another, getting into scrape after scrape and getting out again, with or without a thrashing." Bottom finds himself at the end of the scene stumbling towards Titania's "flow'ry bed," having earlier stumbled through the predicaments posed by the rehearsal of his play and his fellows' flight. The resolution that ends the scene, as is inevitably the case, is actually a new predicament in disguise. This union of lovers cannot hold. Yoking together dullness and wit, boorishness and grace, commonness and courtliness, bestiality and divinity, it provides a perfect emblem of liminal confusion. The next predicament for both characters will be waking up.

One way of describing this alternating rhythm of clowning is to see it as a circle. Always on the move, the clowns never get anywhere; their liminal existence is a state of ceaseless becoming. Like the romantic lovers, both "natural" and "artificial," the clowns indulge endlessly in role-playing, unconscious and conscious. The Dromio twins play each other; Tranio becomes his master; Bottom acts the lover; Touchstone and Feste change their parts with every performance and audience, observing, as Viola puts it, their spectators' "mood," their "quality," and "the time" (*TN* III.i.62–63). The more the clowns are transformed, however, the more they stay the same. They do not discover their folly in a burst of illumination, as happens to some of the lovers at the end of the plays; nor does their experience result in a radical change in status. Touchstone agrees to marry Audrey, but he is still Touchstone. Dogberry remains a man who has suffered losses, and Feste a corrupter of words. Even when reunited with his twin, Dromio of Syracuse turns to the wrong master and asks, "shall I fetch your stuff from shipboard?" (*Err* V.i.409).

Bottom's awakening from his dream epitomizes this immutability. As he slowly comes to his senses and his "rare vision" recedes, Bottom struggles to understand it, but when the truth nears the surface of consciousness, he eases it under: "Man is but an ass, if he go about t'expound this dream" (*MND* IV.i.206–07). As he reaches upwards towards his missing ass's ears, he edges towards the truth again, but this time too he lets it slide away: "Methought I was, and methought I had – but man is but a patch'd fool, if he will offer to say what methought I had" (lines 208–11). Poised between waking and sleeping, reality and dream, Bottom mingles sense and nonsense, collapsing all distinctions in wondrous confusion. Wherever he turns, asininity stares him in the face.

Bottom has been an ass and loved by the Queen of Fairies. Such a paradox makes asininity inescapable. To expound his dream would make Bottom an ass, for he cannot explain the inexplicable. Yet even if he could, he would remain an ass, for this is the content of his dream. Bottom's dream contains the central paradox of the romantic comedies: to know oneself is to know oneself an ass, but to be an ass is not to know oneself. Although he has been "translated" (III.i.119), and touched by a mystery that leaves his senses muddled for the rest of the play, Bottom is not transformed. He returns to Athens Bottom the weaver, and no more is heard of his dream or of the ballad he promises to sing at Thisby's death.

Although touched by transcendence, Bottom is immune to its more profound effects. Mystery speaks through him, as it does through the nonsense of Dromio, Grumio, and Feste, but leaves him essentially unscathed. This immunity of the clown is often expressed as an immunity to romantic love – the incomprehension of natural man to the spiritual fancies of courtly amorists. Moth mocks Armado's love, and Tranio tries to snap Lucentio out of his lover's trance at the sight of Bianca. Occasionally, the clown's imperviousness to things of the spirit takes on a deeper meaning, hinting at the true "natural's" exemption from the realm of the spirit, an exemption that frees him from the knowledge of sin and grace.[38] There are signs of this condition not only in Bottom's role but in Feste's in *Twelfth Night*.

Feste is the "wise man" of a play that celebrates the Epiphany. As we have seen, however, his language occasionally outruns him, hinting at paradoxical and miraculous reversals in normal human affairs. Men do not reach their destinations by wandering, yet Orsino does, and so do Sebastian and Viola. What Feste the skeptic and rationalist ignores, and what his fooling adumbrates, is the potential in life for the miraculous – the potential that the feast of Twelfth Night celebrates. We might excuse Feste a certain skepticism towards the marriages that end the play. But even the wondrous reunion of Sebastian and Viola apparently leaves him untouched. It is Feste who ends the play, alone on the stage, singing a melancholy song that reduces the whole of life to a series of absurd and unpleasant roles. Life's progress, as Feste sings it, is from folly, to knavery, to swaggering, to drunken heads, and through a rain that "raineth every day."

The pleasure of clowning, as Feste's song reminds us, is not without touches of pathos. The clown is a liminal being. At once highly sexed and sexless, self-absorbed and selfless, witty and witless, changeable and constant, he is a figure for the confusion of the liminal stage. As an embodiment of chaos in the midst of a comic rite of passage, the clown is from one perspective an emblem of regression or stasis. While the dynamics of the plays are progressive and integrative, moving through liminality to incorporation, the clown remains fixed in confusion, sometimes outside and alone. When he plays an important part at the end of a comedy, the clown usually reminds us of human recalcitrance, as does the *cipuba* of the Chisungu ceremony or the morris fool at Elizabethan weddings. Such is the case with Bottom's playlet, Touchstone's marriage, and, in a melancholy vein, with Feste's song.

Feste's melancholy lyrics, however, like all the utterances of Shakespeare's clowns, leave us with no fixed and settled point of view, but only with ambiguity and paradox. His song never reaches the apocalyptic ending towards which it seems to move:

> A great while ago the world begun,
> With hey ho, the wind and the rain,
> But that's all one, our play is done,
> And we'll strive to please you every day.   (V.i.405–08)

The final line promises not the end of time but an endless circle of delight. Who makes the promise? Feste the character or Robert Armin the actor? Both are fools. Characteristically, the clown keeps the ball rolling and his true identity in question. His emblem, it seems, is not the line but the circle, and if there is melancholy in circles there is also hope.

The clown's is a natural circle, always the same, but capable of infinite renewal. His circularity is dizzying – always on the move, he never arrives – but his energy is endless. His confusion is a world through which lovers pass en route to marriage. But the true mark of their passage is the knowledge that they carry his confusion within. At those rare and fleeting moments when lovers become one with themselves and with each other in rites of incorporation, they acknowledge their kinship with the clown. "Man is a giddy thing," says Benedick, "and this is my conclusion" (*Ado* V.iv.108–09). In this acknowledgement lies a final paradox of hope and despair: the beginning and the end of Shakespeare's comic rites of passage is folly. To escape from the liminal world is to accept it as one's natural home.

6

Time and Place

"There's no clock in the forest."
(*AYL* III.ii.301)

Rites of passage depend upon a deep connection between our sense of identity and our sense of time and place. To pass from childhood to adulthood, or from a single to a married state, is to take a complicated mental journey through space and time. When the novice leaves his home for the sacred place in the forest, or the betrothed for visits or service within the new family group, he enters realms in which the ordinary laws of time and place are suspended; he finds himself, as van Gennep remarks, both "physically and magico-religiously in a special situation for a certain length of time."[1] Whether the individual returns to a familiar time and place, or, as in the case of marriage, enters a new one, the rites of incorporation insure that the movement is both a return and a renewal. If he enters a familiar world, he finds that his role has changed; if he enters an unfamiliar, he finds that he belongs. The journey is thus both linear and cyclical; as in the seasonal rhythms of nature, identity moves forward in a circle. It is a movement of this kind that Shakespearean comedy celebrates.

We are most conscious of time and place in the comedies, as in life, when the normal routine is disrupted. It is this experience that is captured in the liminal phase. Liminal time is outside the norm, a time out of joint – a "deeply ambiguous 'dreaming time,'" as Roger Grainger observes, "when the past is left behind and the future not yet begun."[2] The liminal place is an alien, often sacred landscape, full of threat and promise, both tomb and womb. The ambiguity of the liminal experience is both temporal and spatial; the transitional state of mind is one of temporary dislocation.

Although I shall be dealing separately with place and time, it should be clear already that the two concepts are closely intertwined. This was even more true in the Elizabethan period, I suspect, than now. The word "space," for example, for moderns almost exclusively a geographical term, denoting area or extension, or even a specific locale, such as outer space, was for Shakespeare almost equally temporal and spatial in its meaning. If one examines a concordance to Shakespeare, one finds that nearly half the references to "space" refer to time. When Antony declares his devotion to Cleopatra with the phrase, "Here is my space" (*Ant* I.i.34), he refers to the land of Egypt. When Berowne reminds Navarre of the terms of his oath, however, he uses "space" to mean "time": "I only swore to study with your Grace,/ And stay here in your court for three years' space" (*LLL* I.i.51–52). This interchangeability of a temporal and spatial vocabulary helps explain the ease with which Shakespeare modulates from one dimension to the other. In a certain sense, place *is* time.

To separate the two concepts, although necessary, is therefore to distort somewhat the nature of the comic experience. This is particularly true of the liminal phase, in which place and time are most obtrusive. The two most persuasive accounts of this phase of the comedies, for example, those of Northrop Frye and C. L. Barber, depend upon metaphors that stress one side of the experience at the expense of the other: Frye's "green world" conveys primarily a sense of place, Barber's "holiday" a sense of time. Although no single metaphor can capture all the implications of the comic experience, that of liminality at least invites us to attend equally to place and time.

In his conception of a "green world," Northrop Frye has provided the most influential account of Shakespeare's use of symbolic geography in the comedies. For Frye the "green world" originates in myths of rebirth and thus "charges the comedies with the symbolism of the victory of summer over winter."[3] In its temporal dimension this world is not only green but golden: "The forest or green world ... is a symbol of natural society, the word natural here referring to the original human society which is the proper home of man, not the physical world he now lives in but the 'golden world' he is trying to regain."[4] Although Frye's schema generates some brilliant insights into the plays, it is difficult to apply, especially since Frye conflates the romantic comedies and late romances into a single genre. If restricted to the romantic comedies, the notion is more plausible for those that invoke natural landscapes, like *A Midsummer Night's Dream* and

As You Like It, than for those, like *The Comedy of Errors*, *The Taming of the Shrew*, and *Twelfth Night*, that do not. Yet the latter plays too depend upon a special sense of place as part of the liminal experience; although they cannot be described as "green" or "golden" worlds, Ephesus, Petruchio's house, and Illyria all resonate with symbolic meaning. And even *A Midsummer Night's Dream* creates a liminal landscape more ambiguous than Frye's idealizing metaphors allow.

In one sense, the very objectivity assigned to place by a metaphor such as the "green world" distorts the experience of the plays. Shakespeare's use of place is too shifty and elusive for such fixity of meaning. His symbolic oppositions are deliberately unstable. Nowhere is symbolic geography more elaborately defined, for example, than in the contrast between Athens and the wood in *A Midsummer Night's Dream*. Athens is a realm of legalism, the wood of license. Athens is a realm of mortals, the wood of fairies. Athens is a court, the wood a natural landscape. Athens serves rationalism, the wood imagination. Athens is a waking, the wood a dreaming world. And the list could be extended. Yet as soon as one presses these antitheses, they begin to dissolve. Laws are tyrannically enforced in the wood as well as in Athens. Fickleness in love is demonstrated in both places. Athens, Hermia tells us, was once a paradise, but her love has turned it into hell; the wood, so often the setting of friendship for Hermia and Helena, becomes the scene of violent quarrels. At the end of the play, moreover, the symbolic oppositions are suspended in paradox: the fairies enter the world of the court to bless the marriages at deep midnight.

What the unstable symbolism of *A Midsummer Night's Dream* reveals is that place in the comedies is as much a psychological as a geographical concept. The Athenian lovers act madly because they are in the wood, and thus subject to Puck's potions, but they are also in the wood because they act madly: they have run away. Geography is both a cause and an emblem of a state of mind. As he rushes into the wood in pursuit of Hermia, Demetrius expresses succinctly this complex interaction of physical and mental landscapes: "And here am I, and wode within this wood,/ Because I cannot meet my Hermia" (II.i.192–93).

Although the whole play takes place in Ephesus, a similar effect is created in *The Comedy of Errors*. Our impression of Ephesus is determined, to a great extent, by the characters who come from outside – Egeon, Antipholus of Syracuse, and his servant, Dromio. For them Ephesus is a bewildering and mainly threatening land – off-bounds to Syracusans, and with a reputation for deception and witchcraft:

> They say this town is full of cozenage:
> As nimble jugglers that deceive the eye,
> Dark-working sorcerers that change the mind,
> Soul-killing witches that deform the body,
> Disguised cheaters, prating mountebanks,
> And many such-like liberties of sin.   (I.ii.97–102)

While Antipholus's experiences confirm his account of the city's reputation – sometimes inducing delight, sometimes despair – they do so not so much because the city is bewitched as because his perception is clouded. His twin brother, very much at home in Ephesus, is equally displaced by his misadventures: locked out of his house, arrested for debt, subjected to the cures of Dr Pinch. Although his wandering takes him no farther than the streets of his own city, Antipholus of Ephesus loses himself as completely as those for whom the city is an alien and enchanted land. The pun in the play's title makes the point: one can "err" with one's legs or mind.

The subjectivity of the liminal landscape needs little demonstration in *As You Like It*, for one's sense of the forest of Arden as a place changes from moment to moment and from character to character. Although the forest looks like a green and golden world from the outside, as in the report of Charles the wrestler, and although the movement into the forest effects the miraculous conversions of both Duke Frederick and Oliver, the actual experience of this strange land varies with the characters who inhabit it. For Orlando it is a place to post verses; for Duke Senior a place to gather wisdom from the book of nature; for Jaques a place to suck melancholy out of songs; for Corin a place to care for sheep; for Silvius a place to lose oneself in an eternity of unrequited love. Like much else in the play, the image of Arden is "as you like it." Or almost. For in this play, as in the others, the liminal landscape is not merely a figment of the imagination. Arden has objective reality, but its reality is not simply objective. Shakespeare's interest lies in the point at which the objective and subjective landscapes intersect. He does not reduce reality to one truth or the other.

The habit of mind that sees in geography a reflection of a mental state, although by no means uniquely Elizabethan, runs counter to the philosophical assumptions that underlie modern dramatic realism. To an audience watching Ibsen's *Hebba Gabler*, place is more likely to be a cause than a symptom of a state of mind. When Hedda stands in her living room, the audience is aware of a mute conflict between the room and the prominent objects it encloses: a portrait, a piano, a case of duelling pistols. The walls belong to George Tesman, Hedda's husband; the objects to General Gabler, her father. The conventions of dramatic realism make clear to an audience that place is objective and imply its causative function: the portrait of General Gabler does not reflect Hedda's disturbed mind but creates it, just as the man himself has created her. In Ibsen's title, indeed, she is still Hedda Gabler; her identity derives from her father, not from her husband. On the Elizabethan stage, by contrast, an audience is immediately aware that geography may be a mental phenomenon: the wood outside Athens and Athens itself exist only in our imagination, aided by a few suggestive props. Shakespeare does not hide this fact but exploits it. When Rosalind arrives in the forest, she looks at a bare stage and says, "Well, this is the forest of Arden" (*AYL* II.iv.15). When Viola lands in Illyria, she surveys the stage and asks, "What country, friends, is this?" (*TN* I.ii.1). Both landscapes are realms of imagination. The Elizabethan genres of allegory and the estate-poem reflect a similar tendency to internalize geography. Spenser's forests in *The Faerie Queene* are mental phenomena, as is the landscape of Penshurst in Ben Jonson's poem. The genre of the estate-poem, as William A. McClung observes, "assigns the virtues of an honourable manor and the vices of a House of Pride to the human beings who alone can bring about such situations."[5] To overstate the case, one might say that for the Elizabethan imagination man creates the place he inhabits, whereas for the modern the place creates the man.

The geography of the liminal phase in the comedies, then, is both internal and external, symptom and cause of the liminal states of mind we have already explored. To see this world as "green," or "golden," a world that represents the victory of summer over winter, gold over iron, human desire over human reality, is to distort the liminal experience. Although Frye recognizes that these landscapes are often dream as well as green worlds, and enchanted as well as golden, the dreams and magic he links them to are those that give us only our desires. In the plays themselves, the alien landscape is far more ambiguous. The dreams are as likely to be nightmares as golden visions – what Theseus calls "the fierce vexation of a dream" (*MND* IV.i.69). Although in the country, Petruchio's house is hardly a green world for Kate, nor is the bewitched world of Ephesus a golden one for Antipholus of Syracuse. And even the forest of Arden, which comes closest of all the comedies to Frye's formula, has nasty weather, churlish landlords, snakes, and lovers who come late for their appointments.

Although Frye offers a useful corrective to moralistic critics, like Sir Philip Sidney, who see only satire in the comic follies of lovers, he errs on the other side by seeing only romance. The crucial point about the liminal world is its ambiguity. Neither simply positive nor negative, creative nor destructive, it is a world in flux. Shakespeare's most common metaphors for liminality capture this ambiguity: magic, for example, can be black or white; dreams can be good or bad; folly can be deranged or inspired; fancy can be deceptive or truthful. To describe the transitional world, we need a word or phrase that conveys these double possibilities. In some sense, we are the victims of changes in the language. Shakespeare's words – magic, dream, folly, fancy – no longer generate the same emotional charge or the same ambivalence. If one were to choose a single word to describe Shakespeare's symbolic landscapes, "enchanted" seems to me preferable to "green" or "golden"; it is more inclusive – even the "green" worlds have magical associations – and more ambiguous. Whatever we call it, the transitional landscape is a setting for dislocation.

The ambiguity of liminal landscapes runs throughout the comedies. In *The Comedy of Errors* Ephesus is variously described as a land of dreams, fairies, mermaids, mists, illusions, and madness. It is a hostile land, for visiting Syracusans are threatened with death, but it is also a benign land, for some Syracusans, at least, are invited to dinner by beautiful women and given golden chains. But even the gifts are bewildering: Antipholus of Ephesus reacts to the gift of the chain by preparing to flee Ephesian witchcraft; Dromio, his servant, reacts to the same chain by desiring to remain in this "gentle nation" and "turn witch" (IV.iv.153–56). In *A Midsummer Night's Dream*, the lovers are separated and united in the same wood, and the symbol of their discord and concord is the magic of Oberon; in the wood grow Diana's bud and Cupid's flower. If Lysander's enchantment takes him out of his reason, Demetrius's returns him to his, or so it seems, for he is never disenchanted once Oberon's potion has restored his original love for Helena. In "Pyramus and Thisby," performed in the final scene, the same wood that is the setting for comic love is the setting for "tragic."

One rarely thinks of Petruchio's bourgeois country house as an enchanted landscape, but it serves the same psychological function. Kate's education, like that of the Athenian lovers, begins with disorientation. Dragged away from her family and her wedding feast, Kate sets out on a journey that shakes her off her horse and out of her senses. In Petruchio's house Kate is subjected to a regimen worthy of the Dr Pinch of *The Comedy of Errors*: she is starved, lectured on continency, denied a wardrobe, and deprived of sleep. In this regard her experience is not ambiguous. Yet this straightforward brutality poses only a minor psychic threat. What unnerves and disorients Kate is Petruchio's insistence that she is not a shrew but "pleasant, gamesome, passing courteous" (II.i.245), and that all he does is done "in reverend care of her" (IV.i.204). "This is the way," he says, "to kill a wife with kindness" (line 208). Mere brutality would stiffen Kate's sense of identity; the combination of brutal methods and kind words dissolves it, until she "Knows not which way to stand, to look, to speak,/ And sits as one new risen from a dream" (IV.i.185–86).

The enchanted landscapes through which Shakespeare's lovers pass en route to marriage, then, are akin to the sacred places of rites of initiation. Like novices, the lovers enter alien realms that both create and reflect their disordered states of mind. The experience is that of a sustained pathetic fallacy, in which distinctions between mind and matter dissolve. Although often located in nature, these landscapes can be anywhere – in Ephesus, Illyria, or Petruchio's country house – for they represent a geography of the mind. Sometimes hostile, sometimes benign, these realms always disorient; their contours are the meandering lines of identities in transition. In such realms anything is possible. In the wood outside Athens, Bottom the weaver becomes both the paramour of a goddess and an ass.

Although hardly as exotic as the journeys taken by Shakespeare's lovers, those of Elizabethan adolescents must have been similarly disorienting. For those sent out to domestic service, apprenticeship, school, university, or travel abroad, adolescence was a distinctly spatial phenomenon. In some cases, of course, the transitional locale was familiar: to serve as apprentice in a neighboring village did not entail severe dislocation. But in others the strangeness of adolescence found its counterpart in a disturbing and exhilarating environment. To move from a small village to an apprenticeship in London, as many young boys did, was to enter a world as bizarre and disorienting as the bush for an African novice. The same might be said of studying at Oxford, Cambridge, or the Inns of Court; of entering the service of the Queen; or of travelling abroad. Although not formal rites of initiation, these journeys served a ritual function and were framed by ceremonies; departures were ceremonious occasions, and returns, in most cases, were marked by the rite of marriage.

Shakespeare's comic settings, unlike those of many of his contemporaries, are foreign and exotic. Their exoticism, however, displaces familiar Elizabethan attitudes and experiences. Contemporary reactions to young men travelling abroad, for example, are expressed in language reminiscent of *The Comedy of Errors* or *A Midsummer Night's Dream*. In *Instructions for Forraine Travell*, James Howell observes that travel abroad "oftentimes makes many to wander from themselves, as well as from their Countrey, and to come back mere *Mimiques*, and so in going farre, to fare worse, and bring back lesse wit, than they carieth forth ..."[6] Although he sees the process as simply destructive, Howell describes it in familiar liminal terms − as wandering and imitating. In *The Scholemaster*, Roger Ascham's objections to travel in Italy are even more strident. For him, a visit to Italy is a visit to Circe's court:

But I am affraide, that over many of our travelers into Italie do not eschewe the way to *Circe's* court: but go, and ryde, and runne, and flie thether, they make great hast to cum to her: they make great sute to serve her: yea, I could point out some with my finger, that never had gone out of England, but onlie to serve *Circes*, in *Italie*. Vanitie and vice, and any licence to ill livyng in England was counted stale and rude unto them. And so, beyng Mules and Horses before they went, returned verie Swyne and Asses home agayne ...[7]

Ascham's response is interesting not only because his sustained metaphor involves both enchantment and metamorphosis but because he senses that such journeys are symptoms as well as causes of disordered states of mind. The asses and swine who return to England were mules and horses before they went. In the wood outside Athens, Bottom's asshead exposes an asininity he brings with him.

Courtship too was associated with spatial dislocations, although not as dramatic or extended as those resulting from travel abroad. Since most courting took place in adolescence, the alien landscapes already discussed provided the settings for the rites of love. Ralph Josselin's five children, as we saw in Chapter 2, all initiated their own marriages, meeting their spouses while away from home, serving as domestics or apprentices. More specifically, certain environments were the natural habitats of love. The experience of holiday release that C. L. Barber so brilliantly describes was associated not only with special times but with special places – places that encouraged love. St Valentine's and May Day both involved a flight of lovers into the forest, and even minor festivals, such as market or fair days, could transform the village square into a setting for romance. In Nicholas Breton's dialogue between a courtier and a countryman, country wooing is described in terms of "dauncing on the green, in the market house, or about the May-poole."[8] Much courting was probably conducted outdoors, as Breton implies, for most Elizabethan houses afforded little privacy.

The most familiar setting for illicit romance, if we can trust the evidence of Phillip Stubbes and Simon Forman, was the garden. At the very least, their accounts show that the traditional associations between gardens and love rested on more than literary convention. Stubbes attacks the common use of gardens for sinful pleasures:

In the Feeldes and Suburbes of the Cities thei have Gardens, either palled, or walled round about very high, with their Harbers and Bowers fit for the purpose. And least thei might bee espied in these open places, they have their Banquetting houses with Galleries, Turrettes, and what not els therin sumpteously erected: wherein thei maie (and doubtlesse doe) many of them plaie the filthie persons. And for that their Gardens are locked, some of them have three or fower keyes a peece, whereof one they keepe for themselves, the other their Paramours have to goe in before them, least happely they should be perceived, for then were all their sporte dasht. Then to these Gardens thei repaire when thei list, with a basket and a boy, where thei, meeting their sweete hartes, receive their wished desires. These Gardens are exelent places, and for the purpose; for if thei can speak with their dearlynges no where els, yet there thei maie be sure to meete them, and to receive the guerdon of their paines: thei know best what I meane.[9]

In his biography of Simon Forman, A. L. Rowse notes how important Avis Allen's locked garden was in her love affair with Forman, and how "numerous these gardens and closes were" throughout London. Forman's diary, in which the word *halek* serves as a code for sexual intercourse, includes entries such as the following:

The 19th of May, Monday, Avis Allen took dislike of me pro halekeros [on account of intercourse], and in nowise would be firm with me again, nor come at me after but by great constraint, etc. The 26th of May we were friends again, p.m. at 30 past 2, being at garden, after we had related all matters between us. Deo gratias!

. . . .

The 12th of March, Friday p.m. 30 past 5, I went to garden, where I found Avis Allen; we became friends again and I did halek, etc., cum illa [with her].

Rowse reports an incident that shows the symbolic role of the garden in Forman's dream life:

He then dreamed he was in a garden with Avis and her friend: they both "strove which should call me to the garden with them." That day he "went to Avis Allen and halek, and had news from Sir William Monson and Steven, my man."[10]

Although both the observation of Stubbes and the practice of Forman suggest the importance of Elizabethan gardens as settings for love, they shed little light on Shakespeare's symbolic geography. If Shakespeare draws upon the psychology of the garden experience for his liminal settings, he does so obliquely; although many of his landscapes are natural, few are literally gardens, and all offer pleasures and perils that are both more sophisticated and more innocent than those described by Stubbes or Forman. Shakespeare's liminal settings have more in common with Terry Comito's description of the psychology of medieval and Renaissance gardens of love:

In sacred places man discovers a special bond with the world. But if the royal garden celebrates man's power in this encounter, the enhancement and perfection of his being, in gardens of love the imagination concedes the helplessness of its rapture and the strangeness of its discovery. ("What does the intellect seek if not to transform all things into itself," Ficino asks, "and what does the will strive to do if not to transform itself into all things?"') Like the fairy pleasances of Celtic tradition, such spots are not just conveniences for lovers but incitements to love, centers of a sometimes dangerous power.[11]

Although Shakespeare's "sacred" or liminal places are not gardens, Comito's description is remarkably apt. The sense of helplessness; of strangeness; of mysterious transformations of the physical into the mental world and vice versa; of enchantment; of a power that is fundamentally ambiguous, potentially destructive or creative – these are the features of liminal experience and the landscape in which it occurs.

There is admittedly a vast social, intellectual, and even geographical gap between Comito's gardens of love and those that Stubbes observed in Elizabethan London. It can be bridged, however, at least to a certain extent, if we consider the implications of a single, prominent feature of almost all Elizabethan gardens, aristocratic or bourgeois – the maze. In the psychology of mazes, Shakespeare's liminal landscapes, neoplatonic gardens of love, and the locked gardens of Stubbes's London intersect.

The popularity of mazes is clear from the large number of Elizabethan and Jacobean garden books that contain both designs and directions for planting, such as Thomas Hill's *The Gardeners Labyrinth* (1577), Gervase Markham's *The English Husbandman* (1635), and William Lawson's *The Countrie Houswifes Garden* (1617). Markham's *Excellent and New Invented Knots and Mazes* (1623) consists entirely of designs. In *A Most Brief and Pleasaunt Treatyse, Teaching howe to Dress, Sowe, and Set a Garden* (1563), Thomas Hill explains the function of mazes in a manner suggestive for Shakespeare's liminal landscapes:

> Here by the way (gentle Reader) I do place two proper Mazes ... as proper adornments upon pleasure to a Garden, that who that lysteth ... may place the one of them ... in that voyde place of the garden that may best be spared ... to sporte them in at times, which mazis being workmanly handled by the Gardiner, shall beutyfye them much, in divisyng foure sondrye fruites to be placed in eche of the corners of the maze, and in the middle of it may be a proper herber decked with roses to be set or els a faire tree of Roses, Mary or other fruyt, at the discrecion of the Gardiner.[12]

If we can assume that courtship was one of the "sports" encouraged by these gardens, then Elizabethan lovers must have occasionally experienced love as a journey not only into nature but into a natural labyrinth. At the center of a maze grown to Hill's specifications might be an arbor of roses; at the center of the labyrinth in the Great Garden at Hampton Court, as described in 1613, was a "small round hill ... called the Venusberg."[13] In the middle of the "mazed world" (II.i.113) of *A Midsummer Night's Dream* is Titania's "close and consecrated bower" (III.ii.7). The kind of delight that mazes afforded Elizabethans is suggested in a speech written by George Peele for the visit of the Queen to Theobalds in 1591. The speaker is a gardener, who describes a maze he has designed, which includes an arbor of eglantine, Elizabeth's special flower. Predictably, the account celebrates her virtues:

The moles destroyed and the plot levelled, I cast it into four quarters. In the first I framed a maze, not of hyssop and thyme, but that which maketh time itself wither with wondering; all the Virtues, all the Graces, all the Muses winding and wreathing about your majesty, each contending to be chief, all contented to be cherished: all this not of potherbs, but flowers, and of flowers fairest and sweetest; for in so heavenly a Maze, which astonished all earthly thoughts' promise, the Virtues were done in roses, flowers fit for the twelve Virtues, who have in themselves, as we gardeners have observed, above an hundred; the Grace[s] of pansies partly-coloured, but in one stalk, never asunder, yet diversely beautified; the Muses of nine several flowers, being of sundry natures, yet all sweet, all sovereign.
   These mingled in a maze, and brought into such shapes as poets and painters use to shadow, made mine eyes dazzle with the shadow, and all my thoughts amazed to behold the bodies. Then was I commanded to place an arbour all of eglantine, in which my master's conceit outstripped my cunning: "Eglantine," quoth he, "I most honour, and it hath been told me that the deeper it is rooted in the ground, the sweeter it smelleth in the flower, making it ever so green that the sun of Spain at the hottest cannot parch it."

What is relevant for my purpose in this description is not the particular symbolism of the plants but the use of the maze both to reflect and create a special state of mind. While the flowers record Elizabeth's wondrous virtues, the maze evokes the wonder appropriate to them: it makes "time itself wither with wondering"; it astonishes "all earthly thoughts' promise"; it makes the gardener's eyes "dazzle with the shadow," and all his "thoughts amazed to behold the bodies." Later, the molecatcher gives an address, assuring the audience that such transcendence is not for the likes of him: "I cannot discourse of knots and mazes: sure I am that the ground was so knotty that the gardener was amazed to see it ... "[14] Mazes, in short, are for amazement.

The maze at Theobalds offered more political than romantic amazement, perhaps, but in the case of Elizabeth politics was conducted by courtship. The experience of a maze, in any event, seems to have been delightful because it transformed into play the often frightening experience of losing oneself. Although bourgeois mazes may have afforded less esoteric delights than those at Theobalds, their psychological effect seems to have been much the same. In his description of a garden in *A New Orchard and Garden*, William Lawson notes that "mazes well framed a man's height, may perhaps make your friend wander in gathering of Berries till he cannot recover himself without your help."[15] Elizabethan adolescents did not need to go to Italy to wander from themselves; they could do so in their own gardens.

Mazes existed not only in Elizabethan gardens but in the open fields. These were turf mazes, or labyrinths, with paths cut into the ground about six inches deep. The origins of these configurations are ancient but obscure. John Aubrey thought they were made by the Danes, but more recent scholarship favors the Romans. Aubrey records that they were used often in the past, "by the young people on Holydaies, and by the School-boyes."[16] The sport consisted of "treading" the maze, but its exact nature is uncertain. That the "amazement" was somehow magical is clear. In *A Midsummer Night's Dream* Titania complains to Oberon that their quarrel has disrupted country sports:

> The nine men's morris is fill'd up with mud,
> And the quaint mazes in the wanton green,
> For lack of tread are undistinguishable.   (II.i.98–100)

In *The Tempest* treading the maze is linked to Prospero's magic. "This is as strange a maze as e'er men trod," says Alonso at the end of the play, "And there is in this business more than nature/ Was ever conduct of" (V.i.242–44). A reference as late as 1908 tells of a maze located on a hillock called "The Fairies' Hill" in Asenby, Yorkshire; the locals recalled having trodden the maze "on a summer's evening and knelt at the centre 'to hear the fairies singing.'"[17] Turf mazes, like those in gardens, then, may have provided in game the kind of spatial dislocations Shakespeare provides in the liminal phase of the comedies.

If Elizabethans associated courtship and adolescence with disorientations that were both geographical and mental, they also linked them to dislocations in time. Adolescence itself is a temporal notion. The old shepherd in *The Winter's Tale* who wishes "there were no age between ten and three-and-twenty, or that youth would sleep out the rest" (III.iii.59–61) conceives of youth as a period in which the normal laws of behavior do not hold. The same is true of the period of courtship. Suspended between childhood and adulthood, the adolescent, particularly the adolescent lover, experiences time as the medium of his confusion. To be uncertain of one's identity is to be unable to place oneself in space or time. It is this sense of a time set apart from the norm – a time interrupted, suspended, or bizarrely unpredictable – that Shakespeare captures in the enchanted realms of the liminal phase.[18]

In *Shakespeare's Festive Comedy*, C. L. Barber shows how the "festive" plays evoke a special sense of time, that of holiday release. Barber's metaphor is most successful for those comedies in which a spirit of play predominates, such as *Love's Labor's Lost* and *As You Like It*. Like Frye's metaphor of the "green" or "golden" world, however, it exaggerates the positive side of the liminal experience. As we have already observed in Chapter 1, Barber's account of *A Midsummer Night's Dream* errs in this direction. One need not go as far as Jan Kott, who says of this play that "in no other tragedy, or comedy" of Shakespeare's, with the exception of *Troilus and Cressida*, is "eroticism expressed so brutally,"[19] but his view offers a useful corrective. As Ruth Nevo observes, the comedies "do not deny the dark side of saturnalia or disinhibition, the ruthless, violent, destructive other face of nature's energies; they occupy always a danger zone of potential radical harm to the individual."[20]

The notion of holiday time, moreover, although it carries with it connotations of re-creation so important in the comedies, does not suggest the extent of the change that takes place. Shakespeare's lovers do not merely return to the work-a-day world after their "holiday" experience; they assume new identities as married adults. While time is suspended, in other words, a great deal happens. As in the process of metamorphosis, which is one of Shakespeare's most common liminal symbols, what seems to be a period of stasis is actually a period of frantic, though invisible, activity. The cocoon is inert; but inside, the larva is becoming a butterfly. In the plays that emphasize the darker side of the comic experience, especially, we often feel that time is not merely suspended but magically accelerated. In these comedies, hypothetical "tragic" futures are played out and somehow exorcised. The process may remind us of the medical rite of the Cuna Indians, which cures the patient by displacing and purging her fears in fiction (p. 10).

In *The Comedy of Errors*, the marriage of Adriana and Antipholus is destroyed and renewed in a single day. Although their misunderstandings are caused by the mistaken identities of the farce plot, the plot itself provides not a random series of misadventures but a precisely graduated descent into chaos. The maze through which both characters wander follows the merciless logic of a troubled marriage. All the confusion of the play arises, literally, because Antipholus is late for dinner; had he been on time his twin would not have been summoned by mistake. Antipholus is late because he is an "errant" husband, and he "errs" because he has a jealous wife. When Antipholus finds himself locked out of his house, he understands the logic of the event: he decides to take revenge on his wife and her lover and to give his wife's chain to the courtesan. As Adriana wanders from one misadventure to the next, she imagines her husband degenerating in stages. The man who comes late for dinner is transformed, in order, into an adulterer, a seducer of his wife's sister, and a lunatic. When she hears Adriana's story at the end of the play, the Abbess finds it psychologically inevitable: "The consequence is then, thy jealous fits/ Hath scar'd thy husband from the use of wits" (V.i.85–86). In the enchanted time of Ephesus, marital journeys that may take years of ordinary time begin and end in a day.

In *A Midsummer Night's Dream* and *The Taming of the Shrew*, time is also magically accelerated while suspended. In the wood outside Athens a single night of dreaming carries the lovers from childhood into adulthood and marriage. What is a chaotic nightmare to the lovers is to the audience a predictable adolescent rite of passage, its steps as foreordained as those of a dance: Lysander betrays Hermia for Helena; Hermia and Helena fall out; Lysander and Demetrius come to blows. When Demetrius awakens from his dream, he remembers his former love for Hermia as something out of the remote past, "an idle gaud,/ Which in my childhood I did dote upon" (IV.i.167–68). In *The Taming of the Shrew*, Kate's "dream" at Petruchio's country house effects a transformation as complete and almost as rapid. Petruchio's methods, like those of modern brainwashing, are calculated to re-structure identity in the briefest possible time.

Even in the forest of Arden, where the characters "fleet the time carelessly, as they did in the golden world" (*AYL* I.i.118–19), Rosalind exercises a magical control over time, using it as a medium to test Orlando and explore her own identity. Their mock-courtship is a playful counterpart to the lovers' nightmare in *A Midsummer Night's Dream*. In this play-time with Ganymede-Rosalind, Orlando lives through a ritual of courtship – "Come, woo me, woo me; for now I am in holiday humor, and like enough to consent" (IV.i.68–69); then a ritual of marriage – "Come, sister, you shall be the priest, and marry us" (lines 124–25); and finally, its after-effects – "maids are May when they are maids, but the sky changes when they are wives" (lines 148–49). The hypothetical future Rosalind makes Orlando live through purges Rosalind of her anxieties and Orlando, presumably, of his fantasies.

This dislocation of time is not unique to the comedies, for in the tragedies as well the time is often "out of joint." But when time is disordered in the tragedies a tragic and irreversible act has made it so. No hypothetical future is unrolled before Hamlet, Macbeth, or Lear. Macbeth lives a nightmare because he has murdered sleep. In the comedies, in contrast, tragedies are mere dreams or mangled playlets. Comic betrayals occur, for the most part, outside of time, in dream, enchantment or play. The characters enact their potential for tragedy in actions that are re-creative, as dream or play may be in actual life. In this sense, the comic experience is like a rite of passage, a curing rite, or an exorcism.

The metaphors of enchantment that often characterize this mysterious comic phenomenon, in which time is simultaneously suspended and accelerated, link it to a familiar folktale motif, that of the supernatural lapse of time in fairyland. In journeys into this strange realm, the laws of mortal time are suspended; humans can spend centuries there which in earthly time amount to no more than a few days. Herla the king, for example, lives with the king of the dwarfs for more than two hundred years, yet upon his return to his earthly realm thinks of the adventure as taking three days.[21] In the romance version of Thomas Rymer, or Thomas of Ercledoun, the hero lives in an elf-castle for more than three years but returns believing three days have elapsed.[22] In the comedies, with their oblique and abbreviated methods of characterization, this mysterious suspended animation of time helps to convince an audience that in the brief two hours of a play identities have been redefined. The enchanted time of the liminal phase, to borrow the words of the Prologue to *Henry V*, turns the "accomplishment of many years/ Into an hour-glass" (lines 30–31).

If from one perspective time is magical in the dreams and games of the liminal experience, from another it is ominously scientific. When Rosalind suspects Orlando's loyalty, she sets him before the court of time: "Time is the old justice that examines all such offenders, and let Time try" (*AYL* IV.i.199–200). This is the familiar figure of Elizabethan proverbs – the Time who "tries all things"; who "tries friends as fire tries gold"; who "tries the truth." Neither hostile nor sympathetic, he is the objective observer, rewarding or punishing depending upon one's abilities to withstand his trials. Rosalind is not only aware of time as a subjective experience, affecting thieves on the way to the gallows differently from maids waiting to be married (III.ii.299-333); she perceives its objective reality. It is Time who takes the measure of a man. Time is Rosalind's touchstone.

The notion that the transitional phase is a time of testing, as we have seen already, is common to rites of initiation and courtship. For Shakespeare's lovers, however, the transitional period is not merely a time of testing but a testing of one's capacity to live in time. Some characters, like Olivia in *Twelfth Night*, reveal their folly in futile attempts to escape time; others, like Proteus in *The Two Gentlemen of Verona*, mimic by their inconstancy time's unceasing flux. The most pressing trials of the comedies, as we have seen already in the case of Proteus, are trials of constancy, for it is time as mutability that is the greatest threat to love. To be fickle in love is to align oneself with the destructive potential in time.

The concern with mutability links the comedies to the sonnets, in which change and decay work to destroy love both from within and without. As an external force, the time of the sonnets is responsible for all destructive change – decay, death, oblivion. It is a "devourer" (19), a "bloody tyrant" (16), a "reaper" (60), a "defacer" (64). The time of the sonnets, in short, is essentially tragic time, against which there are no defenses except, occasionally, poetry and love. Time's destructive power in the sonnets is even more insidious, however, when it works from the inside, undermining constancy. If love affords a way to defeat time, the battle is lost if love itself proves mutable. And the sonnets show repeatedly the inconstancy of love, the inability of lovers to prevent themselves from becoming "Time's fools" (116). Although the poet himself attempts to defy time, asserting his imperviousness to change – "No! Time, thou shalt not boast that I do change" (123) – the development of the sequence attests to the hollowness of his claim, for by the end he, like his friend and his dark lady, is guilty of betrayal. The threats of physical death with which the sonnet sequence begins are finally less disturbing than the psychological instability with which it ends. It is this instability that afflicts the "natural" lovers of the comedies, not the external threats of decay or death.

Those who fare best at living in time in the comedies are the disguised heroines – Julia, Portia, Viola, and Rosalind. Although subject to their own follies, as we have seen, these heroines remain constant in their affection, like the "ever-fixed marks" of sonnet 116, whose love does not "alter when it alteration finds." This capacity in the heroines – and it is shared by the women in *A Midsummer Night's Dream* and *Love's Labor's Lost* – derives from an acceptance of mutability as a fact of life, even in love. Their sensitivity to this fact is often revealed in their attitudes towards oaths. While their lovers swear as readily as they forswear, the women are prone to mock them or resist. When Hermia agrees to meet Lysander in the wood outside Athens, she swears "By all the vows that ever men have broke/ (In number more than ever women spoke)" (*MND* I.i.175–76). And the Princess in *Love's Labor's Lost* demands a full year's penance before she will listen to a "world-without-end bargain" (V.ii.789). Unlike the poet in the sonnets or the young men in the comedies, the heroines neither boast about their constancy nor betray it.

The heroines also have a greater capacity to live in time, to adapt themselves to its natural rhythms. In part this means acting seasonably and patiently. Although such virtues figure in nearly all the comic heroines, Viola in *Twelfth Night* displays them most poignantly, perhaps because her play is to a great extent a play about waiting. Like the feast of the Epiphany to which it alludes, the play creates an atmosphere of expectancy, of time moving towards a moment of sudden fulfillment and illumination. Against this backdrop, Viola's patience as she waits for her brother resonates with larger meanings. Her desire to serve Olivia, to withhold herself from the world until her "occasion" is "mellow" (I.ii.43), reveals her sensitivity to temporal rhythms and her ability to suspend action until she is in phase with them. Shielded by her brother's clothes, Viola greets the future hopefully, trusting in the benignity of time: "What else may hap, to time I will commit ... " (I.ii.60). Although dismayed by the complications brought about by her disguise, she retains her faith: "O time, thou must untangle this, not I,/ It is too hard a knot for me t'untie" (II.ii.40–41).

Viola meets bad fortune with a sustaining belief in time, but she meets good fortune with patient skepticism. When she has reason to believe her brother is alive, she resists hasty conclusions, knowing, unlike Malvolio, the tendency of the imagination to impose its fantasies upon reality: "Prove true, imagination, O, prove true,/ That I, dear brother, be now ta'en for you!" (III.iv.375–76). During the recognition scene at the end of the play, Viola draws out her discovery to a remarkable length, letting the others stand in amazement while she methodically confirms her brother's identity. Even when no doubt remains, she defers an embrace until the time is right:

> If nothing lets to make us happy both
> But this my masculine usurp'd attire,
> Do not embrace me till each circumstance
> Of place, time, fortune do cohere and jump
> That I am Viola ...   (V.i.249–53)

Viola has a sense of occasion in both meanings of the word; like a skillful dramatist, she knows the importance of timing. Her wedding will be held, in Orsino's wonderful phrase, when "golden time convents" (line 381) – a phrase that fuses ideas of wealth, maturity, occasion, and communion. This wedding, however, it is important to stress, will take place outside the world of the play; Shakespeare's golden times, like his golden worlds, are either long gone or deferred, even in the comedies.

Although the comic journeys never quite reach the "golden time" to which Orsino alludes, they head in that direction. While the time of the liminal phase is various and unpredictable, a state of suspended animation or ceaseless flux, the time that drives the comedies to their conclusions is a benign, creative force. The movement is from loss of identity to recovery, from confusion to clarification, from estrangement to familiarity, from adolescent infatuation to mature love. Shakespeare's tragedies end in death, his comedies in marriage; the former enacts the destruction of the individual, the other his perpetuation. Although both genres may lead to insight, tragic time is no less destructive for that – the destruction being all the more powerfully felt because it snuffs out a life in the process of renewal. In the comedies, insight precedes marriage. The overarching motto for comic time might be that of Proteus: "time is the nurse and breeder of all good" (*TGV* III.i.245).

As Susanne Langer has shown, the contrasting endings of tragedy and comedy – death and marriage – make of the former a closed form and the latter an open. According to Langer, however, the openness of the comic ending derives from the tacit assumption that life will be lived "happily ever after."[23] This may be true of sentimental or religious comedy, but it is not true of Shakespearean. Such endings are themselves closed, not open. Shakespeare's marriages are beginnings. Not that we assume unhappiness. In contrast to his histories, which are also open forms, the comedies rarely invite us to contemplate the future. While the histories end with images of an anxious and uncertain time to come, images that strike all the more forcibly because they hint at civil dissension and civil wars as inevitable as truth, the comedies point no farther than the wedding day. The comedies end on beginnings, but they remain discreetly silent about futures they invite us to meet with hope.

Both the comedies and tragedies hint occasionally at an ultimate transcendence of time, although such gestures are especially subtle and oblique in the comedies. *King Lear* concludes on an apocalyptic note, while *Othello* and *Macbeth* open out to eternities of damnation. Whenever a sense of infinity hovers over comic endings, as in the theophany of *As You Like It* or the apocalyptic overtones of *Twelfth Night*,[24] it serves more to remind us that we remain in time than that we shall eventually escape. Had Shakespeare wished to evoke more strongly a sense of timelessness at the end of the comedies, he had in marriage a perfect symbol, for central to the wedding ceremony is the idea that earthly marriages prefigure the marriage of Christ with his Church at the end of time. In his "Epithalamion," Spenser evokes this feeling of transcendence by concluding the poem with the prospect not only of begetting children but of begetting saints. In Shakespeare's comedies, however, marriage is not a shadow of an atemporal union but a substantial union in time. The epiphanies that sometimes end the comedies may suspend time in moments of wonder, but we are never allowed to forget that it is our natural element.

Implicit in Proteus's conception of time as the "nurse and breeder of all good" is a notion of maturing. As Leo Salingar observes, one of the distinctive marks of Shakespeare's comic endings is their "suggestion of harmonisation with the natural order."[25] All the comedies, especially those in which nature figures most directly, convey a sense of growth appropriate to rites of initiation. The progression from infatuation to married love is also a progression from adolescence to maturity. In *Love's Labor's Lost* the young aristocrats begin and end the play out of harmony with time. Having failed to ripen in love, the young men, as the Princess tells Navarre, must be exposed to winter unprepared:

> If frosts and fasts, hard lodging and thin weeds
> Nip not the gaudy blossoms of your love
> But that it bear this trial, and last love;
> Then at the expiration of the year,
> Come challenge me...　　　　　　　(V.ii.801–05)

Although the play ends not like a comedy, for "Jack hath not Gill" (V.ii.875), the metaphor assures us that the frosts of winter will yield to new, perhaps less "gaudy" blossoms in the spring. The songs at the end of the play re-enforce this faith in the goodness of the seasonal cycle and in man's capacity to live harmoniously, if not perfectly, within it.

In *A Midsummer Night's Dream*, the parallels between the youthful escapades of Theseus and Hippolyta and those of the young lovers make the process of maturing a dominant motif. The frenetic haste which prompts Lysander and Hermia to flee into the woods finds its middle-aged counterpart in the courtly romanticism with which Theseus chides the moon for delaying his wedding:

> She lingers my desires,
> Like to a step-dame, or a dowager,
> Long withering out a young man's revenue.   (I.i.4–6)

Here we have the shadow of a lover's impatience, not the thing itself. When Lysander awakens in the wood to fall madly in love with Helena, he sees his irrationality, ironically, as evidence of his new maturity: "Things growing are not ripe until their season,/ So I, being young, till now ripe not to reason . . ." (II.ii.117–18). As the lovers awaken from their dream, struggling to come to terms with their experience, the prospect of maturity returns. When Demetrius looks back upon his betrayal of Helena, it seems as remote as a childhood memory:

> My love to Hermia
> (Melted as the snow) seems to me now
> As the remembrance of an idle gaud,
> Which in my childhood I did dote upon . . .   (IV.i.165–68)

The tentativeness alone indicates that this time the feeling of maturity is at least not ridiculous. Although the play leaves us with no illusions about human (or elvish) constancy, it assures us that "ripening" into "reason" is a natural, if unconscious and ultimately inexplicable, process. Even the story that the lovers tell Hippolyta "grows to something of great constancy" (V.i.26).

Although maturing is a natural, even normal process in Shakespeare's comic world, it is not inevitable, as the playlet of "Pyramus and Thisby" in *A Midsummer Night's Dream* so ludicrously reminds us. Even in the comedies that develop most explicitly the sense that time is a "nurse and breeder of all good," there is an element of risk. In the chaos of liminal time, as we have seen, anything can happen. In *As You Like It*, Touchstone observes that "from hour to hour, we ripe and ripe,/ And then from hour to hour, we rot and rot" (II.vii.26–27), but only the rotting strikes us as inexorable.

Susanne Langer defines comedy as a realm of Fortune, tragedy as a realm of Destiny – the former imaging life as a circle, constantly renewing itself, the latter as a line, with a beginning, middle and end.[26] If by Fortune we mean good Fortune – the coincidences that bring sets of twins to the same city, that cause plots to be overheard by the watch, that bring bad brothers to blessed hermits – Langer's observation is just. In an Elizabethan context, however, the word *Fortune* is problematic, for its connotations are more often negative than positive. After he slays Tybalt, Romeo calls himself "Fortune's fool" (*Rom* III.i.136). Despite her proverbial instability, moreover, the goddess Fortuna had become by the end of the sixteenth century an emblem of regular and mechanical motion,[27] an implication perhaps inescapably present in the image of the wheel. In *Richard III*, when the old Queen Margaret gloats over the fact that the "course of justice" has "whirl'd about" (IV.iv.105), she is thinking of Fortune's wheel not as an arbitrary and capricious force but as a force of even-handed and mechanical retribution. Comic time too brings its revenges, but it does so, as Feste reminds Malvolio in *Twelfth Night*, with the motion of a "whirligig" (V.i.376), a spinning top. The difference between the potentially ominous and regular motion of the wheel and the playful and erratic motion of the top suggests the essential difference between tragic and comic Fortune.

Chance or *luck* may seem better words than *Fortune* to characterize the unpredictability of comic time, but even these words carry negative as well as positive connotations: luck may be good or bad. Even when good, moreover, luck implies an absence of design that is alien to the comedies. Although the comic world may seem to be ruled by chance to those within it, especially during the chaotic time of the liminal phase, the audience retains a secure faith in an underlying design. The reliance on conventional plot formulas and the heightened theatrical self-reflexiveness so characteristic of Shakespeare's comedies create in audiences, if not in the characters onstage, a belief in comic destiny. This destiny works differently from tragic destiny, however. Whereas the tragedies map out clearly the steps in the causal sequence that bring the hero to his destruction, the comedies throw audiences off balance, dizzying them with confusions, and even tricking them occasionally with appearances of gods or abbesses or ships out of nowhere. Despite this confusion, audiences of the comedies know that "Jack will have Gill," if only next year. Beatrice and Benedick are made for each other; Sebastian and Viola must be reunited; Egeon cannot be executed, especially in a play entitled *The Comedy of Errors*. While the comic characters become hopelessly muddled in the flux of liminal time, their audiences, slightly dizzy, await clarification and communion.

The ability to sense a design underlying the chaos of events and to shape one's response accordingly is a characteristic of the disguised heroines, as we have seen in the case of Viola. Although analogous, the audience's faith is not quite the same. While the heroines believe in time or providence, the audience believes in art, in its compact with the dramatist. In tragedy, both audience and hero fix their eyes on Fate or Destiny; in comedy, the heroine may fix her eyes on time, as Viola does, but the audience is searching for the dramatist. In the comedies, the playwright is his own *deus ex machina*.

The plays that most emphasize chance, such as *The Comedy of Errors*, *Twelfth Night*, and *Much Ado About Nothing*, act out the familiar proverb, "Truth is the daughter of time." As Samuel C. Chew has shown, emblems of Time leading his daughter, Truth, out of a cave into the sunlight were popular throughout the Renaissance. Elizabeth herself played the role of Truth in a tableau vivant during her coronation procession in 1559.[28] From this perspective, Time is not so much the Maturer as the Revealer, he who brings truth to light and confounds error. He achieves this end not through a gradual ripening but through a sudden illumination, as when Sebastian discovers Viola or Claudio another Hero. In *Much Ado About Nothing*, Shakespeare stretches our faith in this capacity of time as far as he ever does in the comedies, dragging out the bumbling of the watch until we begin to fear that Truth will perish in her cave; although Dogberry and his fellows eventually confound Don John's plot, they owe as much to Borachio's impatience as their own investigative efforts.

The revelation of truth at the end of the comedies implies a sense of progress, since recognition marks the creation of a new identity. As in rites of initiation, however, this forward motion in time conveys also the feeling of a return. The experience is defined in both temporal and spatial terms. Time seems to have been reversed: in *The Merchant of Venice*, three of Antonio's sunken ships sail into harbor; in *The Comedy of Errors*, the twins go happily off to their own baptismal feast; in *As You Like It*, the Duke regains his daughter and his dukedom. Although this feeling of time's reversability is present at the end of the late romances as well, it is muted there by reminders of inexorable decay: Prospero returns to Milan, but to make every third thought his grave, and Hermione comes to life again, but with grey hair. Spatially, the renewals of the comedies are accentuated by symbolic geography. The return to Athens in *A Midsummer Night's Dream*, to the court in *As You Like It*, or to Kate's home in *The Taming of the Shrew* all convey a sense of beginning again, not in a vicious but a benign and re-creative circle. In the symbolic geography of the tragedies, in contrast, there are no returns: Othello never leaves Cyprus, nor does Antony escape Egypt, although he attempts to die like a Roman there. Comic progress moves in a circle – of reversals, renewals, rebirths, and reunions. Shakespeare's comedies, then, move to the rhythm of rites of initiation and marriage. Theirs is a paradoxical motion, combining the implications of the circle and the line. The entry into an enchanted world, whether Ephesus or the forest of Arden, is both a physical and mental event, in which spatial and temporal disorder embody the confusion of adolescent love. Enchanted landscapes are ambiguous, labyrinthine places; even if one holds a thread, as do the disguised heroines, the experience is bound to be amazing. Enchanted times are also bewildering, whether magically suspended and accelerated or in unnerving flux. If "there's no clock in the forest," and no path but a maze, there is no self either. Yet the chaos of the liminal world is ultimately regenerative. To journey into it is to be renewed and re-oriented. "Journeys end," Feste's song assures us, "in lovers meeting,/ Every wise man's son doth know" (*TN* II.iii.43–44); the experience of wise men cannot be ignored, particularly in a play that celebrates the feast of the Epiphany. The comedies end not only with lovers meeting, moreover, but with weddings, ritual events in which time begins again and strangers are made at home.

7

Incorporations

"One feast, one house, one mutual happiness"
(*TGV* V.iv.173)

It is a truism that comedies end in marriage. This should not obscure Shakespeare's remarkable dependence on the convention, however, or his originality in exploiting it. With the exception of *Love's Labor's Lost*, in which the marriages are deferred for a year, all the romantic comedies end with wedding celebrations onstage or off. *Much Ado About Nothing* concludes with the couples on their way to church; *As You Like It* with a spectacle that is both wedding and masque; and *The Taming of the Shrew* and *A Midsummer Night's Dream* with wedding feasts. Even in those endings that focus upon recognitions rather than the festivities that will follow, the familiar rituals of marriage – exchanging of oaths, kissing, handfasting, dancing – play a prominent role. More than any other comic dramatist, ancient or modern, Shakespeare brings the wedding day onstage, making the festive occasion part of the theatrical experience.

The importance of marriage rites in the comedies reflects their status in Elizabethen society. Charles Phythian-Adams's observations upon marriage in late medieval Coventry hold true for Elizabethan England as well: "Marriage ... represented the most important single step in an individual's career. Not only did it mark the late transition to a socially superior age-group from menial dependency in a household that was not necessarily that of a person's origin, but it also signalised the creation of a new domestic unit that was familial, economic, and social in its implications. The pledging was thus both private and public."[1] With the abolition of many of the communal rituals of the church after the Reformation, and with the increasing hostility of religious reformers to seasonal festivals such as those of May Day or Twelfth Night, the traditional rites of passage of birth, marriage, and death probably took on for most Elizabethans an increasing emotional significance. And of these traditional rites marriage was the most complicated, elaborate, and extensive.

Although Puritan and Anglican reformers objected vigorously to the noise, drunkenness, and lewdness of some wedding celebrations, none urged their abolition. The Puritan William Gouge even insists that such festivities are not only lawful but essential:

> Though upon the forenamed consecrating of marriage it be in regard of the substance thereof fully consummate, yet for the greater solemnity of so honourable a thing, it is very requisite that further there be added a *civill celebration* of it: under which I comprise all those lawfull customes that are used for the setting forth of the outward solemnitie thereof, as meeting of friends, accompanying the Bridegroome and Bride both to and from the Church, putting on best apparell, feasting, with other tokens of rejoycing: for which we have expresse warrant out of Gods word.[2]

It goes without saying that this endorsement extends only to what Bullinger calls "convenient and honest mirth."[3] Nonetheless, the fact that even Puritans approved of *"civill celebration"* suggests the strength of feeling Shakespeare could draw upon by recreating not only the religious but secular rites of marriage.

Weddings are essentially rites of incorporation – the means by which a man and woman are united to each other and to their social group. In *The Rites of Passage* Arnold van Gennep divides them into two categories: the personal, which join husband and wife, and the collective, which bind the pair to society. As van Gennep recognizes, the two kinds overlap considerably; some rituals, like feasting, are both personal and collective at the same time. It is useful to separate them, however, for their relative weight in any given society tells something important about its values. Typical of personal rites are eating together; washing each other; exchanging gifts, such as bracelets, clothes, or rings; and the binding or touching of each other, as in kissing, embracing, or joining hands. The most potent personal rite, sexual consummation, usually takes place in private. Collective rites include the exchange of gifts and visits but usually center upon the two great public occasions of feasts and religious ceremonies. Most of the societies van Gennep draws upon emphasize collective rites; the social rather than the individual dimension of marriage predominates.[4]

In a broad sense, one can say the same of Elizabethan weddings, especially if one contrasts them to those of the eighteenth century or beyond. Lawrence Stone presents convincing evidence that Elizabethans generally stressed the social function of marriage, Augustans its private pleasures.[5] With their emphasis upon genealogy, kinship, and parental control, Elizabethans probably experienced less often and less intensely the intimate domestic life that Stone finds characteristic of the "companionate" marriage of the eighteenth century. Although Stone never considers the marriage rituals of either period, a comparison of representative wedding days might support his thesis. Certainly the striking contrast between Thomas Deloney's description of a bourgeois wedding in the late sixteenth century and François Misson's of one in the late seventeenth century suggests a profound change in attitude towards marriage as a social institution.

Although fictitious, Deloney's description of the wedding of his titular hero in *Jack of Newbury* conforms to Elizabethan practice. Since some of the customs he records will become important later, the passage is worth quoting at length:

So the marriage day beeing appointed, all things were prepared meet for the wedding, and royal cheere ordained; most of the Lordes, Knights, and Gentlemen therabout, were invited thereunto: the Bride being attired in a Gowne of sheepes russet, and a kertle of fine wosted, her head attired with a billiment of gold, and her haire as yellow as golde hanging downe behind her, which was curiously combd and pleated; according to the manner in those dayes, shee was led to Church betweene two sweet boyes, with Bride laces and Rosemary tied about their silken sleeves, the one of them was sonne to Sir *Thomas Parrie*, the other to Sir *Francis Hungerford*. Then was there a faire Bride-cup of silver and gilt caried before her, wherein was a goodly branch of Rosemary gilded very faire, hung about with silken Ribonds of all colours: next was there a noyse of Musicians that played all the way before her: after her came all the chiefest maydens of the Countrie, some bearing great Bride Cakes, and some Garlands of wheate finely gilded, and so shee past unto the Church.

It is needelesse for mee to make any mention heere of the Bridegroome: who being a man so well beloved, wanted no companie, and those of the best sort, beside divers Marchant Strangers of the Stilyard, that came from London to the Wedding. The marriage being solemnized, home they came in order as before, and to dinner they went, where was no want of good cheere, no lacke of melodie: Rhennish Wine at this wedding was as plentifull as Beere or Ale, for the Marchants had sent thither ten Tunnes of the best in the Stilyard.

This wedding endured ten dayes, to the great reliefe of the poore, that dwelt all about ... [6]

The elaborateness of the ceremony, the complexity of its symbolic details, and its length are all impressive to the modern reader; most striking, however, is its public nature. Most of the "Lordes,

Knights, and Gentlemen" in the neighborhood attend, even though it is a bourgeois wedding, and two sons of knights lead the bride. The merchants are well represented, not only by their presence but by their "ten Tunnes" of "Rhennish Wine." The friends of the bride and groom wear their favors and accompany them in the procession, which doubtless draws crowds of onlookers, attracted by the "noyse of Musicians." The feasting extends not only to the invited guests but to the "poore, that dwelt all about," who for ten days share in the celebrations of their betters. The crowded vitality of such occasions is captured in a remarkable contemporary painting, the "Fête at Bermondsey." The painting portrays the festive table, bride-cup and bride-cakes, musicians, and representatives of all social classes. Even the villagers in the background, going about their normal affairs, are linked visually to the feast; there are no boundaries separating the invited from the uninvited.[7]

François Misson visited England at the end of the seventeenth century and recorded the marriage customs of the Anglican bourgeoisie living in or near London; his slice of society therefore corresponds very closely to Deloney's. What he found, however, differs remarkably. He begins his account by noting that the publication of the banns may be dispensed with for a fee, and that many couples take advantage of the system: "To proclaim Bans is a Thing no Body now cares to have done; very few are willing to have their affairs declar'd to all the World in a publick Place, when for a Guinea they may do it *snug*, and without noise ... " "Persons of quality," he observes, "and many others who imitate them, have lately taken up the Custom of being marry'd very late at Night in their Chamber, and very often at some Country House." At such weddings the bride and groom feast for a few days, but without much noise, and only with close relations. Although it is still customary to distribute ribbons widely as favors, some of the gentry have taken to avoiding it, to save expense. Public weddings, while they still exist, are "extraordinary weddings. The ordinary ones ... are generally incognito." In the latter, the bride and groom, accompanied by two groomsmen and bridesmaids, get their license, are married, feast quietly at a tavern or friend's house, "and return Home at Night as quietly as Lambs."[8] In a letter to William Temple, Dorothy Osborne expresses an attitude that seems implicit in this radical change in fashion: "the truth is I could not indure to bee Mrs. Bride in a Publick wedding to be made ye happiest person on Earth."[9]

Although Stone views the greater individual liberty and domestic intimacy of eighteenth-century marriages as distinct social advances, to juxtapose accounts of the weddings in both periods is to become aware of the danger of simple judgments. If there was a gain in personal intimacy in eighteenth-century marriages, it seems to have been purchased at the expense of social ties. In Misson's description, marriage is no longer the center of a network of communal bonds, encompassing the lowest and highest orders of society, but a private affair, restricted to families and close friends. What Elizabethans gained in strong collective bonds, moreover, was not necessarily lost in personal relationships, for the ceremonies that bound husband and wife together in both periods were essentially the same. Husband and wife were at the center of the wedding rites, both secular and religious, and the tie that joined them was that of love, freely given. Unless we are prepared to dismiss the wedding oath and other such rites as "empty ritual," we must assume that even in Elizabethan society the personal rites of marriage carried moral and psychological weight.

Given the dominance of arranged marriages in the sixteenth and seventeenth centuries, the personal rituals of courtship and marriage may have served more to stimulate affection than reflect it. We have already observed this possibility in the courtship of Sir Simonds D'Ewes and Anne Clopton (p. 70). The effect of the ring ceremony upon Lady Mildmay suggests the psychological importance of a will to love: "My father-in-law gave me this posie in my wedding ring, *maneat inviolata fides*, which in the very instant of my marryage I received most religiously with a full resolution by the grace of God to performe the same unto the ende of my lyfe." The impersonality of Lady Mildmay's marriage arrangements, moreover, supports Stone's thesis; the father-in-law who gave the ring seems to have been more interested in the match than his son, who refused the marriage until "his father told him, yf he did not marry me, he should never bring any other woman into his house."[10] Dorothy Osborne, whose hostility towards public marriages reflected late seventeenth-century tastes, also opposed the familiar argument that marriage itself can create love: "I shall never bee perswaded that marriage has a Charme to raise love out of nothing, much lesse out of dislike."[11] That she denies the argument with a metaphor drawn from magic may tell us something about the psychological potential of the marriage rite in Elizabethan times. Whatever their effects, it is clear that Elizabethan weddings, in contrast to those Misson observed at the end of the seventeenth century, articulated an ideal of union that was at once personal and communal, in the widest possible sense.

The elaborate and varied details of Elizabethan weddings have been thoroughly described elsewhere, and their full cultural significance lies outside our scope.[12] It may be useful, however, to highlight their dramatic potential by surveying some of their most important features. As is clear from Deloney's description, the central events of a wedding, excluding the consummation, consisted of the procession to and from the church, the religious ceremony, and the feast. Another important ritual preceded the wedding, however, that of the betrothal, the chief ceremonies of which were repeated as part of the marriage service.

Although betrothal, or "handfasting," was essentially a personal rite, its significance was such that the more serious families attempted to make it as public as possible. *De praesenti* betrothals consisted of unconditional oaths to marry and were therefore legally binding, conferring conjugal rights, as we know from *Measure for Measure.* Hence these ceremonies were usually conducted by a priest, generally in the home but sometimes at church. The central rites were those that joined the couple: the exchange of vows to marry, the joining of hands, the kiss, and the conferral or exchange of rings. The families and witnesses participated by ratifying the formal arrangements for dowry and jointure and by sharing in a ceremonial toast. The potential dignity and emotional power of such occasions is conveyed by the priest's words in *Twelfth Night,* when he describes the betrothal of Olivia and Sebastian as

> A contract of eternal bond of love,
> Confirm'd by mutual joinder of your hands,
> Attested by the holy close of lips,
> Strength'ned by interchangement of your rings,
> And all the ceremony of this compact
> Seal'd in my function, by my testimony . . .   (V.i.156–61)

In this case, the solemnity of the language is ironic, for neither partner knows the other. Between the betrothal and the wedding, the personal rites of courtship continued and no doubt intensified: the man wearing his betrothed's favors – her handkerchief, perhaps, or ribbon – and drinking her health in public; the pair exchanging gifts, such as portraits, rings, handkerchiefs, gloves, bracelets, or posies (nosegays of flowers wound about with a line or two of verse).

The wedding day consisted of an elaborate series of personal and collective rites. When the Queen visited Kenilworth in 1575, the local villagers entertained her with a wedding procession and traditional wedding game, that of tilting at the quintain. Robert Laneham described the procession in a letter to a friend, and his account, though condescendingly mock-heroic, fleshes out that provided by Thomas Deloney in *Jack of Newbury*. Laneham's attention to symbolic detail, in particular, illustrates how avidly wedding rituals, like other pageants or visual displays, were "read" for their significance. The leader of this procession was the bridegroom. He was followed by his companions, ranged two by two, each of whom wore "blu buckeram bridelace upon a braunch of green broom (cauz rozemary iz skant thear) tyed on hiz leaft arme (for a that syde lyez the heart)." Blue is for constancy, rosemary for remembrance, and the lace would have been tied in a true-love-knot. The men were followed by morris dancers – "according too the auncient manner, six dauncerz, Mawdmarion, and the fool." Behind them came three women, carrying "thrée speciall spisecakes of a bushell of wheat." After them marched a young man (in Laneham's untranslatable phrase, a "loovely loober woorts") bearing the bride-cup, which Laneham describes with great zest. It was "foormed of a sweet sucket barrell, a faire turnd foot set too it, all seemly besylverd and parcell gilt, adourned with a bea[u]tiful braunch of broom, gayly begilded for rosemary: from which, too brode brydelaces of red and yelloo buckeram begilded, and galauntly streaming by such wind az thear waz (for hée carried it aloft)." The use of a "sucket," or sweetmeat, barrel unfortunately attracted swarms of flies, which the poor cupbearer swatted manfully en route. At the end of the procession came the bride, whom Laneham describes as a "stale stallion and a wel spred," and her dozen bridesmaids, equally appealing, ranged two by two behind her.[13] Laneham does not mention the traditional strewing of flowers, the bride's garland, or the musicians, whose function may have been fulfilled on this occasion by the morris dancers. The ceremony in the church is familiar to most readers and is set forth in detail in the *Book of Common Prayer*. The personal union of bride and bridegroom was effected by the joining of hands, the exchange of vows, and the placing of the ring on the fourth finger of the bride's left hand; the compact was sealed by the marriage sermon, which outlined the duties of husband and wife, re-enforcing the mutual understanding and acceptance achieved in courtship. The congregation served as witnesses and participated in prayers for the welfare of the couple. The priest's blessings and the required taking of communion united the couple not only to each other and the congregation but to God. Although not a sacrament, the ceremony centered upon a conception of marriage as, in the priest's words, "the mystical union, that is betwixt Christ and his Church."[14] In becoming mystically "one flesh," man and wife participated in the marriage of Christ with his Church at the end of time.

At the conclusion of the ceremony in the church, the priest bestowed upon the groom a kiss of benediction, which he passed on to the bride. At this point too the couple joined their companions in a ceremonial toast, the bride-cup being passed around, filled with wine and small pieces of bread or cake; these are the "sops" that Petruchio throws in the sexton's face when he marries Kate (*Shr* III.ii.174). Although a serious part of the ritual, the toast no doubt relaxed the participants, providing a transition between the solemnity of the service and the high spirits of the procession homeward.

Wedding feasts, as Deloney's description reveals, usually extended for days, and sometimes for weeks. Much of the merriment was casual and spontaneous, but the customary activities included games, sports, dancing, and, in noble households, masques and plays. On the wedding day the bride and groom were at the center of attention – the bride presiding over the feast and dancing with all the male guests, the groom sometimes serving. The bride-cake played an important role in fertility rites: the bride and groom kissed over it, and guests passed crumbs through their own wedding rings and sprinkled them over the couple. The bedding of the couple was itself a ceremonial affair, including a ritual undressing by their respective companions, a procession to the bedchamber, the drinking of a sack posset, and various games, such as sewing of the sheets, untying the bride's garter, and flinging her stocking. At this stage in the evening, if not before, occurred the bawdy singing that so offended the ears of religious reformers. On the morning after the consummation, the bride and bridegroom were often awakened by a gentler music. The absence of a honeymoon clearly made even the consummation something of a collective rite.

An Elizabethan wedding day thus dramatized a union that was at once personal and collective, sexual and spiritual, secular and religious. The exchange of vows, the joining of hands, the giving of the ring, the consummation − all made of husband and wife "one flesh." In their union, the entire community participated − in the procession to and from the church; in the religious ceremony; in the feasting, dancing, and games; and even in the preliminary rites of consummation. Both couple and community, moreover, participated in the religious mystery by means of which they became spiritually one with God, a union prefiguring the final and permanent marriage of Christ and his Church. Some weddings, certainly, were no more than "empty" rituals, pageants for the consolidation of money and power; others, from the evidence of contemporary moralists, were little more than licensed riots. But the ideal was a rite that was socially and personally meaningful, solemn and joyful. It is given permanent expression in Spenser's celebration of his own marriage, his "Epithalamion."

In comparing these rites of incorporation to the endings of Shakespeare's comedies, however, it is important to remember that the significance of a wedding lies in the full event, not merely in the abstract ideal it embodies. Since ideals are never actualized, weddings, like all ritual events, are inescapably ironic. In varying degrees, the experience is one of emotional involvement, often profound, and of detachment, occasionally unsettling. The sneeze that interrupts the ring ceremony, the notorious incompatibility of the pair, the discomfort of the two families are all part of the event's meaning and feeling. Boisterous vulgarity, melancholy withdrawal, and hostility were presumably as common to Elizabethan weddings as to Shakespeare's comic endings. If such discords were too clamorous, neither weddings nor comedies could survive, but without them weddings would be impossible and comedies escapist fantasies. The ritual patterns that Shakespeare re-creates have the texture of ritual events, not idealized myths. Because they are traditional, they provide Shakespeare with a relatively fixed set of social meanings and emotions; because no ritual event is the same, they provide a wide range of ironies and emotional tones. Only close studies of single plays can suggest their remarkable individuality.[15]

The various modes of incorporation that end the comedies, as we shall see, depend heavily upon the ceremonies of the wedding day. Before Shakespeare's comic heroes and heroines are united, however, a more internalized experience of incorporation often occurs – a flash of recognition that marks the integration of the self. Understanding of oneself and one's partner, as we have seen, is the explicit end of rites of courtship and is re-enforced in the marriage sermon; its counterpart in traditional comic form is the moment of recognition. When such moments occur, they are powerful conductors of comic joy; their absence is the most telling of comic ironies.

In classical comedy recognitions make marriage possible not because they alter a character's sense of self but his social status. When there is confusion over a person's identity in New Comedy, as Leo Salingar observes, the source is "not primarily his psychological identity, his inner self, but his birth, his original name and status."[16] Mistresses become wives, as in Terence's *Self-Tormentor*, when it is discovered that they are not slaves but the eligible daughters of family friends. In Shakespeare's comedies, however, marriage never depends upon such reversals; his interest is in the psychology, not the sociology of love. Even in *The Comedy of Errors* and *Twelfth Night*, plays which end in classical recognitions, the revelations are important primarily for their psychological effect. Viola withholds her identity until her brother appears, not because her social status is in question but because she will not know herself until she knows his fate; when she identifies Sebastian, she identifies herself, speaking her name for the first time in the play. The twins of *The Comedy of Errors* experience a similar burst of illumination.

Most of the comic recognitions, unlike those in *The Comedy of Errors* and *Twelfth Night*, which anticipate the late romances, stress romantic love rather than family reunion. Recognitions precede marriage. Implicit in this pattern, as Shakespeare develops it, is a conception of knowledge as itself a mode of incorporation, a union of the self with the self and another. In marriage one achieves both spiritual and carnal knowledge. The most condensed example of the paradox that underlies this pun on "knowing" occurs not in the comedies but in the witty and grotesque travesty of union in "Venus and Adonis." As Venus presses on remorselessly in her efforts to seduce her reluctant partner, he pleads,

> If any love you owe me
> Measure my strangeness with my unripe years;
> Before I know myself, seek not to know me ...   (lines 523–25)

Venus will not be denied, however, or delayed; she folds him in so tight an embrace that "Incorporate then they seem, face grows to face" (line 540). Adonis is "known" before he "knows" himself, and the symbol of that sexual and spiritual confusion is a hermaphroditic union. In the comedies, as we have seen, such confusion is part of the liminal experience. The comic plots, one might say, set right the disastrous union of Venus and Adonis by moving towards self-knowledge and, in marriage, an incorporation that is both physical and spiritual.

The emblem of recognition in Shakespeare's comedies is thus not the bracelet or ring that in classical comedy identifies the social status of the wearer but an unmasking, as at the end of *Much Ado About Nothing* or *Love's Labor's Lost*. In the plays with disguised heroines, this usually takes the form of a change in costume, the resumption of female attire marking the heroine's "discovery" in both senses of the word. For the heroines, whose education is conscious and cumulative, the unmasking symbolizes less a sudden revelation than a fulfillment – a new acceptance of themselves and their roles. For their future husbands, however, the Orlandos and Orsinos, disclosure is illumination; in an instant, they know their wives and their own folly.

The degree of insight Shakespeare permits his heroes, or at least permits them to articulate, varies considerably, providing actors and directors with a wide range of comic tonalities. The two extremes might be represented by the two guiltiest fools in the comedies, Proteus in *The Two Gentlemen of Verona* and Claudio in *Much Ado About Nothing*. When Julia unmasks, Proteus confesses his folly and moralizes his story: "O heaven, were man/ But constant, he were perfect" (V.iv.110–11). When Hero unmasks, Claudio says, "Another Hero!" (V.iv.62). Is this rapt adoration, bewilderment, or guilty surprise? The compositor of the 1623 Folio may have been the first to exploit Shakespeare's deliberate open-endedness, for he changed the Quarto's punctuation to a question mark.

Although it is also difficult to penetrate Orsino's mind at the end of *Twelfth Night*, in the course of the long recognition scene he seems to progress from astonishment to insight. The first stage is amazement: "One face, one voice, one habit, and two persons,/ A natural perspective, that is and is not!" (V.i.216–17). Then, joyful anticipation: "I shall have share in this most happy wrack" (line 266). Then, the adoption of a new role: "Here is my hand – you shall from this time be/ Your master's mistress" (lines 325–26). And finally, as the full meaning of his folly dawns, a subtle readjustment:

> Cesario, come –
> For so you shall be while you are a man;
> But when in other habits you are seen,
> Orsino's mistress, and his fancy's queen.   (lines 385–88)

The earlier ambiguity in "master's mistress" – who is in authority? – is accentuated in the phrase "fancy's queen." Orsino ends the play, as he began it, thinking about the imagination. Has the "fancy" that was "so full of shapes" and "high fantastical" (I.i.14–15) found a ruler? Or is Orsino's "fancy" still king, and Cesario (the king), its queen? Such ambiguities are responsible for much of the emotional density of Shakespeare's comic endings. To iron them out, in criticism or onstage, is to diminish their comic truth.

What is recognized at these moments of illumination is thus difficult to define, at least without reducing insights to platitudes and the plays to moral tracts. But the recognitions resolve dramatic plots, and plots are in some sense psychological configurations. C. L. Barber suggests that the "festive" comedies end in a special kind of "clarification": a "heightened awareness of the relation between man and 'nature' – the nature celebrated on holiday."[17] Although in many ways persuasive, Barber's view shies away from the obvious fact that all of the romantic comedies, even those that are most "festive," center on the experience of love. The "clarifications" that occur primarily define that experience. Although the nature of love's folly varies from character to character, its most common form, as in the sonnets, is mutabilit the inconstancy that Proteus laments when he says, "O heave were man/ But constant, he were perfect" (*TGV* V.iv.110–11). Most of the comic heroes, if they discover anything, discover their foolish capacity to "err" in love and, to their mingled shame and joy, the capacity of their future spouses to remain true.

The insights of the heroines include not only knowledge of error but faith in truth. To call such insights "clarifications" is to some extent misleading, for the word suggests an easy rationality that is alien to the experience, which is mysterious and paradoxical. Perhaps the phrase that best captures this sense of mystery is Helena's, in *A Midsummer Night's Dream*. As she awakens with the other lovers after their strange and haunting vision, Helena looks at Demetrius and finds him "like a jewel,/ Mine own and not mine own" (IV.i.191–92). This experience of the "parted eye," as Hermia calls it, "when everything seems double" (lines 187–88), occurs at the moment of awakening, when illusion blends with reality.[18] The mysterious ease with which the boundaries between the two realms dissolve, the rapidity with which "mine own" can become "not mine own," is central to the experience of this play and others. Characteristically, Shakespeare tightens the insight into paradox: it is not that Demetrius was once Helena's, then betrayed her, and now is hers again – though this is what the plot enacts – but that Demetrius is simultaneously hers and not hers; everything not only seems but is double. Loving, it seems, is accepting this duplicity.

The Comedy of Errors concludes with a similar paradox, expressed in Adriana's discovery of her husband's twin: "I see two husbands, or mine eyes deceive me" (V.i.332). She errs, of course, for she sees one husband and a brother-in-law. The Duke's question, however, which follows immediately upon her exclamation, hints at a paradox that may make one husband two:

> One of these men is genius to the other:
> And so of these, which is the natural man,
> And which the spirit? Who deciphers them?   (lines 333–35)

In the nightmarish convolutions of the plot, Adriana has indeed had two husbands – one who betrayed her and went mad in the process, and another who remained true. The former, we might say, is the natural man; the latter, the spiritual. In recovering Antipholus, Adriana not only discovers and accepts her own error, but indirectly, the duality of her husband. The duplicity she earlier feared, and that prompted her possessiveness, proves true in a way she could not have imagined. The play's central symbol of this union of the natural and spiritual is the Phoenix, the name of the home to which the couple returns to celebrate a "gossip's feast" (V.i.406) and, presumably, to renew their marriage.

This paradox of the "parted eye" is played out with astonishing complexity in the symmetrical plot of *Much Ado About Nothing*. The reversals of Claudio and Benedick, upon which the play is structured, end in a love that, for Benedick, at least, combines two certainties – betrayal and truth. Claudio begins the play as the naive, conventional romantic – "Can the world buy such a jewel?" (I.i.181); Benedick, as the worldly skeptic – "Yea, and a case to put it into" (line 182). Claudio's volte-face occurs with Hero's "betrayal," a shock that transforms him into a cynic:

> For thee I'll lock up all the gates of love,
> And on my eyelids shall conjecture hang,
> To turn all beauty into thoughts of harm,
> And never shall it more be gracious.   (IV.i.105–08).

Benedick, meanwhile, having been duped in the opposite direction, struggles to become the romantic, a reversal he completes when he accepts Beatrice's demand to "Kill Claudio" (line 289). To prove his love, Benedick wipes conjecture from his eyes and commits himself to Beatrice's "soul" rather than his own suspicions that Claudio has been wronged by Don John:

> *Benedick.* Think you in your soul the Count Claudio
>   hath wrong'd Hero?
> *Beatrice.* Yea, as sure as I have a thought or a soul.
> *Benedick.* Enough, I am engag'd, I will challenge him.   (lines 328–32)

Benedick's capitulation is simultaneously the play's most romantic and comic event, for his expression of faith in Beatrice, which redeems him from Claudio's fault, is absurdly misplaced; his earlier skepticism is more appropriate to the occasion. When Claudio and Benedick meet again in Act V, scene i, they have exchanged roles: Claudio is the cynic and wit, refusing to take anything Benedick says seriously; Benedick is the sentimentalist, playing in deadly earnest the role of challenger.

To compound the confusion, Benedick eventually discovers that his faith in Beatrice's "soul" is itself based upon an illusion –

the fiction invented by his friends and played out for his benefit in the garden. If Benedick's faith is founded upon illusion, however, so is Claudio's skepticism, for he too is the victim of a deception. The deceptions, moreover, are in some sense truthful lies; like Hamlet's play to catch the conscience of the king, they enact scenarios that reveal their audiences to others and themselves. By the end of the play, these paradoxical interactions of truth and fiction, faith and skepticism, have created for both the major characters and the audience a kind of intellectual vertigo. At the end of *The Two Gentlemen of Verona*, Proteus can deliver a simple homily on constancy; at the end of *Much Ado About Nothing*, Benedick can only say, "man is a giddy thing, and this is my conclusion" (V.iv.108–09). In Benedick's case it is hard to tell insight from bewilderment.

Implicit in the working out of these paradoxes, as the fictions of *Much Ado* suggest, is an analogy between love and poetry, both of which depend upon an ordering of the fancy, or imagination. Immature lovers, as we have seen, like inferior poets, are swallowed up by their fictions, losing themselves in endless fantasies. The mark of a mature lover, and true poet, it seems, is an ability to believe and disbelieve simultaneously, to hold the opposed worlds of truth and fiction in a precarious balance. It is partly for this reason that the comedies are so self-reflexive, the terms of love becoming so easily terms of art. The most concise statement of this complex relationship occurs in *A Midsummer Night's Dream*, when Hippolyta muses over the credibility of the lovers' narrative:

> But all the story of the night told over,
> And all their minds transfigur'd so together,
> More witnesseth than fancy's images,
> And grows to something of great constancy;
> But howsoever, strange and admirable.   (V.i.23–27)

Here the language of love and fiction coalesce, the truth of each becoming the same truth and subject to the same test. Both the lovers and their stories are harmoniously united, bound by a power greater than mere fancy, and both the "story" and "their minds" grow to "something of great constancy." Through their dream, and its telling, the lovers achieve a unity that transcends fancy and aspires to the condition of great art – constancy. The arts of love and poetry are in this sense ultimately one. The appropriate response to such a union – and Hippolyta's is more appropriate than Theseus's – is neither belief nor disbelief but wonder, for it is "strange and admirable." In George Puttenham's delightfully expressive epithet, paradox is "the wonderer."[19] And wonder, as Bacon observes, is "the *seed* of knowledge."[20] The insights that occur at the ends of the comedies may ultimately clarify, but their immediate effect is less simply rational.

Although the comic recognitions are modes of incorporation, to call them rites would be misleading; many are internalized and even inarticulate. More ritualistic, and more potent dramatically, are the stylized gestures of union that figure so prominently in the final scenes. These ceremonies often achieve a cumulative impact. In many of the plays, they set right earlier travesties of union that symbolize the disorder of the liminal phase – the marriage of Petruchio and Kate, for example, or Bottom's amour with Titania, or Rosalind's mock-marriage with Orlando. In the rituals that conclude the plays, we often discover the proper forms of ceremonies that were earlier inverted, parodied, or interrupted. The potential effects of these dramatic patterns may be illustrated by three of the most important personal rites of incorporation – the giving of chains, rings, and kisses.

One of Shakespeare's additions to Lodge's *Rosalynde*, his source for *As You Like It*, is the chain that Rosalind gives to Orlando at their first meeting, after he has defeated Charles the wrestler and disclosed his identity. As Rosalind places the chain around Orlando's neck, her gesture recalls the earlier grasp of the wrestler, and her words re-enforce the image: "Sir, you have wrastled well, and overthrown/ More than your enemies" (I.ii.254–55). Both lovers have been "overthrown" by love, and Orlando's chain, which he wears from that point on, is a constant reminder of a bond more powerful than the arms of a wrestler.

The circle that joins Orlando and Rosalind widens at the end of the play to include all the couples united by Hymen: "Here's eight that must take hands/ To join in Hymen's bands" (V.iv.128–29). The witness of this "handfasting," Hymen assures us, is heaven:

> Then is there mirth in heaven
> When earthly things made even
> Atone together.   (lines 108–10)

The personal rite has become collective, the romantic gesture a social and religious bond. The durability of the bond is called in question by the presence of Audrey and Touchstone, but only Jaques stands outside the circle, and even he blesses each couple in turn, mimicking Hymen's rite of union with his own, by no means hostile, rite of separation.

As a ritual of bonding, the giving of a chain plays an even more important role in *The Comedy of Errors*. Although we are not told why Antipholus of Ephesus has decided to commission a chain for his wife, the combination of her savage possessiveness and his irresponsibility makes it likely that the gift is an attempt to bring harmony into a dissonant marriage. For this marital relationship, a chain is an ironically apt symbol. Throughout the play, the fate of the chain mirrors the fate of the marriage. Having been locked out from dinner, Antipholus determines to give the chain to the courtesan "to spite my wife" (III.i.118); for his wife and her "confederates" (IV.i.17), he replaces the chain with a rope. When he refuses to pay the goldsmith for a chain he has not received (it has been given to the wrong twin), Antipholus is arrested on a "bond," and then subjected to the ministrations of the aptly named Dr Pinch, which consist of being bound with Dromio and thrust into a dark cellar. As a direct consequence of commissioning a chain for his wife (the plot has the logic of nightmare), Antipholus finds himself in the dark, "gnawing with my teeth my bonds in sunder" (V.i.250). When the play's many confusions are finally resolved, the chain, now the property of Antipholus of Syracuse, can be returned to Adriana and join her to the proper twin. As a symbol of a renewed marriage, it will presumably pinch neither party. Shakespeare, however, with customary tact, avoids the sentimental gesture that would complete the pattern: there is no stage direction indicating that Antipholus should place the chain around his wife's neck. If it occurs – and there is no reason we shouldn't imagine it – the gesture takes place discreetly off-stage.

As this sketch suggests, the chain in *The Comedy of Errors* is merely the most visible symbol of bonding, a motif that recurs throughout the play, appearing in the repeated references to the various contracts at issue – marriage bonds, dinner engagements, promissory notes – and in the misfortunes of the twin servants, who are bound to their masters and therefore bound to suffer. In the final scene, Antipholus of Syracuse stands on stage with his father, Egeon, for the first time in the play: the one wears

Adriana's chain, the other is tied and on his way to execution. Egeon's plight reminds Dromio of his and his master's recent escape from Dr Pinch:

> Ourselves we do remember, sir, by you;
> For lately we were bound as you are now.
> You are not Pinch's patient, are you, sir?   (V.i.293–95)

Like his married son, Egeon discovers that his marriage has been renewed and his bonds redefined. "Whoever bound him," says his newly restored wife, "I will loose his bonds,/ And gain a husband by his liberty" (V.i.340–41).

The paradox that, rightly viewed, even marriage bonds confer freedom is enacted wittily by the Dromio twins as they leave the stage and bring the play to its close. Since the bonds of law and custom dictate that the elder take precedence, each defers politely to the other, but this results in a stand-off. Instead of drawing lots to determine their status, they resolve the problem with a gesture:

> We came into the world like brother and brother;
> And now let's go hand in hand, not one before another.
>
> (V.i.425–26)

This "handfasting" of the twins confirms a new kind of bond, based on the equality of love. The relationship between the competing bonds of law and love is explored in many of the comedies, most searchingly, perhaps, in *The Merchant of Venice*.

Chains did not figure in Elizabethan wedding ceremonies, but they are particularly effective comic symbols because they can be used to convey both the romantic and anti-romantic possibilities in bonding. As a symbol of marital union in *The Comedy of Errors*, the chain carries some of the associations of less theatrical emblems, such as the yoke or clog. Marriage, Bullinger observes in *The Christen State of Matrimonye*, is called in Latin a "conjugium/ a joyning or yoking together/ like as when two oxen are coupled under one yoke, they beare or draw together like burthen and waight."[21] Cesare Ripa's emblem for matrimony, reproduced in the *Riverside Shakespeare* (p. 317), is a female figure wearing not only a yoke but a clog. In *Much Ado About Nothing*, Don Pedro predicts Benedick's fate with the phrase, "'In time the savage bull doth bear the yoke'" (I.i.261). The only character in Shakespeare callous enough to apply one of these emblems to his spouse is Bertram in *All's Well That Ends Well*,

who announces the arrival of Helena with, "here comes my clog"
(II.v.53).

The most potent and romantic symbol of marriage for Elizabethans was the ring. At betrothal ceremonies, as we have seen,
the couple exchanged rings, or the woman received one from the
man, which she customarily wore on her right hand until the
wedding, when it was transferred to the fourth finger of the left
hand. Contemporary commentators on marriage stress
repeatedly the symbolic importance of the wedding ring. In *An
Heptameron of Civill Discourses*, George Whetstone describes
the "close joyning of the ringe" as a "figure of true unitie of the
married: betweene whom, there should be no division in desire,
no difference in behaviour."[22] In his *Laws of Ecclesiastical Polity*,
Richard Hooker defends the ring ceremony against Puritan objections, calling the ring an appropriate symbol of "faith and
fidelitie."[23] The most complete account of its symbolic value
occurs in Henry Swinburne's *A Treatise of Espousals*. Swinburne
notes that the ring is "a Sign of all others, most usual in Spousals
and Matrimonial contracts." The shape of a ring, he explains,
signifies that the couple's "mutual love and hearty affection
should roundly flow from one to the other, as in a Circle, and that
continually, and for ever." The ring is worn on the fourth finger of
the left hand, according to Swinburne, who adopts the traditional
view, because the "*Vena amoris*" in that finger goes directly to the
heart; to encircle it with a ring, therefore, signifies "that the love
should not be vain or fained, but as they did give their Hands to
each other, so likewise they should give their Hearts also, where-
unto that Vein is extended." Swinburne condemns his contemporaries for their new fashion of wearing rings merely for display
or as love-tokens; when "every skipping Jack, and every flirting
Jill" wear rings, he complains, they trivialize the symbol.[24]

Even more impressive testimony of the importance of the
wedding ring comes from the contemporary form of the object
itself. To be effectual, a ring needed to be no more than a plain
circle, and not even of gold. Yet Elizabethans delighted in its
possibilities for infinite elaboration. Rings could be made not only
of gold, a symbol of purity, but with verses inscribed in them; such
"poesy," or "posy," rings extended the visual symbol of union
into the verbal domain. More elaborate still were "gimmal" rings,
which could be interlocked as one or separated into as many as

eight. At betrothal ceremonies, such rings were often divided among the participants and witnesses, to be rejoined upon the bride's finger at the wedding, thus extending the bond between bride and bridegroom to their closest friends.[25] This tendency to expand the personal into a collective rite is characteristic of nearly all of Shakespeare's comedies. Gimmal rings could also have posies inscribed in them, even a different line of verse for each one; sometimes too they were made in symbolic shapes, such as a pair of hands clasping a heart. It was theoretically possible, then, to bind bride, bridegroom, and friends with a ring symbolizing perfect union in its metal (gold), its shape (circle), its structure (clasped hands), its inscription ("love me, and leave me not"), and its position on the hand. It is not surprising that Spenser's "Epithalamion" enacts an endless circle or that Shakespeare exploits rings so consistently in the comedies.

Rings circulate throughout the plays, their various misplacings and replacings charting the course through liminal confusion to marital union. When Antipholus gives his wife's chain to the courtesan in *The Comedy of Errors*, he takes a ring in exchange, returning it apologetically after he and his wife are reunited. In *The Two Gentlemen of Verona*, Proteus sends the disguised Julia to give away her own betrothal ring to his new love, Silvia. In *Twelfth Night*, Olivia gives away two rings – one to Viola-Cesario, the other to Sebastian, a more fitting recipient. Rings also prove difficult to handle in *The Merchant of Venice*. Although passed around with considerable frequency in the comedies, all of the rings eventually find their way to their rightful owners. Shakespeare achieves his subtlest effects not merely by exploiting the conventional symbolism of rings but by drawing upon the marriage ceremony itself. As the words of the ritual make clear, the giving of the ring effects not only a spiritual but a sexual and economic union: "With this ring I thee wed: with my body I thee worship: and with all my worldly goods I thee endow."[26] To my knowledge, no contemporary commentator discussed the sexual implications of placing a finger through a ring while saying "with my body I thee worship," but surely the custom of passing crumbs of bride-cake through rings to insure fertility made comment unnecessary. The phrase excited considerable controversy during the period, but only for doctrinal reasons; the problem was the word "worship," which Puritans rejected as idolatrous and Anglicans, like Richard Hooker, tried to redefine as "honour."[27] The giving of a ring in the comedies often takes its full meaning from the words and actions of the wedding rite; it is potentially a giving of the whole self – spiritual, sexual, and economic.

In *The Comedy of Errors* Antipholus of Ephesus receives a ring from the courtesan, in exchange for his wife's chain. The ring is an appropriate symbol of the sexual and economic ambiguities in Antipholus's extra-marital relationship. The exchange of chain for ring is a commercial transaction, as is sex for a courtesan. The distracted woman spends much of the play trying to recover her ring, expressing her dismay in unconscious innuendo, as when she complains that "a ring he hath of mine worth forty ducats" (IV.iii.83), or tells Adriana that her husband "all in rage to-day/ Came to my house, and took away my ring" (IV.iv.137–38). When Antipholus returns the ring to the courtesan in the final scene, he does so under the watchful eyes of his wife.

The notion that one gives all in giving a ring underlies the problematic ending of *The Two Gentlemen of Verona*. The climax of the play contrasts two gestures of love for Proteus, that of Valentine and that of Julia. Valentine seems to give Proteus all, but Julia gives the ring. Having discovered that Proteus loves Silvia (even to the point of attempted rape), Valentine yields his claim to her in an absurdly exalted gesture of pure friendship: "And that my love may appear plain and free,/ All that was mine in Silvia I give thee" (V.iv.82–83). At this, Julia swoons. When she recovers, she makes a curious apology: "O good sir, my master charg'd me to deliver a ring to Madam Silvia, which (out of my neglect) was never done" (lines 88–90). Her "neglect" refers to her wooing of Silvia, which was done "so coldly" (IV.iv.106) that Silvia refused to accept Proteus's ring. While Valentine has apparently sacrificed all for Proteus, Julia has served both him and herself. It is her gesture of selflessness, so human in its hesitation, that the play celebrates, not Valentine's sterile heroism. It is Julia who returns Proteus to himself and her ring to his hand.

The threefold symbolism of the wedding ring figures most prominently, and most paradoxically, in *The Merchant of Venice*. When Bassanio passes the test of the caskets, Portia responds with a ceremonious gesture that recalls the spiritual, sexual, and economic bonds of the marriage oath:

> But now I was the lord
> Of this fair mansion, master of my servants,
> Queen o'er myself; and even now, but now,
> This house, these servants, and this same myself
> Are yours – my lord's – I give them with this ring ...
>
> (III.ii.167–71)

Bassanio, however, breaks his oath, giving his ring to the "lawyer" who has saved Antonio. Upon his return to Belmont, he discovers that his spiritual error has had sexual consequences. As Portia reminds him, the wearer of a wedding ring has full conjugal rights: "by this ring, the doctor lay with me" (V.i.259). Gratiano's punning couplet, which concludes the play, is characteristically simple-minded but not inappropriate. As the couples retire to consummate their marriages, the sexual significance of the rings predominates: "Well, while I live I'll fear no other thing/ So sore, as keeping safe Nerissa's ring" (lines 306–07). The ring of *All's Well That Ends Well* also has sexual potency, for Helena gets back her husband only after she produces both his ring and his child.

Like the ring, the kiss symbolizes both sexual and spiritual union. The neoplatonic notion of the kiss as an exchange of souls was widespread in the period, and Shakespeare himself draws upon it explicitly in the death scenes of *Romeo and Juliet* and *Othello*. In the earliest days of the Church, the wedding kiss seems to have been interpreted as a mingling of souls, and certainly the Elizabethan ceremony gives that impression, for the kiss was passed from priest to bridegroom to bride.[28] Petruchio is thus rather worse than indecorous when he kisses Kate's lips with "such a clamorous smack/ That at the parting all the church did echo" (III.ii.178–79). Although Shakespeare shies away from the metaphysics of kissing in the comedies, he uses it consistently to mark the ceremonious pledging of love – as when Proteus and Julia are betrothed in *The Two Gentlemen of Verona*, or Viola and Sebastian in *Twelfth Night*, or when Bassanio is instructed by the note in the leaden casket to claim Portia with "a loving kiss" (III.ii.138).

The symbolic potential of a kiss is amply illustrated by a textual crux in *Much Ado About Nothing*. At the very end of the play,

Beatrice and Benedick mark their final capitulations to love by exchanging a kiss. The line which indicates this action – "Peace, I will stop your mouth" (V.iv.97) – is assigned by most editors to Benedick, although both the Quarto and Folio texts assign it to Leonato. The emendation thus relies upon a critical judgment, that it makes more sense for Benedick to initiate his own kiss than for Leonato to bring the two lovers together. While this view is certainly plausible, the logic of the scene, not to mention textual authority, makes a strong case for Leonato. At this point there is hardly any need for Benedick to stop Beatrice's mouth, for she has already finished speaking; their dialogue has been rigorously symmetrical, almost stichomythic, and she has just balanced his equivocal offer of love with her own. If anyone needs silencing at this moment, it is probably Benedick, who is preparing the next attack in a skirmish that threatens to become another war. In an earlier scene, moreover, when a kiss is also proposed as a means of bringing lovers together, Hero and Claudio, it is initiated not by one of the lovers but by Beatrice, an observer: "Speak, cousin, or (if you cannot) stop his mouth with a kiss, and let not him speak neither" (II.i.310–11). A move from Leonato would complete this pattern.

More importantly, to have Leonato step in and bring Beatrice and Benedick together is the most fitting end to a courtship that began with a similar gesture in the garden. The bond between these two lovers is not merely personal, despite their strident individualism, but social; without the intercession of their friends, both lovers might have continued their flirtatious warfare to eternity. At this last moment in the play, it seems dramatically apt to insinuate that they might still do so. The gesture of Leonato, if it is his gesture, heightens our sense that love is paradoxically the most personal and social of emotions. Benedick himself makes this point, with unconscious irony, when he asserts that he will oppose himself to the whole of society while fulfilling its designs upon him: "In brief, since I do purpose to marry, I will think nothing to any purpose that the world can say against it, and therefore never flout at me for what I have said against it; for man is a giddy thing, and this is my conclusion" (V.iv.104–09). Whichever version one prefers, to stage this simple gesture of a kiss is to determine to a great extent the thrust of the entire play.

The title of the musical version suggests the importance of

kissing in *The Taming of the Shrew*. Petruchio says "Kiss me, Kate," three times in the play, each one marking a stage in the development of their love. The first occurs in their parody of a betrothal. Having described how Kate has hung about his neck to win his love, Petruchio joins hands with her in a handfasting that elicits the astonishment of those present. "Was ever match clapp'd up so suddenly?" asks Gremio (II.i.325). As Petruchio exits, he demands a kiss – "And kiss me, Kate, we will be married a' Sunday" (line 324). Whether the kiss is only threatened or enacted is not clear, but in either case it is not a gesture of peaceful union. The climax of this travesty of romantic ritual occurs at the wedding ceremony, when Petruchio's "clamorous smack" makes the church echo (III.ii.178). At this stage in their relationship, the kiss is a form of assault.

When Petruchio next demands a kiss, in Act V, scene i, he and Kate are in the streets of Padua, returning to Kate's home for the wedding of Bianca and Lucentio. On this occasion the kiss is a test of Kate's new obedience and freedom from social constraints. Kate refuses so bold a gesture at first; when she finally yields, she signifies her acceptance of Petruchio and her social liberation. The kiss in the streets celebrates a private compact that transcends social convention.

Petruchio's final demand for a kiss converts the gesture into a genuine offer of love. As Kate concludes her homily of obedience at the wedding feast, she turns to the other wives and exhorts them to follow her in an act of complete submission to their husbands:

> place your hands below your husband's foot;
> In token of which duty, if he please,
> My hand is ready, may it do him ease.   (V.ii.177–79)

As she offers to humble herself, Petruchio prevents her with, "Why, there's a wench! Come on, and kiss me, Kate" (line 180). Without a hint of sentimentality from either partner, Kate's rite of submission is transformed into a rite of love. Even as Kate bows to convention she defies it, joining with Petruchio to celebrate a victory that belongs to them both. In contrast to Beatrice and Benedick, whose kiss seems to acknowledge both their love and their dependence on society, Kate and Petruchio acknowledge their love but turn their wits upon the world at large. "Come Kate," says Petruchio, "we'll to bed"; and, turning to the other new husbands, "We three are married, but you two are sped" (lines 184–85). *The Taming of the Shrew* is unique among the comedies for this cool, although not unfriendly, split between personal and collective union.

In most of the comedies, personal concord creates social communion. To compare the wedding feast in *The Taming of the Shrew* with that in *A Midsummer Night's Dream*, for example, is to become aware of the breadth of Shakespeare's comic vision. Although not without qualifying ironies, chiefly in the limited understandings of the mortals, Theseus's feast is a flawless rite of incorporation. Bottom has returned to his companions in time to honor the Duke's marriage with their play; the lovers are married and in accord; Theseus and Hippolyta preside graciously over the festivities; and even the fairies, united once again, offer their blessing. Egeus, whose opposition to the marriage of Hermia and Lysander has been overruled, is either absent or (the stage directions are ambiguous) a silent observer. The jests of the aristocrats at the expense of the actors are exchanged with such discretion, or are perhaps overheard with such insensitivity, that they enhance the festive atmosphere; in *Love's Labor's Lost* the same jests create dissonance. The final scene of *A Midsummer Night's Dream* thus shows a whole world in concord, as does the crowded canvas of the "Fête at Bermondsey"; the painting, however, omits the fairies.

In *The Taming of the Shrew* not only are the fairies excluded, but, as we have seen, the social bonds are brittle. Jesting figures in this banquet too, but it is not vented harmlessly on uncomprehending actors. The married couples create their own entertainment, which, instead of strengthening social bonds, sets the nerves on edge. The skirmishing begins with Hortensio's bride attacking Kate: "Your husband, being troubled with a shrew,/ Measures my husband's sorrow by his woe" (V.ii.28–29). As Kate remarks, the widow's meaning is "a very mean meaning" (line 31). The sport that ensues, though all in good fun, produces real losers, and not just economically; the defeated couples go to bed with signs of trouble on the horizon. In their case insight does not bring about incorporation. The play's conclusion ironically reverses the relative positions of the couples, for Kate and Petruchio emerge with the most successful marriage. It reverses as well the conventions of wedding feasts. This banquet, which celebrates the wedding of

Bianca and Lucentio, seals the union of Kate and Petruchio; the earlier banquet, which celebrated the wedding of Kate and Petruchio, confirmed the betrothal of Bianca and Lucentio, who presided in their absence. It is typical of the play's ironic attitude towards social convention that the couples are happiest at the wedding feast of others, and that their own are rites of separation. *The Taming of the Shrew* and *A Midsummer Night's Dream* are in many respects the opposite extremes of Shakespeare's comic spectrum.

Although only these two comedies end with actual wedding feasts, the ceremony is promised at the end of nearly all the others, imparting to their reconciliations and reunions an anticipatory atmosphere of festivity. Valentine's invitation to Proteus to share "One feast, one house, one mutual happiness" (*TGV* V.iv.173) expresses the dominant mood. To reverse the mood, as Shakespeare does in the anti-comic ending of *Love's Labor's Lost*, the ceremonies need only be reversed: the King looks forward to an "austere insociable life" in "some forlorn and naked hermitage" (V.ii.799,795), and Berowne to a "twelvemonth in a hospital" (line 871), where his witticisms will fall upon deaf ears. Even this ending does not deny festivity, however, but merely defers it for one year. In the more conventional endings, festivity is introduced not only by anticipation but by the inclusion of wedding entertainments – in particular, dancing and drama. Like the personal rites of union we have already examined, these social rites are subtly expressive of the couples and communities they bind together.

In *The Governor*, Sir Thomas Elyot addresses the sensitive issue of whether dancing should be included in the education of a gentleman. He will not bore his readers, he says, with what they know already, that dancing symbolizes marriage: "And forasmuch as by the association of a man and a woman in dancing may be signified matrimony, I could in declaring the dignity and commodity of that sacrament make entire volumes, if it were not so commonly known to all men, that almost every friar limiter carrieth it written in his bosom."[29] Instead of reiterating this familiar text, Elyot demonstrates the value of dancing with an allegory of his own invention, a detailed description of the basse dance, or measure, as a definition of the virtue of prudence. Whether there is any relation between prudence and marriage he does not say.

John Davies's poem, "Orchestra," is another familiar and more provocative source for Elizabethan attitudes towards dancing at weddings. In the myth that Antinous tells Penelope, the world is created when Love persuades the elements to dance:

> *Dauncing* (bright Lady) then began to be,
> When the first seedes whereof the world did spring,
> The Fire, Ayre, Earth and Water did agree,
> By Loves perswasion, Natures mighty King,
> To leave their first disordred combating;
>   And in a daunce such measure to observe,
>   As all the world their motion should preserve.
>
> Since when they still are carried in a round,
> And changing come one in anothers place,
> Yet doe they neyther mingle nor confound,
> But every one doth keepe the bounded space
> Wherein the daunce doth bid it turne or trace:
>   This wondrous myracle did Love devise,
>   For Dauncing is Loves proper exercise.[30]

The conception of the dance in this passage is remarkably appropriate to the dancing that ends the comedies. In a broad sense, as we have seen, the structure of the comedies, like that of rites of passage, mimics the process of creation – the transformation, brought about by love, of chaos into order. The cosmic scope of Davies's imagery is particularly relevant to plays like *A Midsummer Night's Dream* and *As You Like it*, which extend earthly unions in metaphysical directions. Davies's notion of dancing as a union that preserves individuality – the elements "neyther mingle nor confound" – parallels Shakespeare's more paradoxical vision of lovers as both two and one; in both cases identity is not lost in love but completed. The final line of the passage may contain a sexual innuendo; if so, it is appropriate, for it would anchor, as Shakespeare does, the generative powers of the universe in those of man himself. The dancing that ends the comedies is in all senses a creative act.

Since neither allegories nor myths are social events, it is important to compare the visions of Elyot and Davies with some descriptions of actual dancing. Bullinger's account of dancing at sixteenth-century weddings, though sour, is probably not inaccurate:

After the bancket and feast/ there begynneth a vayne/ madd/ and unmanerly fayshion. For the bryde must be brought in to an open dauncyng place. Then is there such a renninge/ leapinge/ and flynging amonge them/ then is there such a lyftinge up and discoveringe of the damesels clothes and of other wemens apparell/ that a man might thinke/ all these daunters had rast [?] all shame behinde them/ and were become starke madde .... Then must the poore bryd kepe foote with all dauncers/ and refuse none/ how scabbed/ foule/ droncken rude and shamels [*sic.*] so ever he be.[31]

Phillip Stubbes, who does not restrict his observations to weddings, reacts even more violently, especially to the custom of kissing during a dance: "What clipping, what culling, what kissing and bussing, what smouching and slabbering one of another, what filthie groping and uncleane handling is not practised every wher in these dancings?"[32] Shakespeare uses this custom in *Henry VIII*. When the King takes Anne Boleyn as his dancing partner, he says, "I were unmannerly to take you out,/ And not to kiss you" (I.iv.95–96). The lack of "smouching and slabbering" in this episode does not entirely discredit Stubbes; behind Henry's elegant manners lie common intentions. Given the range of possibilities in both kissing and dancing, it is probably safe to assume that Elizabethan weddings were varied enough to offer something for both idealists and realists in all social classes.

At the end of *A Midsummer Night's Dream*, the separate dances of the "hempen homespuns" and the fairies hold sense and spirit in perfect balance. The dancing begins at the end of "Pyramus and Thisby," with two members of Bottom's company performing a bergomask, a clownish country dance which, according to Curt Sachs, "presents the characteristic alternation of fleeing and yielding, of denial and surrender ... of all wooing dances."[33] Sometimes these rough courtship dances were accompanied with bawdy lyrics; Thomas Morley refers to bergomask songs as a "wanton and rude kind of music."[34] Whether this particular bergomask is sung is uncertain: Bottom invites Theseus "to hear a Bergomask dance," but he also invites him to "see the epilogue" (V.i.353); his senses have been muddled since he awakened from his dream.

With words or without, the dance, like the play the rustics have just performed, mimics the story of the lovers, but this time with comical rather than tragical mirth. Although it parodies the lovers' courtships, the dance functions more as celebration than satire. A fertility rite of a coarse and homespun kind, it brings to the play something of the sexual mirth so prominent at weddings and so objectionable to the moralists: "Sathan hath so woven his owne impuritie, with the pure Ordinance of God, that a Mariage, is accounted no Mariage, if it be not solemnized with beastly and profane Songs, Sonnets, Jiggs, indited by some hellish Spirit, and chaunted by those, that are the publique incendiaries of all filthy lusts; and these are ordinarily made in the scorne and derision of this Holy Estate, to delight and solace the Guests withall."[35] Shakespeare's bergomask "solemnizes" the wedding with sexual "delight."

The form of the fairies' dance is not specified, but it is clearly intended to complement the bergomask. Alan Brissenden suggests that the fairies dance a carole, "in which the dancers link hands and move to the music of a song, usually sung by themselves." This dance would be particularly appropriate, he says, because in the Middle Ages the carole was used "in religious ritual and in such ceremonies as blessing the bounds of the parish."[36] The ritual of blessing the bed, performed by the fairies, was itself a familiar medieval ritual, discontinued after the Reformation. Whatever its precise form, the dance of the fairies not only celebrates the order of the earthly marriages but the reunion of the fairy community, effected earlier in the reconciliation of Titania and Oberon, itself marked by a dance. Since the dissension among the fairies throws all nature out of balance, disordering the seasons so that the "mazed world . . . knows not which is which" (II.i.113–14), their dancing, like that in Davies's myth, creates the world anew, transforming chaos into harmony. As in Davies's myth, too, the elements of the scene as a whole "neyther mingle nor confound": fairies dance with fairies, homespuns with homespuns; Bottom stays where he belongs. Each world celebrates the marriages in its own terms, contributing its distinctive grace and charm.

The dance that concludes As You Like It effects an even broader social communion, for in joining the four couples it brings together aristocrats and commoners, shepherds and courtiers, all sharing the blessing of Hymen. The ambiguity of the Duke's directions for the dance has caused uncertainty about its kind. Taking his cue from the Duke's call for "rustic revelry" (V.iv.177), John H. Long suggests a "rustic measure," such as the "hay."[37] Taking theirs from the Duke's instructions, "With measure heap'd in joy, to th' measures fall" (line 179), Walter

Sorell and Alan Brissenden prefer a stately dance of the court, sometimes called a "measure," the pavane.[38] The ambiguity of the Duke's language is intentional, it seems to me, and sets the atmosphere of the dance rather than its precise form. The attempt is to create a synthesis of the courtly and rustic, the civilized and the pastoral, of the kind that is achieved by the stylized rusticity of the songs that end *Love's Labor's Lost*. The "measure" of the dance, moreover, is not limited to the married couples or to Arden; it will return to the court, according to the Duke, where all "Shall share the good of our returned fortune,/ According to the measure of their states" (lines 174–75). Even Jaques's rejection of the dance is not seriously disruptive, for he too accepts the value of measure, only of a different kind – "I am for other than for dancing measures" (line 193).

Although the dance at the end of *Much Ado About Nothing* has neither the social nor metaphysical inclusiveness of those in *A Midsummer Night's Dream* or *As You Like It*, it too serves as a rite of incorporation, marking the new order among the couples and in the society as a whole. The dance reverses the implications of an earlier dance in Act II, scene i, transforming its gestures of separation into gestures of communion. In the former dance, the participants are all masked and mutually deceived, the unconscious victims both of Don John, who plots to undo them even as they execute their figures, and their own follies. The latter dance coincides with the announcement of Don John's capture, and the dancers are unmasked, undeceived, and on their way to be married.

In keeping with the play's realistic and satiric tone, however, this dancing is not without hints of discord. Leonato objects to it as a violation of convention, which dictates dancing after weddings, not before. When Benedick overrules him, the social symbolism of the dance becomes slightly equivocal. Benedick's urgency, moreover, implies that its personal symbolism is also equivocal. Why should he desire so strongly to dance *before* his wedding? On the one hand, Benedick's gesture reveals his characteristic defiance of convention, expressed even as he proves his conventionality by accepting marriage. On the other, it reveals his anxiety about his future as a married man; it is not everyone who needs a dance to "lighten" (V.iv.118) his heart on his wedding day. As he approaches marriage, Benedick does not look forward to a lifetime of dancing. "Get thee a wife," he says to Don Pedro, "There is no staff more reverent than one tipp'd with horn" (lines 122–24). If the dance called for is a pavane, Benedick at least may be too unsettled to achieve the required stateliness and grace. The dance that concludes *Much Ado About Nothing* is equivocal both as a psychological and as a social symbol.

In *A Midsummer Night's Dream*, Theseus proposes not only dancing but masques or plays to "wear away this long age of three hours/ Between our after-supper and bed-time" (V.i.33–34). Although "Pyramus and Thisby" is the only literal rendering of such a wedding entertainment in the comedies, several endings include adaptations. The wager that concludes *The Taming of the Shrew* is a spontaneous game, but it turns into a dramatic performance. The show of the Nine Worthies in *Love's Labor's Lost* nearly becomes a betrothal pageant but founders with the entry of Marcade. In the final scene of *As You Like It*, a masque and wedding are combined. Although Shakespeare uses a variety of devices to evoke the atmosphere of traditional wedding entertainments, they all have in common the social expressiveness developed most fully in the aristocratic masque.

Like masques, the entertainments that end the comedies are not autonomous works of art, independent of the place and occasion of their performance, but celebrations of both, sometimes tinged with unconscious irony. The Jonsonian masque, observes Stephen Orgel, "attempted from the beginning to breach the barrier between spectators and actors, so that in effect the viewer became part of the spectacle. The end toward which the masque moved was to destroy any sense of theater and to include the whole court in the mimesis – in a sense, what the spectator watched he ultimately became."[39] The ease with which masque-world and audience came together can be seen at a glance in the famous portrait of Sir Nicholas Unton, one section of which depicts his wedding masque.[40] At the head of her court, Diana moves in procession from the acting area to the banqueting table and presents the mistress of the household with a scroll. It is this organic connection between spectacle and social milieu that makes Shakespeare's wedding entertainments such subtle and complicated rites of incorporation.

Theseus's entertainment, although a play rather than a masque, evokes most directly the atmosphere of such courtly occasions.

The performance of "Pyramus and Thisby" joins the extreme ends of society in a shared theatrical experience – Bottom and his fellows delighting in the chance to honor the Duke's wedding, display their virtuosity, and perhaps win a pension in the bargain; the court delighting in the players' ineptitude and their own wit. The "tragedy" performed is ostensibly no more suitable for the occasion than the pageant of the nine Muses mourning for the death of learning, which Theseus earlier rejected as "not sorting with a nuptial ceremony" (V.i.55); its effects, however, run counter to its intentions, and its theme relates to the occasion in ways that escape the attention of the court. The obliviousness of the lovers to the irony of watching a "tragic" version of their own experience comments subtly on their own as well as the players' limitations. It may comment as well on the difficulties of the genre, for eye-witness accounts of Jonson's masques show that such failures of the imagination were not uncommon.[41] It is important not to overstate the ironies, however, for the virtue of such performances, as Theseus is well aware, lies in the spirit of communion they create: "never any thing can be amiss,/ When simpleness and duty tender it" (V.i.82–83).

If the performance of "Pyramus and Thisby" celebrates the new social concord in Athens, the pageant of the Nine Worthies in *Love's Labor's Lost* symbolizes the social discord in Navarre. Intended as a celebration of love, to "congratulate the Princess at her pavilion in the posteriors of this day" (V.i.88–89), as Armado puts it, the pageant actually promotes confusion and disharmony. Having been caught out in the folly of their disguise as Russians, the aristocrats bring forth the pageant, as Berowne admits, to salvage some of their pride. When the King protests that the pageant will shame them, Berowne replies, "We are shame-proof, my lord; and 'tis some policy/ To have one show worse than the King's and his company" (V.ii.512–13). Not only do the young men fail to see the ironic relevance of the pageant's theme to their own aspirations, both academic and amatory, in which they have been as "o'erparted" (line 584) as Nathaniel in the role of Alexander, but they exercise their wits with such callous self-indulgence that they cause pain to those who are trying to give them pleasure. Their behavior finally provokes from Holofernes a deserved, and surprisingly dignified, rebuke: "This is not gener-ous, not gentle, not humble" (line 629). The broken pageant is thus a figure for the young men's ignorance; until they learn charity, they cannot understand love. Berowne, the worst offender because the wittiest, is sent off to learn that

> A jest's prosperity lies in the ear
> Of him that hears it, never in the tongue
> Of him that makes it ...   (lines 861–63)

The persistency with which Shakespeare tests romantic love against charity has much in common with his contemporaries' insistence on generosity to the poor at weddings. "Mariage feasts are abused," says William Gouge, "when the needy and distressed are not remembred therein."[42] Before he is married, Berowne will serve a year in a hospital.

The entertainment that closes the wedding feast of *The Taming of the Shrew* puts Kate in the role of model wife. As in her earlier sport with old Vincentio, who was "amaz'd" at their "strange encounter" (IV.v.54), Kate takes a conspiratorial delight in her role, for although she must work within fixed guidelines, she may improvise at will. In both cases her submission is required by her director, but her flair for hyperbole is her own. By her final performance, she understands her role so well that she needs only the slightest cues. Productions of the play that omit the Christopher Sly episodes at the beginning diminish the delightful theatricality of the ending, not only by losing the play outside the play but by losing the parallels between Sly's role and Kate's. Both characters are given the option of clinging to a familiar but demeaning identity – as beggar and shrew – or of accepting a new one that offers freedom, fulfillment, and acceptance of certain rules. For Sly these include learning to drink sack, call his wife "madam," and restrain his sexual passion, lest he fall into his dreams again; for Kate, they include learning to call the sun the moon and her husband lord. Both enjoy their new roles, but only Kate's enjoyment is fully conscious; she becomes the accomplished actress, living simultaneously within her role and without. Kate's climactic performance, however, although it surprises her spectators, does not please them all. Her wedding entertainment, as we have seen, is more personal than collective rite.

If *The Taming of the Shrew* ends with the most unsentimental wedding entertainment in the comedies, *As You Like It* ends with the most romantic. With the entrance of Hymen, the play suddenly shifts in mode, from drama into masque. And yet the masque is presented as a real event: a god has descended, as far as we know, and the spectacle he creates is a rite of marriage. This magical event is the most compressed and complete rite of incorporation in the comedies; it is at once a moment of recognition, a marriage, a wedding masque, and a theophany. The moment is also the most wondrous in the comedies, for it is the only time a character catches the audience by surprise. To end the play, Rosalind need only change her clothes; instead, she proves herself a true magician and introduces Hymen. As always, however, Shakespeare allows us to feel the full magic of the moment without yielding to enchantment. Jaques's gesture of withdrawal runs counter to the masque's romantic idealism, as does the presence of Audrey and Touchstone within its inner circle. Even more important is our continuing awareness that in this play we are being permitted a glimpse of life as we like it. When the mysterious *"still music"* announces the entrance of Hymen (V.iv.108.s.d.), Touchstone has just completed describing his method of preventing duels. Touchstone's art, like Shakespeare's, depends upon a willingness to entertain fictions: "Your If is the only peacemaker; much virtue in If" (lines 102–03).[43]

In various ways, all of these wedding entertainments suspend the dramatic illusion. When a play turns into a masque, or when a play-within-a-play mimics the main plot, or when a character knowingly performs a new role, the gap between actors and audience narrows, and we become newly conscious of the theatricality of art and life. In an audience this awareness is the counterpart of the recognition achieved by characters like Helena, who awaken from their "dreams" to see with "parted eye." The experience of love, as we have seen, like the experience of art, depends upon a disciplined imagination, a willingness to believe and disbelieve at the same time. The effect of this theatrical self-consciousness is not merely a heightened sense of paradox but an extension of the communal bonds established within the plays to encompass the audience. For the most part, this effect is indirect: the presence of festivity onstage makes us conscious of the plays themselves as festive occasions, and of ourselves as not merely observers but participants in a re-creative entertainment. Sometimes, as when Rosalind in her epilogue offers to kiss the men in the audience, the gesture is direct. Although the comedies never become masques – never dissolve the boundaries between art and life, players and audience – their endings welcome us to the feast. Our applause, as Puck implies at the end of *A Midsummer Night's Dream*, becomes a gesture of incorporation: "Give me your hands, if we be friends,/ And Robin shall restore amends" (V.i.437–38).

If Shakespeare's endings involve us in their festivities, however, they also induce a comic catharsis. We experience not only the delight that arises from comic communion but the detachment that accompanies our awareness of its incompleteness and fragility. If we are to call Shakespeare a "magician" or "mythmaker," as Philip Edwards observes, we must resist the idealizing tendencies of those metaphors: "The 'festive comedies' do not really end in clarification and in a resolution of the opposing forces of holiday and everyday. A strong magic is created: and it is questioned."[44] In part, this questioning is provoked by "outsiders," like Jaques or Malvolio, who in various ways resist insight and incorporation. But their recalcitrance is merely its most tangible form. The subtler questionings lie within the dramatized rites themselves – in the inevitable discrepancy between ritual form and human reality.

As abstract forms, weddings, like comedies, aspire towards total harmony of being. Their "magic," to adopt Edwards's term, lies in the glimmerings they provide of such transcendence, as when the placing of a ring encloses a whole community, if only for a moment, in a circle of love. As events, however, weddings generate inescapable ironies, conscious to all but the most naive or drunken guests. The double vision that results, although inevitable, is accidental and uncontrolled. In the comedies, this duality is present by design – in equivocal recognitions, hesitant marriages, and hints of social discord. To respond to the whole of Shakespeare's comic experience is to align ourselves with the comic heroines, whose maturity enables them to love with "parted eye." Shakespeare's comedies fulfill two strong human desires – for perfection and for truth. They offer no golden worlds, merely hopeful ones, enclosed in gestures of affection.

8
Conclusion

As a comic dramatist, Shakespeare stands alone. His distinctive comic tendencies, of course, are not without precedent or parallel. His focus on the comedy of courtship and marriage; his separation of his central characters from their familiar social setting; his treatment of their psychic turmoil as the main obstacle to their fulfillment in love; his depiction of that turmoil through the motifs of role-playing and disguise; his development of the paradoxes of clowning; his use of symbolic dislocations in place and time; his exploitation of the rites and customs of marriage – taken singly, these tendencies can be found, to some degree, in other comic dramatists. Taken together, however, they add up to a unique comic form, stable enough to be defined yet flexible enough to permit endless variation. Throughout this essay, I have sought to enrich our understanding and appreciation of this form by highlighting its resemblance to that of rites of passage. The presence of this ancient and universal structure in Shakespeare's romantic comedies, I have suggested, helps explain their distinctive and peculiarly deep imaginative appeal.

To understand how this ritual structure might have been available to Shakespeare, I have ventured into Elizabethan social history. In many respects, Shakespeare's stylized and conventional art imitates but displaces the familiar life around him. A wide variety of social phenomena work their way into the remote and exotic worlds of the romantic comedies: the practice of sending out adolescents; the psychology of imitation; stereotypes of adolescent and courting behavior; popular notions of time and place; customs of fooling, both onstage and off; and the elaborate and extensive ceremonies of marriage. In pursuing these rites and customs of adolescence, courtship, and marriage, I have explored territories only recently charted by social historians and still largely ignored by literary critics and scholars. The importance of such pursuits to our understanding of Shakespeare has recently been urged by Maynard Mack. Observing that Shakespeare "keeps up an elusive but fascinating traffic between the world of history and the world of art," Mack suggests that "our chances of learning more about his achievement in the latter depend in large part on our learning more about the former."[1]

Much has been learned about Elizabethan social life in the past decade; many of the sources for this study have only become available within the past five years, some in the few years since Mack's article. Yet much remains unknown, even within the limited territory I have surveyed. Elizabethan adolescence, with its striking initiatory customs, continues to be a mysterious social phenomenon, with profound implications for the society as a whole. The psychology of imitation, which seems so central to Elizabethan culture, has attracted little study outside literary or pedagogical contexts. The nature of Elizabethan courtship remains highly problematic, its practical and romantic strands difficult to disentangle, and its relation to class divisions obscure. The role of ritual in this highly ritualistic society has scarcely been examined.

It is not merely the world of history that demands the critic's attention, however, but, as Mack suggests, the traffic between that world and Shakespeare's art. As in rites of passage, crossing the intersections poses the greatest dangers. The tendency among social historians is to stay on their own side of the street, ignoring literature as an untrustworthy reflector of social realities. Yet plays, like parish records, are social documents, and while their relation to social life may be more oblique and difficult to define, it may also be more significant. The tendency among literary historians, to judge from past Shakespearean scholarship, is to fall into the opposite error – to reduce works of literature to their social context, finding in them mere reflections of social conventions or dominant ideas. Though opposed, these tendencies converge: both derive from a limited view of the creative process. History becomes art, but in doing so is transformed. The challenge of the historical critic, and perhaps the critical historian, is to clarify that transformation.

Shakespeare's romantic comedies, as we have seen, do not merely reflect the structure of an Elizabethan rite or set of social customs. These may have suggested such a structure to Shakespeare, in shadowy and fragmentary outline, but it is he who created it, giving shadows substance and fragments dramatic form. Every study of Shakespeare, like that of any great artist, must end by recognizing the mystery of imagination. The marvel of Shakespeare's is that his forms are not only Elizabethan but universal. In re-creating the social patterns of his age, he gave "local habitation" to one of the most ancient and universal patterns of human experience – that of rites of passage. This dynamic structure makes Shakespeare's romantic comedies at once unique, Elizabethan, and universal.

The pursuit of the origins, nature, and effects of Shakespeare's comic art thus extends far beyond the world of Elizabethan England that Mack urges us to explore. Yet this should come as no surprise. Shakespeare's universality itself is unique. If Elizabethan social history may shed light on Shakespeare's responsiveness to his world, primitive ritual may illuminate the contours of his imagination and help explain our own world's responsiveness to his plays. In his tribute to the First Folio, Ben Jonson called Shakespeare the "Soule of his age." Jonson also asserted, however, "He was not of an age, but for all time." Jonson's claim of immortality may have seemed in his own day mere hyperbole; in ours, which sees Shakespeare studied and performed in every region of the world, it begins to look like fact.

Notes

1 Introduction: Comic Rites

1 Shakespearean comedy has been defined from many different perspectives. The two most influential critics of the genre, C. L. Barber and Northrop Frye, offer radically different views. In *Shakespeare's Festive Comedy* (Princeton: Princeton Univ. Press, 1959), Barber isolates a sub-genre, the "festive" comedies, within the set of plays culminating in *Twelfth Night*; in *A Natural Perspective* (New York: Columbia Univ. Press, 1965), Frye groups the "romantic" comedies and late romances into a single, inclusive genre. For surveys of twentieth-century criticism of the comedies, see John Russell Brown, "The Interpretation of Shakespeare's Comedies: 1900–1953," *Shakespeare Survey* 8 (1955), 1–13; M. M. Mahood, "Shakespeare's Middle Comedies: A Generation of Criticism," *Shakespeare Survey* 32 (1979), 1–13; and Wayne A. Rebhorn, "After Frye: A Review-Article on the Interpretation of Shakespearean Comedy and Romance," *Texas Studies in Literature and Language* 21 (1979), 553–82.

2 In "The Father and the Bride in Shakespeare" (*PMLA* 97 [1982], 325–47), Lynda E. Boose interprets Elizabethan weddings as separation rites marking "the separation of the daughter from the interdicting father" (p. 326). Although I view weddings, with van Gennep, as centering upon incorporation, I find Boose's account of this dimension of the rite and its role in the plays she examines insightful and persuasive.

3 Van Gennep's study was originally published in French in 1909. The edition I have used is *The Rites of Passage*, trans. Monika B. Vizedom and Gabrielle L. Caffee (Chicago: Univ. of Chicago Press, 1960). For surveys that demonstrate the extent of van Gennep's influence, see Eliot D. Chapple and Carleton S. Coon, *Principles of Anthropology* (New York: Henry Holt, 1942), pp. 484–506; Edward Norbeck, *Religion in Primitive Society* (New York: Harper and Brothers, 1961), pp. 138–64; and Monika Vizedom, *Rites and Relationships: Rites of Passage and Contemporary Anthropology*, Sage Research Papers in the Social Sciences 4 (Beverly Hills, Calif.: Sage Publications, 1976).

4 I restrict the term "initiation" throughout to those rites which define the passage through adolescence into adulthood. The term "puberty rites" is misleading, as van Gennep points out, because "physiological puberty and 'social puberty' are essentially different and only rarely converge" (p. 65); this is especially true for Elizabethan society, in which the most significant mark of adulthood was marriage, which for most people occurred in the late twenties. The phrase "initiation rites" is also ambiguous, since it can refer to entrance into secret societies, for example, or political office; with rites of this kind, however, I am not concerned. The

descriptions of rites that follow are selected from *Rites of Passage*, pp. 65–145.

5 Max Gluckman, *Custom and Conflict in Africa* (Oxford: Basil Blackwell, 1965), p. 119.

6 Van Gennep, *Rites*, p. 18.

7 "Variations on a Theme of Liminality," in Sally F. Moore and Barbara G. Myerhoff, eds., *Secular Ritual* (Assen/Amsterdam: Van Gorcum, 1977), pp. 37–38.

8 Van Gennep, *Rites*, pp. 138–39.

9 *Shakespeare and the Traditions of Comedy* (Cambridge: Cambridge Univ. Press, 1974), p. 283.

10 *Feeling and Form* (New York: Charles Scribner's Sons, 1953), pp. 328, 331.

11 Van Gennep, *Rites*, p. 182.

12 For a useful review of the major theoretical perspectives brought to bear on reproductive ritual, which includes puberty rites, see Karen Ericksen Paige and Jeffery M. Paige, *The Politics of Reproductive Ritual* (Berkeley: Univ. of California Press, 1981), pp. 1–42.

13 *The Andaman Islanders* (New York: Free Press of Glencoe, 1964), p. 234. Vizedom traces Radcliffe-Brown's influence in *Rites and Relationships*, pp. 14–20.

14 Gluckman, *Custom and Conflict*, p. 119.

15 *Order and Rebellion in Tribal Africa* (London: Cohen and West, 1963), pp. 118, 126.

16 *Essays on the Ritual of Social Relations* (Manchester: Manchester Univ. Press, 1962), pp. 46–47.

17 Vizedom, *Rites*, pp. 46–47.

18 Frye, *Natural Perspective*, p. 72.

19 Salingar, *Traditions*, p. 172.

20 Vizedom, *Rites*, p. 44.

21 *Structural Anthropology*, 1, trans. Claire Jacobson and Brooke G. Schoepf (New York: Basic Books, 1963), pp. 187, 198.

22 For stimulating discussions of Shakespeare's comedies as cathartic and curative structures, see Ruth Nevo, *Comic Transformations in Shakespeare* (London: Methuen, 1980), pp. 216–27, and Sherman Hawkins, "The Two Worlds of Shakespearean Comedy," *Shakespeare Studies* 3 (1967), 70–73.

23 *Symbolic Wounds*, rev. ed. (Glencoe, Ill.: Free Press, 1954), p. 70.

24 Bettelheim, *Wounds*, p. 150. Although he refers to neither Jung nor Bettelheim, Victor Turner finds in the Ndembu circumcision rite a similar pattern: "The novice dies to be transformed or transmuted, and attain to a higher quality of existence. This is death to the indistinct and amorphous state of childhood . . . in order to be reborn into masculinity and personality" (*Ritual of Social Relations*, p. 173).

25 Bettelheim, *Wounds*, p. 147.

26 *Infant and Child in the Culture of Today* (New York: Harper and Brothers, 1943), pp. 292–93; Vizedom notes the resemblance between van Gennep's schema and that of Gesell and Ilg in *Rites and Relationships*, p. 8.

27 *Rites and Symbols of Initiation*, trans. Willard R. Trask (New York: Harper and Row, 1958), pp. 4–7. Eliade's account of the liminal

experience as a symbolic re-enactment of the creation of the world out of primordial chaos is highly suggestive, and I shall draw on it later. His views apply only to initiation rites, however, and the pattern he defines seems less universal than he implies; his evidence is taken from a few Australian tribes, chiefly the Kamilaroi. Anthropologists have generally ignored his thesis.

28 See Norbeck, *Religion*, pp. 164–68. The festive reversals characteristic of such rites are explored from a variety of perspectives in Barbara A. Babcock, ed., *The Reversible World* (Ithaca, N. Y.: Cornell Univ. Press, 1978).

29 *Anatomy of Criticism* (Princeton: Princeton Univ. Press, 1957), pp. 163–86; *Natural Perspective*, p. 73.

30 Barber, *Festive Comedy*, pp. 6–10.

31 Van Gennep, *Rites*, pp. 189–90.

32 Gluckman, *Order and Rebellion*, pp. 131–35.

33 Salingar, *Traditions*, p. 16.

34 Barber, *Festive Comedy*, p. 119.

35 Salingar, *Traditions*, p. 222.

36 John Dover Wilson, *Shakespeare's Happy Comedies* (London: Faber and Faber, 1962), p. 162; Peter G. Phialas, *Shakespeare's Romantic Comedies* (Chapel Hill: Univ. of North Carolina Press, 1966), p. 243; David Young, *The Heart's Forest* (New Haven: Yale Univ. Press, 1972), p. 68; Margaret Boerner Beckerman, "The Figure of Rosalind in *As You Like It*," *Shakespeare Quarterly* 29 (1978), 44.

37 Barber, *Festive Comedy*, p. 238.

38 See my article "Rosalynde and Rosalind," *Shakespeare Quarterly* 31 (1980), 42–52.

39 For some useful distinctions between ritual and drama, written from an anthropological perspective, see Max and Mary Gluckman, "On Drama, and Games and Athletic Contests," in Moore and Myerhoff, eds., *Secular Ritual*, pp. 227–37.

40 The only other sustained account of Shakespeare's plays as rites of passage, Marjorie Garber's *Coming of Age in Shakespeare* (London: Methuen, 1981), takes this approach. Garber's interesting study focuses on characterization, not dramatic structure, and cuts across generic lines.

41 *Renaissance Self-Fashioning* (Chicago: Univ. of Chicago Press, 1980), pp. 4–5.

42 *The Forest of Symbols* (Ithaca, N.Y.: Cornell Univ. Press, 1967), p. 19.

43 "Religion and Ritual: The Definitional Problem," *British Journal of Sociology* 12 (1961), 159.

44 Edmund R. Leach, "Ritual," in the *International Encyclopedia of The Social Sciences*, ed. David L. Sills (Macmillan and The Free Press, 1968), XIII, 524. For further reviews of the definitional problems, see Jack Goody, "Against 'Ritual,'" in Moore and Myerhoff, eds., *Secular Ritual*, pp. 25–35, and Gilbert Lewis, *Day of Shining Red* (Cambridge: Cambridge Univ. Press, 1980), pp. 1–38.

45 See Terence Hawkes, *Structuralism and Semiotics* (London: Methuen, 1977), pp. 123–50.

46 *Natural Symbols*, 2nd ed. (London: Barrie and Jenkins, 1973), pp. 19–39.

47 Douglas, *Natural Symbols*, p. 16.

48 See Frank Aydelotte, *Elizabethan Rogues and Vagabonds* (1913; rpt. London: Frank Cass, 1967), pp. 26–30.
49 *The Cult of Elizabeth* (London: Thames and Hudson, 1977), p.16.
50 William Camden, *The History of... Princess Elizabeth*, ed. Wallace T. MacCaffrey (Chicago: Univ. of Chicago Press, 1970), p. 29.
51 *A Catechisme or Christian Doctrine* (1599; rpt. Menston, Yorkshire: Scolar Press, 1969), pp. 142–43.
52 *A Directory for the Publique Worship of God* (London, 1644), p. 35.
53 *The Book of Common Prayer 1559*, ed. John E. Booty (Charlottesville: Univ. Press of Virginia, 1976), p. 20.
54 *The Description of England*, ed. Georges Edelen (Ithaca, N.Y.: Cornell Univ. Press, 1968), p. 34.
55 J. S. Purvis, ed., *Tudor Parish Documents of the Diocese of York* (Cambridge: Cambridge Univ. Press, 1948), p. 150.
56 *Pasquil's Palinodia* (London, 1619), sig. B3.
57 *The Early Stuarts, 1603–1660*, 2nd ed. (Oxford: Clarendon Press, 1959), p. 203.
58 *The Puritan Way of Death* (New York: Oxford Univ. Press, 1977), pp. 101, 111.
59 Alan Macfarlane, *The Family Life of Ralph Josselin* (Cambridge: Cambridge Univ. Press, 1970), p. 53. For general surveys of the customs surrounding birth, marriage and death, see Lu Emily Pearson, *Elizabethans at Home* (Stanford: Stanford Univ. Press, 1957); Phillis Cunnington and Catherine Lucas, *Costume for Births, Marriages, and Deaths* (London: Adam and Charles Black, 1972); and John Brand, *Observations on Popular Antiquities* (London: Chatto and Windus, 1913).
60 *Farming and Account Books* (London: Surtees Society, 1857), pp. 116–17.
61 *The World We Have Lost* (New York: Scribner's, 1965), p. 97.
62 *The Family, Sex and Marriage in England, 1500–1800* (New York: Harper and Row, 1977), p. 181.
63 Michael MacDonald, *Mystical Bedlam* (Cambridge: Cambridge Univ. Press, 1981), pp. 88–89. Napier, an Anglican clergyman, practiced medicine from 1597 to 1634. MacDonald analyzed over two thousand of his medical accounts and found that "almost 40% of the men and women who described their anxieties and dilemmas to Napier complained about the frustrations of courtship and married life" (p.88).
64 See Macfarlane, *Family Life*, pp. 205–10, and Stone, *Family*, pp. 107–09.
65 "Age and Authority in Early Modern England," *Proceedings of the British Academy* 62 (1976), 226.
66 Quoted in Steven Watson, *A History of the Salters' Company* (London: Oxford Univ. Press, 1963), pp. 46–47.
67 Quoted in M. H. Curtis, "Education and Apprenticeship," *Shakespeare Survey* 17 (1964), 69.
68 "The London Apprentices as Seventeenth-Century Adolescents," *Past and Present* 61 (1973), 149–61.
69 "English Youth Groups and *The Pinder of Wakefield*," *Past and Present* 76 (1977), 127–33.
70 "Rule and Misrule in the Schools of Early Modern England," The Stenton Lecture, 1975 (Reading: Univ. of Reading, 1976).

71 "Latin Language Study as a Renaissance Puberty Rite," *Studies in Philology* 56 (1959), 103–24.
72 Wallace Notestein observes that early seventeenth-century playwrights may have helped create the more liberal attitudes towards women that emerged at the end of the century; see "The English Woman, 1580–1650," in J. H. Plumb, ed., *Studies in Social History* (London: Longmans, Green, 1955), p. 103. For a provocative but one-sided argument that Elizabethan playwrights created a feminist theater, see Juliet Dusinberre, *Shakespeare and the Nature of Women* (London: Macmillan, 1975).

2 Separations

1 Arnold van Gennep, *The Rites of Passage*, trans. Monika B. Vizedom and Gabrielle L. Caffee (Chicago: Univ. of Chicago Press, 1960), pp. 15–25.
2 Henry Best, *Farming and Account Books* (London: Surtees Society, 1857), p. 116.
3 See Lawrence Stone, *The Family, Sex and Marriage in England 1500–1800* (New York: Harper and Row, 1977), pp. 107–12, and Alan Macfarlane, *The Family Life of Ralph Josselin* (Cambridge: Cambridge Univ. Press, 1970), pp. 205–10.
4 *A Relation ... of the Island of England*, trans. Charlotte A. Sneyd (London: Camden Society, 1847), pp. 24–25.
5 *English Works*, ed. W. A. Wright (Cambridge: Cambridge Univ. Press, 1904), pp. 222–37.
6 Macfarlane, *Family Life*, pp. 92–98.
7 A. L. Rowse, *Simon Forman* (London: Weidenfeld and Nicolson, 1974), pp. 274–75; see also pp. 267–78.
8 James M. Osborn, ed., *The Autobiography of Thomas Whythorne* (London: Oxford Univ. Press, 1962), p. 10.
9 Alan Macfarlane, ed., *The Diary of Ralph Josselin 1616–1683* (London: Oxford Univ. Press, 1976), pp. 446–47.
10 *The Truth of Our Times* (1638; facs. rpt. New York: Columbia Univ. Press, 1942), pp. 10–11.
11 Ludovicus Vives, *The Office and Duetie of an Husband*, trans. Thomas Paynell (London, c. 1553), sig. L4^v.
12 W. Carew Hazlitt, ed., *Old English Plays* (London, 1874), II, 280.
13 J. Payne Collier, ed., *Illustrations of Old English Literature* (London, 1866), I, 7.
14 *The Puritan Family* (Boston, 1944), p. 28.
15 *The Puritan Way of Death* (New York: Oxford Univ. Press, 1977), pp. 57–61.
16 Stone, *Family*, p. 108.
17 Stannard, *Way of Death*, p. 63.
18 "The Two Worlds of Shakespearean Comedy," *Shakespeare Studies* 3 (1967), 68.
19 John E. Booty, ed., *The Book of Common Prayer 1559* (Charlottesville: Univ. Press of Virginia, 1976), p. 297. For an insightful analysis of this scene against the background of the Anglican marriage ceremony, see Arthur Kirsch, *Shakespeare and the Experience of Love* (Cambridge: Cambridge Univ. Press, 1981), pp. 42–46.
20 Van Gennep, *Rites*, p. 130.

21 For a reproduction and account of the "Young Man amongst Roses," see Roy Strong, *The Cult of Elizabeth* (London: Thames and Hudson, 1977), pp. 56–83. The woodcut by Rowlands and the other Hilliard portrait are reproduced in *The Riverside Shakespeare*, p. 216 and plate 5.

3 Natural Transitions

1 *A Nest of Ninnies*, in J. P. Feather, ed., *The Collected Works of Robert Armin*, I (1608; facs. rpt. New York: Johnson Reprint Corp., 1972), sig. B2ᵛ.

2 *Rites of Passage*, trans. Monika B. Vizedom and Gabrielle L. Caffee (Chicago: Univ. of Chicago Press, 1960), p. 18.

3 *The Family, Sex and Marriage in England 1500–1800* (New York: Harper and Row, 1977), p. 108.

4 *The Good and the Bad* (1616), in Alexander B. Grosart, ed., *Works* (Edinburgh: Edinburgh Univ. Press, 1879), II, 14.

5 Quoted in Samuel C. Chew, *The Pilgrimage of Life* (New Haven: Yale Univ. Press, 1962), p. 161.

6 *Micro-cosmographie* (1628), ed. Edward Arber (London, 1868), p. 51.

7 *The Differences of the Ages of Mans Life* (London, 1633), p. 121.

8 James M. Osborn, ed., *The Autobiography of Thomas Whythorne* (London: Oxford Univ. Press, 1962), pp. 12–13.

9 *Ibid.*, p. 21.

10 James E. Savage, ed., *The "Conceited Newes" Of Sir Thomas And His Friends* (1616; facs. rpt. Gainesville, Fla: Scholar's Facsimile, 1968), pp. 77–79.

11 Lawrence Babb shows that the conventional mark of falling in love on the Elizabethan stage was "to freeze into statuesque abstraction and to gaze in wide-eyed and speechless wonder at the newly beloved"; see *The Elizabethan Malady* (East Lansing: Michigan Stage College Press, 1951), p. 172.

12 Useful general discussions of Elizabethan conceptions of the imagination are provided in Ruth L. Anderson, *Elizabethan Psychology and Shakespeare's Plays*, University of Iowa Humanistic Studies III, 4 (Iowa City, 1927); J. B. Bamborough, *The Little World of Man* (London, 1952), pp. 36–41; and William Rossky, "Imagination in the English Renaissance: Psychology and Poetic," *Studies in the Renaissance* (1958), 49–73. For the role of imagination in magic, see D. P. Walker, *Spiritual and Demonic Magic from Ficino to Campanella* (London, 1958), pp. 76–80, and Edward Berry, "Prospero's 'Brave Spirit,'" *Studies in Philology* 76 (1979), 36–48. On the importance of imagination in adolescence, see Anderson, *Elizabethan Psychology*, p. 38.

13 *Autobiographies* (London: Macmillan, 1955), p. 477; *Mythologies* (London: Macmillan, 1959), pp. 333–34.

14 "Latin Language Study as a Renaissance Puberty Rite," *Studies in Philology* 56 (1959), 107.

15 Foster Watson, trans., *Vives: On Education* (1913; rpt. Totowa, N. J.: Rowman and Littlefield, 1971), p. 64.

16 William Harrison Woodward, *Desiderius Erasmus Concerning the Aim and Method of Education* (New York: Teacher's College, Columbia Univ., 1964), p. 189.

17 *English Works*, ed. William Aldis Wright (Cambridge, 1904), pp. 206–20.
18 *Ibid.*, p. 183.
19 *Ibid.*, p. 200.
20 Woodward, *Erasmus*, p. 164.
21 *The Institutio Oratoria*, trans. H. E. Butler (Cambridge, Mass.: Loeb Classical Library, 1958), I.ix.1–3, and II.vii.1–5.
22 *Th'overthrow of Stage-Plays* (London, 1599), p. 19. For a penetrating study of Puritan opposition to the stage, see Jonas Barish, *The Antitheatrical Prejudice* (Berkeley: Univ. of California Press, 1981), pp. 80–131.
23 Wright, ed., *English Works*, pp. 267–68.
24 *Timber, or Discoveries*, ed. Ralph S. Walker (Syracuse, N. Y.: Syracuse Univ. Press, 1953), pp. 86–87. For an excellent study of Jonson's conception of imitation, see Richard S. Peterson, "Imitation and Praise in Ben Jonson's Poems," *English Literary Renaissance* 10 (1980), 265–99. General surveys of the literary idea of imitation are provided in Harold Ogden White, *Plagiarism and Imitation During the English Renaissance* (1935; rpt. New York: Octagon Books, 1965), and J. W. Pigman III, "Versions of Imitation in the Renaissance," *Renaissance Quarterly* 33 (1980), 1–32.
25 Woodward, *Erasmus*, p. 173.
26 I quote Pigman's translation in "Versions of Imitation," p. 24; a more formal translation is provided by Izora Scott in *Ciceronianus* (1908; rpt. New York: AMS Press, 1972), p. 58.
27 Watson, trans., *On Education*, pp. 197–98.
28 *Role-playing in Shakespeare* (Toronto: Univ. of Toronto Press, 1978), pp. 11–20.
29 Alan Macfarlane, ed., *The Diary of Ralph Josselin* (London: Oxford Univ. Press, 1976), pp. 1–2.
30 Quoted in Frank Livingstone Huntley, *Sir Thomas Browne* (Ann Arbor: Univ. of Michigan Press, 1962), p. 8.
31 *The Autobiography of a Hunted Priest*, trans. Philip Caraman, S. J. (New York: Doubleday, 1955), p. 217.
32 *Life of Sir Philip Sidney*, ed. Nowell Smith (1907; rpt. Ann Arbor: University Microfilms, 1964), pp. 128–30. Of the authenticity of the death scene, Roger Howell says, "Greville's account is the only authority for it, and he was not an eyewitness, but the magnanimity displayed by the wounded knight was so in keeping with his character and what the twentieth century would call his image that it would be rash to reject it outright as a fabrication"; see *Sir Philip Sidney* (London: Hutchinson, 1968), p. 256.
33 Lewis Soens, ed., *Sir Philip Sidney's "Defense of Poesy"* (Lincoln: Univ. of Nebraska Press, 1970), p. 31.
34 *Erotomania* (Oxford, 1640), p. 118.
35 G. C. Moore Smith, ed., *The Letters of Dorothy Osborne to William Temple* (Oxford, 1928), p. 146.
36 James Turner, ed., *Love Letters* (London: Cassell, 1969), p. 26.
37 Barbara Winchester, *Tudor Family Portrait* (London: Jonathan Cape, 1955), p. 65.
38 John G. Nichols, ed., *The Autobiography of Anne Lady Halkett*, Camden Society n. s. 13 (London, 1875), pp. 4–19.

39 J. O. Halliwell, ed., *The Autobiography and Correspondence of Sir Simonds D'Ewes* (London, 1845), I, 316. Lawrence Stone describes D'Ewes's courtship in *Family*, pp. 187–89.

40 Ephesians 5:31; I quote from Lloyd E. Berry, ed., *The Geneva Bible: A Facsimile of the 1560 Edition* (Madison: Univ. of Wisconsin Press, 1969).

41 *Comic Transformations in Shakespeare* (London: Methuen, 1980), p. 28.

42 *Civilization and Its Discontents*, trans. James Strachey (New York: W. W. Norton, 1961), p. 13.

43 *Shakespeare and the Experience of Love* (Cambridge: Cambridge Univ. Press, 1981), p. 69.

44 Baldesar Castiglione, *The Book of the Courtier*, trans. Charles S. Singleton (Garden City, N. Y.: Doubleday, 1959), p. 350.

45 *Rites and Symbols of Initiation*, trans. Willard R. Trask (New York: Harper and Row, 1958), pp. 6, xiii–xiv. Eliade depends upon the descriptions in R. H. Matthews, "The Bora Initiation Ceremonies of the Kamilaroi Tribe," *Journal of the Royal Anthropological Institute* 24 (1895), 411–27, and 25 (1896), 318–39.

46 Robert G. Hunter develops this idea in *Shakespeare and the Comedy of Forgiveness* (New York: Columbia Univ. Press, 1965), pp. 88–92.

47 Nevo, *Comic Transformations*, p. 67.

4 Artificial Transitions

1 Gordon Donaldson, ed., *The Memoirs of Sir James Melville of Halhill* (London: Folio Society, 1969), p. 39.

2 *James the Fourth*, ed. Norman Sanders (London: Methuen, 1970), p. xliv.

3 *Gallathea*, ed. Anne B. Lancashire (Lincoln: Univ. of Nebraska Press, 1969), III.ii.35–39.

4 *Disguise Plots in Elizabethan Drama* (New York: Columbia Univ. Press, 1915), pp. 61–99. Most critical discussions of female disguise in the comedies focus on a particular play or character. Some useful general studies are Muriel C. Bradbrook, "Shakespeare and the Use of Disguise in Elizabethan Drama," *Essays in Criticism* 2 (1952), 159–68; Peter Hyland, "Shakespeare's Heroines: Disguise in the Romantic Comedies," *Ariel* 9 (1978), 23–39; Nancy K. Hayles, "Sexual Disguise in 'As You Like It' and 'Twelfth Night,' " *Shakespeare Survey* 32 (1979), 63–72; and Robert Kimbrough, "Androgyny Seen Through Shakespeare's Disguise," *Shakespeare Quarterly* 33 (1982), 17–33.

5 *Role-playing in Shakespeare* (Toronto: Univ. of Toronto Press, 1978), p. 40.

6 *The English Gentlewoman* (London, 1631), pp. 120, 130–31.

7 William Cecil, Lord Burghley, "Certain Precepts for the Well Ordering of a Man's Life" (c. 1584), in Louis B. Wright, ed., *Advice to a Son* (Ithaca, N. Y.: Cornell Univ. Press, 1962), p. 9.

8 *A Discourse of Marriage and Wiving* (London, 1615), p. 4.

9 J. O. Halliwell, ed., *The Autobiography and Correspondence of Sir Simonds D'Ewes* (London, 1845), I, 319. Lawrence Stone develops this courtship at length in *The Family, Sex and Marriage in England 1500–1800* (New York: Harper and Row, 1977), pp. 187–89.

10 *A Godlie Forme of Household Government* (London, 1612), p. 109.

11 *A Preparative to Mariage* (1591; facs. rpt. Norwood, N. J.: Walter J. Johnson, 1975), p. 59.

12 W[illiam] W[hately], *A Bride-Bush or A Wedding Sermon* (1617; facs. rpt. Norwood, N. J.: Walter J. Johnson, 1975), p. 45.

13 *A Care-Cloth or the Cumbers and Troubles of Marriage* (1624; facs. rpt. Norwood, N. J.: Walter J. Johnson, 1976), pp. 45–46, 68.

14 *A Modest Meane to Mariage*, trans. Nicholas Leigh (London, 1568).

15 John Brinsley, *Ludus Literarius* (London, 1612), p. 212; see also pp. 214–22.

16 James M. Osborn, ed., *The Autobiography of Thomas Whythorne* (London: Oxford Univ. Press, 1962), pp. 73–79.

17 For these and other cures, see Robert Burton, *The Anatomy of Melancholy*, ed. Floyd Dell and Paul Jordan-Smith (New York: Tudor Publishing Co., 1938), pp. 777–96.

18 See the Arden edition of the play, edited by John Russell Brown (London: Methuen, 1964), p. 113n.

19 *The Honestie of this Age* (London, 1614), p. 35.

20 Frederick J. Furnivall, ed., *Anatomy of Abuses in England*, New Shakespeare Society Series VI, nos. 4, 6 (London, 1877–79), p. 73.

21 *The Description of England*, ed. Georges Edelen (Ithaca, N. Y.: Cornell Univ. Press, 1968), p. 147. Harrison's critique is essentially the same in the 1577 version; see the edition of Frederick J. Furnivall (London: New Shakespeare Society, 1877) I, 170–71.

22 Quoted in Louis B. Wright, *Middle-Class Culture in Elizabethan England* (1935; rpt., Ithaca, N. Y.: Cornell Univ. Press, 1958), p. 493.

23 *Hic-Mulier, or the Man-Woman* (London, 1620), sigs. C2^v, B2.

24 *Haec-Vir, or the Womanish-Man* (London, 1620), sig. B3.

25 *Shakespeare and the Nature of Women* (London: Macmillan, 1975), p. 234.

26 *Hic-Mulier*, sig. B3.

27 *Shakespeare's Festive Comedy* (Princeton: Princeton Univ. Press, 1959), p. 242.

28 Frederick J. Furnivall, ed., *Robert Laneham's Letter*, New Shakespeare Society Series VI, no. 14 (London, 1890), pp. 26–32; see also John Brand, *Observations on Popular Antiquities* (London, 1877), p. 102.

29 "Women on Top: Symbolic Sexual Inversion and Political Disorder in Early Modern Europe," in Barbara A. Babcock, ed., *The Reversible World* (Ithaca, N. Y.: Cornell Univ. Press, 1978), pp. 147–90.

30 *Custom and Conflict in Africa* (Oxford: Basil Blackwell, 1965), p. 116.

31 Quoted in Peter Burke, *Popular Culture in Early Modern Europe* (London: Temple Smith, 1978), p. 202.

32 Davis, "Women on Top," p. 183.

33 *Chisungu* (New York: Grove Press, 1956), pp. 73–74.

34 Albert Feuillerat, ed., *The Prose Works*, I (1912; rpt. Cambridge: Cambridge Univ. Press, 1962), 78.

35 See Mark Rose, "Sidney's Womanish Man," *Review of English Studies*, n. s. 15 (1964), 353–63.

36 W. H. D. Rouse, ed., *Shakespeare's Ovid* (New York: W. W. Norton, 1961), IV, 477–78.

37 "Spenser's Hermaphrodite and the 1590 *Faerie Queene*," *PMLA* 87 (1972), 195,

38 *Symbolic Wounds*, rev. ed. (New York: Collier Books, 1962), pp. 34, 113, 147–48. Mircea Eliade provides a similar interpretation of sex reversal, although from a religious perspective, in *Rites and Symbols of Initiation*, trans. Willard R. Trask (New York: Harper and Row, 1958). According to Eliade, "the religious meaning of these customs is this: the novice has a better chance of attaining to a particular mode of being – for example, becoming a man, a woman – if he first symbolically becomes a totality. . . . The androgyne is considered superior to the two sexes just because it incarnates totality and hence perfection" (p. 26). The difficulty with this interpretation, I find, aside from the scarcity of anthropological evidence to support it, is that it blurs the distinction between totality as chaos and totality as mystical perfection. Bettelheim's view, that sexual confusion is creative and leads eventually to sexual integration, seems more in keeping with anthropological evidence and is certainly more appropriate to the theory of rites of passage. Anthropologists have been generally sympathetic to Bettelheim's theory: see M. G. Marwick, "The Study of Ritual," *African Studies* 16 (1957), 181–87, and Karen Ericksen Paige and Jeffery M. Paige, *The Politics of Reproductive Ritual* (Berkeley: Univ. of California Press, 1981), pp. 11–14. Anthropologists seem to have ignored Eliade's views for the most part; the only review I have been able to locate, that of Dorothy Libby in *American Anthropologist* 61 (1959), 688–89, is hostile. Jan Kott uses Eliade to support his interpretation of Rosalind's "androgyny" in *As You Like It*; see *Shakespeare Our Contemporary*, trans. Boleslaw Taborski (New York: Norton, 1964), pp. 289–92.

39 John E. Booty, ed., *The Book of Common Prayer 1559* (Charlottesville: Univ. Press of Virginia, 1976), p. 292.

40 *The Shakespeare Inset* (London: Routledge and Kegan Paul, 1965), p. 76.

41 Dusinberre, *Nature of Women*, pp. 265–67.

5 Natural Philosophers

1 J. B. Leishman, ed., *The Three Parnassus Plays* (London: Nicholson and Watson, 1949), pp. 129–31.

2 *Shakespeare and the Popular Tradition in the Theater*, ed. Robert Schwarz (Baltimore: Johns Hopkins Univ. Press, 1978), p. 186.

3 Ronald B. McKerrow, ed., *The Works of Thomas Nashe*, rev. ed., ed. F. P. Wilson (Oxford: Basil Blackwell, 1958), III, 341.

4 Lewis Soens, ed., *Sir Philip Sidney's "Defense of Poesy"* (Lincoln: Univ. of Nebraska Press, 1970), p. 49.

5 In an insightful essay, G. L. Evans observes that the scene in which Dogberry wishes he had been "writ down an ass" (*Ado* IV.ii) may have been written by Kemp himself; if not, Evans suggests, it was written by Shakespeare "in absolute and well-judged servility to the known values of Kemp's comic genius"; see "Shakespeare's Fools: The Shadow and the Substance of Drama," in Malcolm Bradbury and David Palmer, eds., *Shakespearean Comedy*, Stratford-upon-Avon Studies 14 (London: Edward Arnold, 1972), 146. Although the scene may have been written by Kemp, it was apparently played by Robert Armin after Kemp's departure from the company; see Charles S. Felver, *Robert Armin, Shakespeare's Fool*, Kent State Univ. Bulletin, Research Series V (Kent, Ohio: Kent State Univ. Press, 1961), 11.

6 Weimann, *Popular Tradition*, p. 11.
7 Felver, *Armin*, pp. 21–24.
8 *Ibid.*, pp. 39–56.
9 *Feeling and Form* (New York: Charles Scribner's Sons, 1953), p. 342.
10 *The Trickster* (London: Routledge and Kegan Paul, 1956), p. 155.
11 C. G. Jung, *Four Archetypes*, trans. R. F. C. Hull (Princeton: Princeton Univ. Press, 1959), p. 140; Jung's essay also appears as Part Five in Radin's *Trickster*.
12 Radin, *Trickster*, pp. 151–54.
13 Elsie C. Parsons and Ralph L. Beals, "The Sacred Clowns of the Pueblo and Mayo-Yaqui Indians," *American Anthropologist* 36 (1934), 506–07. See also Julian H. Steward, "The Ceremonial Buffoon of the American Indian," *Michigan Academy of Science, Arts, and Letters* 14 (1930), 187–207; Verne F. Ray, "The Contrary Behavior Pattern in American Indian Ceremonialism," *Southwestern Journal of Anthropology* 1 (1945), 75–113; and Edward Norbeck, *Religion in Primitive Society* (New York: Harper Brothers, 1961), pp. 206–12.
14 *The Medieval Stage*, I (London: Oxford Univ. Press, 1903), 325.
15 Sandra Billington, " 'Suffer Fools Gladly': the Fool in Medieval England and the Play *Mankind*," in Paul V. A. Williams, ed., *The Fool and the Trickster* (Cambridge: D. S. Brewer, 1979), pp. 36–54.
16 *Shakespeare's Festive Comedy* (Princeton: Princeton Univ. Press, 1959), p. 25.
17 *Chisungu* (New York: Grove Press, 1956), p. 88.
18 *The Elizabethan Jig* (1929; rpt. New York: Dover, 1965), pp. 432–36; for discussions of the fool's role in wooing dances, see pp. 7, 18–19, 249–53.
19 Frederick J. Furnivall, ed., *Robert Laneham's Letter*, New Shakespeare Society Series VI, no. 14 (London, 1890), pp. 22–23.
20 McKerrow, ed., *The Works of Thomas Nashe*, I, 83.
21 See Robert Hillis Goldsmith, *Wise Fools in Shakespeare* (Liverpool: Liverpool Univ. Press, 1958), p. 4, and the drawings in Francis Douce, *Illustrations of Shakespeare* (London: Thomas Tegg, 1839), plate III.
22 Enid Welsford, *The Fool* (1935; rpt., Gloucester, Mass.: Peter Smith, 1966), p. 171; see also pp. 159–72.
23 *The Ritual Process* (Chicago: Aldine Publishing Co., 1969), p. 110.
24 Clarence H. Miller, ed., *The Praise of Folie*, trans. Sir Thomas Chaloner (London: Oxford Univ. Press, 1965), p. 15.
25 *The Fool and His Scepter* (Evanston, Ill.: Northwestern Univ. Press, 1969), pp. 13–22.
26 Goldsmith, *Wise Fools*, pp. 1–5.
27 *Praisers of Folly* (Cambridge, Mass.: Harvard Univ. Press, 1963), pp. 91–100.
28 Miller, ed., *Praise of Folie*, p. 15.
29 The ass was associated with licentiousness in the medieval Feast of Fools and is linked to sexual potency in the Old Testament and elsewhere; see Beryl Rowland, *Animals with Human Faces* (Knoxville: Univ. of Tennessee Press, 1973), pp. 22–23, and Ad deVries, *Dictionary of Symbols and Imagery* (Amsterdam: North-Holland Publishing Co., 1974), pp. 26–29. Apuleius's *The Golden Ass*, a possible source for *A Midsummer Night's Dream*, contains an adventure in which the hero, who has been

transformed into an ass, is seduced by a rich matron of Corinth. The episode combines innocent affection and sexual abnormality in a manner not unlike that of Titania's wooing of Bottom; see *The Golden Asse of Lucius Apuleius*, trans. William Aldington (London: Chapman and Dodd, [1925]), X, 46.

30 *Shakespeare and the Traditions of Comedy* (Cambridge: Cambridge Univ. Press, 1974), p. 172.

31 Welsford, *Fool*, p. 160; see also pp. 141–42, 215.

32 Miller, ed., *Praise of Folie*, p. 120.

33 J. P. Feather, ed., *The Collected Works of Robert Armin*, I (New York: Johnson Reprint Corp., 1972), B3.

34 Willeford, *Fool and His Scepter*, p. 26.

35 A source for this discussion of time, Ecclesiastes 2 and 3, in *The Geneva Bible*, allows a glimpse at the working of Shakespeare's imagination. Both sections in Ecclesiastes focus on the transitoriness of life and our inability to know or control the future. The topic headings for both sections stand side by side, in large type, on facing pages. One reads, "Who knoweth his heire"; the other, "Tyme for all things." See the facsimile edition of Lloyd E. Berry (Madison: Univ. of Wisconsin Press, 1969), pp. 277–78.

36 *Collected Works*, I, C3ᵛ.

37 *The Forest of Symbols* (Ithaca, New York: Cornell Univ. Press, 1967), p. 97.

38 See Miller, ed., *Praise of Folie*, pp. 48–49.

6 Time and Place

1 Arnold van Gennep, *The Rites of Passage*, trans. Monika B. Vizedom and Gabrielle L. Caffee (Chicago: Univ. of Chicago Press, 1960), p. 18.

2 *The Language of the Rite* (London: Darton, Longman, and Todd, 1974), p. 117. Anthropological accounts of rites of passage rarely explore the implications of their temporal and spatial symbolism. On the general neglect of time among anthropologists, see Leonard W. Doob, "Time: Cultural and Social Anthropological Aspects," in Tommy Carlstein et al., eds., *Making Sense of Time* (London: Edward Arnold, 1978), pp. 56–65. Mircea Eliade's conception of the liminal stage of initiation rites as a return to primordial chaos is suggestive, as we have seen (p. 78), but is based on slender evidence; this pattern does not figure in the comedies, moreover, with the possible exception of the hints of a "golden world" in *As You Like It*. See *Rites and Symbols of Initiation*, trans. Willard R. Trask (New York: Harper and Row, 1958), pp. 6, xiii–xiv.

3 *Anatomy of Criticism* (1957; rpt. New York: Atheneum Press, 1967), p. 183.

4 *A Natural Perspective* (New York: Harcourt, Brace, and World, 1965), p. 142.

5 *The Country House in English Renaissance Poetry* (Berkeley: Univ. of California Press, 1977), pp. 182–83.

6 *Instructions for Forraine Travell* (1642; rpt. Westminster: A. Constable, 1895), p. 63.

7 William Aldis Wright, ed., *English Works* (Cambridge: Cambridge Univ. Press, 1904), p. 228.

8 *The Court and Country* (1618), in Alexander B. Grosart, ed., *Works* (Edinburgh, 1879), II, 7.

9 Frederick J. Furnivall, ed., *Anatomy of Abuses in England*, New Shakespeare Society Series VI, nos. 4, 6 (London, 1877—79), p. 88.

10 *Simon Forman* (London: Weidenfeld and Nicolson, 1974), pp. 55, 290, 294, 60.

11 *The Idea of the Garden in the Renaissance* (New Brunswick, N. J.: Rutgers Univ. Press, 1978), p. 90.

12 *A Most Brief and Pleasaunt Treatyse* (1563; rpt. Herrin, Ill.: Trovillion Private Press, 1938), cap. IV.

13 Quoted in Roy Strong, *The Renaissance Garden in England* (London: Thames and Hudson, 1979), p. 53.

14 Alexander Dyce, ed., *The Dramatic and Poetical Works of Robert Greene and George Peele* (London, 1861), pp. 578—79.

15 *A New Orchard and Garden* (1617; rpt. London: Cresset Press, 1927), p. 64.

16 *Three Prose Works*, ed. John Buchanan-Brown (Fontwell, Sussex: Centaur Press, 1972), p. 287.

17 W. H. Matthews, *Mazes and Labyrinths* (London: Longmans, Green, 1922), p. 77. David Ormerod discusses the relevance of the myth of Theseus, the labyrinth, and the minotaur to one Shakespearean comedy in "*A Midsummer Night's Dream*: The Monster in the Labyrinth," *Shakespeare Studies* 11 (1978), 39—52. Giles Fletcher's poem, "A Lover's Maze," illustrated ineptly the conventional connection between love and amazement; see Lloyd E. Berry, ed., *The English Works of Giles Fletcher, the Elder* (Madison: Univ. of Wisconsin Press, 1964), pp. 115—18.

18 Most of the critical discussions of time and place in Shakespeare occur in studies of individual plays. Useful general accounts of Shakespearean conceptions of time are provided in Ricardo J. Quinones, *The Renaissance Discovery of Time* (Cambridge, Mass.: Harvard Univ. Press, 1972), and, especially, Frederick Turner, *Shakespeare and the Nature of Time* (Oxford: Clarendon Press, 1971).

19 *Shakespeare Our Contemporary*, trans. Boleslaw Taborski (New York: W. W. Norton, 1964), p. 218.

20 *Comic Transformations in Shakespeare* (London: Methuen, 1980), p. 224.

21 Edwin S. Hartland, *The Science of Fairy Tales* (1891; rpt. Detroit, Mich.: Singing Tree Press, 1968), pp. 178—80; see also pp. 161—254.

22 Francis J. Child, *The English and Scottish Popular Ballads* (Boston: Houghton Mifflin, 1882), I, 321. Although she does not mention the motif of fairy time, Anne Paolucci argues that Shakespeare exploits a similar temporal disorientation in *A Midsummer Night's Dream*; see "The Lost Days in *A Midsummer Night's Dream*," *Shakespeare Quarterly* 28 (1977), 317—26.

23 *Feeling and Form* (New York: Charles Scribner's Sons, 1953), pp. 333—34.

24 See Barbara K. Lewalski, "Thematic Patterns in *Twelfth Night*," *Shakespeare Studies* 1 (1965), 178—79.

25 *Shakespeare and the Traditions of Comedy* (Cambridge: Cambridge Univ. Press, 1974), pp. 13—14.

26 Langer, *Feeling and Form*, p. 331.

27 See Willard Farnham, *The Medieval Heritage of Elizabethan Tragedy* (Berkeley: Univ. of California Press, 1936), pp. 340–51.

28 *The Pilgrimage of Life* (New Haven: Yale Univ. Press, 1962), p. 19.

7 Incorporations

1 *Desolation of a City: Coventry and the Urban Crisis of the Late Middle Ages* (Cambridge: Cambridge Univ. Press, 1979), p. 86.

2 *Of Domesticall Duties* (1622; facs. rpt. Norwood, N. J.: Walter J. Johnson, 1976), p. 206.

3 H. Bullinger, *The Christen State of Matrimonye* (1541; facs. rpt. Norwood, N. J.: Walter J. Johnson, 1974), sig. G6^v.

4 *The Rites of Passage*, trans. Monika B. Vizedom and Gabrielle L. Caffee (Chicago: Univ. of Chicago Press, 1960), pp. 132, 117.

5 See *The Family, Sex and Marriage in England, 1500–1800* (New York: Harper and Row, 1977), pp. 4–9 for a summary of Stone's view.

6 Merritt E. Lawlis, ed., *The Novels of Thomas Deloney* (Bloomington: Indiana Univ. Press, 1961), pp. 28–29.

7 The painting is reproduced in David Bevington, ed., *The Complete Works of Shakespeare*, 3rd ed., (Glenview, Ill.: Scott, Foresman, 1980), pp. 22–23. Whether it represents an actual wedding or a generalized view of wedding festivities is unclear; for an interpretation, see Erna Auerbach and C. Kingsley Adams, comps., *Paintings and Sculpture at Hatfield House* (London: Constable and Co., 1971), pp. 53–55.

8 M. Misson's *Memoirs and Observations in His Travels over England*, trans. Mr. Ozell (London, 1719), pp. 183, 349–52; the work was published in French in 1698.

9 G. C. Moore Smith, ed., *The Letters of Dorothy Osborne to William Temple* (Oxford, 1928), p. 169.

10 Rachel Weigall, ed., "The Journal of Lady Mildmay, circa 1570–1617," *Quarterly Review* 215 (1911), 122–23.

11 Smith, ed., *Letters*, p. 10.

12 The most complete descriptions are in Chilton L. Powell, *English Domestic Relations, 1487–1653* (1917; rpt. New York: Russell and Russell, 1972), pp. 1–60, and Lu Emily Pearson, *Elizabethans at Home* (Stanford: Stanford Univ. Press, 1957), pp. 279–362; for details of the wedding day, I have found Pearson's work especially useful. General discussions of marriage customs in Shakespeare's plays are provided in Margaret Loftus Ranald, "'As Marriage Binds, and Blood Breaks': English Marriage and Shakespeare," *Shakespeare Quarterly* 30 (1979), 68–81, and in two articles by Ann Jennalie Cook: "The Mode of Marriage in Shakespeare's England," *Southern Humanities Review* 11 (1977), 126–32, and "Wooing and Wedding: Shakespeare's Dramatic Distortion of the Customs of His Time," in *Shakespeare's Art from a Comparative Perspective*, ed. Wendell M. Aycock (Lubbock: Texas Tech Press, 1981), pp. 83–100.

13 Frederick J. Furnivall, ed., *Robert Laneham's Letter*, New Shakespeare Society Series VI, no. 14 (London, 1890), pp. 21–24.

14 John E. Booty, ed., *The Book of Common Prayer 1559* (Charlottesville: Univ. Press of Virginia, 1976), p. 290.

15 Alexander Leggatt is particularly sensitive to the tonal range of the comedies; see *Shakespeare's Comedy of Love* (London: Methuen, 1973).

16 *Shakespeare and the Traditions of Comedy* (Cambridge: Cambridge Univ. Press, 1974), p. 126.

17 *Shakespeare's Festive Comedy* (Princeton: Princeton Univ. Press, 1959), p.8.

18 For stimulating explorations of this motif, see Robert B. Schwartz, "Shakespeare's Parted Eye: Approaches to Meaning in the Sonnets and Plays," *Dissertation Abstracts* 40 (1978), 3324A (Univ. of Virginia), and "Approaching the Sonnets: Shakespeare's Parted Eye," *Wascana Review* 17, no. 2 (1982), 51–65.

19 George Puttenham, *The Arte of English Poesie* (1589; facs. rpt. Menston, Yorkshire: Scolar Press, 1968), p. 189.

20 *The Works of Francis Bacon*, ed. James Spedding, R. L. Ellis and D. D. Heath. 14 vols. (London, 1857–74), III, 266.

21 Bullinger, *Matrimonye*, sig. A6ᵛ.

22 *An Heptameron of Civill Discourses* (London, 1582), sig. X3.

23 W. Speed Hill, ed., *The Works of Richard Hooker* (Cambridge, Mass.: Harvard Univ. Press, 1977), II, 404.

24 *A Treatise of Espousals* (London, 1686), pp. 207–09; the work was written in about 1600.

25 For illustrations of gimmal rings, see R. Chambers, ed., *The Book of Days* (London: Ward R. Chambers, 1932), I, 220–22.

26 Booty, ed., *Common Prayer 1559*, p. 293.

27 Hill, ed., *Hooker*, II, 404–06; see also Stone, *Family*, p. 522.

28 See Nicholas James Perella, *The Kiss Sacred and Profane* (Berkeley: Univ. of California Press, 1969), pp. 158–243 (especially pp. 231–34) and p. 40.

29 *The Book named The Governor*, ed. S. E. Lehmberg (London: Dent, 1962), p. 77.

30 Robert Krieger, ed., *The Poems of Sir John Davies* (Oxford: Clarendon Press, 1975), p. 94.

31 Bullinger, *Matrimonye*, sigs. G5ᵛ–G6.

32 Frederick J. Furnivall, ed., *Anatomy of the Abuses in England*, New Shakespeare Society Series VI, nos. 4, 6 (London, 1877–79), p. 155.

33 *World History of Dance*, trans. Bessie Schönberg (New York: Norton, 1937), p. 367.

34 Thomas Morley, *A Plain and Easy Introduction to Practical Music*, ed. R. Alec Harman (London: Dent, 1952), p. 296.

35 William Bradshaw, *A Mariage Feast* (London, 1620), p. 4.

36 Alan Brissenden, *Shakespeare and the Dance* (London: Macmillan, 1981), p. 45.

37 John H. Long, *Shakespeare's Use of Music* (Gainesville: Univ. of Florida Press, 1955), p. 160.

38 Walter Sorell, "Shakespeare and the Dance," *Shakespeare Quarterly* 8 (1957), 368; Brissenden, *Shakespeare and the Dance*, p. 54.

39 *The Jonsonian Masque* (Cambridge, Mass.: Harvard Univ. Press, 1967), p. 6.

40 The portrait is reproduced in *The Riverside Shakespeare* (pl. 4) and discussed in detail by Roy Strong in *The Cult of Elizabeth* (London: Thames and Hudson, 1977), pp. 84–110. Strong argues that the scene in

question could not represent a wedding because the central female figure is wearing black. The painting of the "Fête at Bermondsey" poses the same problem, although its details make it unmistakably a wedding feast. Black may seem an unlikely choice for a wedding, but Elizabethan brides wore various colors; given the context that Strong creates for Unton's memorial portrait, it would be even more unlikely for Unton's widow to omit their wedding.

41 Orgel, *Jonsonian Masque*, pp. 67–80.

42 Gouge, *Domesticall Duties*, pp. 206–07.

43 For an insightful discussion of the role of this conditional in the play, see Maura Slattery Kuhn, "Much Virtue in *If*," *Shakespeare Quarterly* 28 (1977), 40–50.

44 *Shakespeare and the Confines of Art* (London: Methuen, 1968), p. 70.

8 Conclusion

1 "Rescuing Shakespeare," *International Shakespeare Association Occasional Paper No. 1* (Oxford: Oxford Univ. Press, 1979), 30.

Index